THE
LOGIC
OF
FREEDOM

THE LOGIC OF FREEDOM

Free Will, Human Nature, and the Rational Argument for a Genuinely Free World

LAURA DAVIDSON

Austro-Libertarian Publishing, LLC
Spokane, WA

ISBN-13: 979-8-9879057-2-2 (Hardcover)
ISBN-13: 979-8-9879057-1-5 (Paperback)
ISBN-13: 979-8-9879057-0-8 (E-Book)

Library of Congress Control Number: 2023903887

Disclaimer: This book analyzes a variety of concepts in the natural and social sciences and reaches various philosophical conclusions. Nothing in this book should be construed as financial, legal, medical, or mental health advice. The content of this book is not intended to be used, nor should it be used, as a means of self-help or personal guidance. All ideas and opinions expressed are for informational purposes only. Although every effort has been made to ensure the accuracy of the information presented at the time of publication, the author and the publisher assume no responsibility for errors, inaccuracies, omissions, or any other inconsistencies and disclaim any liability to any party for any loss, damage, or disruption that may result from the ideas, opinions, or statements contained in this book.

Published by Austro-Libertarian Publishing, LLC

Acknowledgements

I would like to express my deep and sincere gratitude to my friend and mentor Professor Walter Block for his invaluable guidance and encouragement over the years, without whom I would probably never have written this book. In our many conversations, Walter has consistently inspired me with his intellect, his wit, and his sense of humor, and has given me the motivation and confidence necessary to tackle this project and many others.

In addition, I am extremely grateful to Dr. David Gordon, who graciously agreed to review this work, and who provided me with a number of helpful insights. I cannot thank him enough for his generosity in sharing his expansive knowledge and expertise with me.

I also owe a debt of gratitude to many of the academic staff at the Ludwig von Mises Institute who through their scholarly writings have had an indelible effect on my thinking and intellectual life.

Finally, I would like to thank my family and friends who have provided me with encouragement, love, and comfort in the course of my studies.

Table of Contents

Introduction

How free are we really? It is a common belief among many people today, especially in the scientific community, that because the brain is composed of matter, it follows that human thoughts are generated by a process governed by physical laws. After all, the brain's operation is a biological process, and biological mechanisms can in theory be reduced to chemical processes, and these in turn can be explained in the language of physics. Therefore, say many scientists, the brain is like a machine, a very complicated machine to be sure, but in the end its operation can be explained in the same way we use to describe the workings of a computer. It is true its complexity prevents us from being able to know exactly how it works at present, but it is only a matter of time before we have the right tools and technology. When we do, we will not only be able to describe how the brain thinks, but we will also be able to predict *what* it will think.

If all of this is true, if the operation of the brain really can be explained entirely in this reductionist manner, then this would imply its output – the mind – is governed by a fully deterministic process. It would mean everything we think, everything we dream, all the memories we have, and all our desires and choices are determined by specific causes in a one-to-one relationship. It would mean we have absolutely no free will.[1] Neuroscientists argue over the way in which they believe the deterministic process occurs, but most agree

---

[1] The term "free will" is a pleonasm, since the word "will" seems to contain the concept of "free." However, since almost everyone uses the term "free will," I shall continue to use it in this book.

free will is simply an illusion. Evolution has given us a mind that thinks it is free, they say, precisely so we do not become too despondent, apathetic, and nihilistic. But in reality, we are merely very complicated automatons, preprogrammed to respond in a mechanistic way to external stimuli.

However, if we really do not have free will, then this has grave consequences for the meaning of our lives in general and ethics in particular. For how can we be held morally responsible for anything we do? Every action, no matter how small, requires a thought that precedes it, and that thought reflects a choice we make according to our scale of values. But if all our choices are made for us by physical processes that are fully determined, then how can we ever be held liable or culpable for any immoral act?

The determinist position leads inevitably to moral perspectives that include relativism and nihilism, which can be used as excuses for instituting all manner of political actions anathema to human freedom. For if our will is not free, then it would seem we have no need to live in a free society. Why have freedoms at all if everything we think and do originates, not within us, but from events outside of our control in a strictly physical process? One response might be that social freedoms are nevertheless necessary to make us feel better about our lives, to mollify us, and to keep us from thinking we are slaves. But if this is correct, the reality is inescapable: we *are* slaves, and life becomes a pointless exercise.

The position taken in this book is that the determinists are wrong. We do have genuine free will. Our thoughts and choices are *not* made for us in a strictly mechanistic process governed by the laws of physics, and they are *not* an illusion. This does not mean everything we do is governed by the will, of course. Clearly there are autonomic and reflexive behaviors where the will does not operate or is very limited. In addition, there are many situations where we are influenced in our decisions by external circumstances and by instinct. Human nature plays a major role. However, to the extent we have alternatives and are able to choose, we alone control our will. And I contend this means that as free-thinking beings possessed of reason, it is our natural right to live in a society where we are free to exercise our will without physical interference, on the condition that we are *not* free to threaten or interfere physically with anyone else. And this right exists, *not* to provide us with the illusion of freedom as some claim, but rather because to be able to act in such a manner without inhibitory force is affirmative of life, and life has meaning.

A truly free society allows for the maximum possible freedom for every individual. But it does not mean that people are free to engage in physical aggression. On the contrary, it means that the law demands that every person should be free *from* physical aggression, provided of course they do not initiate or threaten violence themselves. Unfortunately, this is not the case today, because in every jurisdiction around the world, even in democratic societies, the law itself often codifies aggressive acts whereby individuals suffer great physical harm to their person or property.

Most people are led to believe from an early age that it is justifiable for the government to enact various laws that violate the will of the individual under many different circumstances. Allegedly, the laws exist for the greater good, but very often they benefit a privileged few at the expense of the many. These laws are always coerced under a physical penalty of some kind, whether in the form of a fine or imprisonment. If a street gang were to engage in this kind of coercion, it would clearly be criminal, but because the government does it, it is deemed to be justified.

However, in a society grounded in genuine liberty, this would not be the case. Indeed, to be free from this kind of aggression is exactly what it means to live in a truly free society. The only kind of laws which would exist would be those that *protect* person and property from aggressive interference, such as those prohibiting murder, rape, kidnapping, assault, robbery, theft, and fraud, etc.

Natural law philosophers have long extolled the virtues of a genuinely free system, and many books have been written on this subject. Their authors have shown how such a society would almost certainly be fairer, more egalitarian, more moral, less utopian, and definitely less violent than any community governed by the kind of political systems that exist today. While I concur with many of their claims, that is not the purpose of this book. Rather, I wish to provide a rational justification for the existence of the free society and to demonstrate logically – from first principles – why human beings are meant to be free, what it means for human happiness, and why a system based on genuine freedom is the only political philosophy in keeping with our humanity and the laws of nature. It starts with proving we have free will.

Part 1 (chapters one to four) endeavors to provide the proof that our will is free. I draw on a variety of different subjects – including evolutionary biology, philosophy of mind, and physics – to support the case. However, the crux of the argument is a logical one, in that I believe the concept of free will can be deduced axiomatically from self-evident propositions in conjunction with a few empirical observations concerning human cognition and understanding. In order to accomplish this task, I first examine in more detail the different views concerning determinism, indeterminism, compatibilism and free will. Most arguments that purport to show why human beings have free will rely on the inconsistencies involved with the alternative positions. But while pointing out the deficiencies in competing points of view is necessary, it is not sufficient to prove conclusively that the will is free.

Next, I consider the nature of consciousness. Philosophers have long debated whether the human mind is composed of the same substance as matter – the monist position – or whether the mind is a completely separate entity, which is the dualist point of view. The monist perspective would tend to imply a physical explanation for all thoughts and choices, and hence that determinism is true. The dualist standpoint would seem to be required if free will exists, but then the question arises, how can matter – the brain – give rise to a mind that is *not* matter, and where does the mind exist?

It is clear that we are not the only animal species to possess consciousness. So how did consciousness evolve, and in particular, how did we evolve free will from more primitive ancestral species that lacked it? The answers will provide the necessary perspective to view human understanding and decision-making *not* as something that has arisen in isolation, detached from our ancestral environment, but rather as a level of awareness that has come about in a gradual process over time. This is important because, while human beings are unique in having a will, we cannot deny there are other aspects of our thought processes that are influenced by our evolutionary past which we have in common with other animal species.

In chapter four, I arrive at the heart of the issue and answer the central question of why we have free will. Traditionally, it has been assumed by most philosophers that there are only two ways in which to derive knowledge. On the one hand, there exist empirical fact-based statements derived from observations and experience. On the other hand, there are propositions deduced logically which are not fact-based, but which give rise merely to tautologies. This epistemological duality was first definitively claimed by the 18th century Scottish thinker David Hume, who at the end of his work *An Enquiry Concerning Human Understanding* famously declared:

> Does it contain any abstract reasoning concerning quantity or number? No. Does it contain any experimental reasoning concerning matter of fact and existence? No. Commit it then to the flames: for it can contain nothing but sophistry and illusion.[2]

Unfortunately, this view has persisted among many philosophers since Hume and is the dominant mode of thought regarding the

---

[2] Hume, David (2018) [1748] *An Enquiry Concerning Human Understanding* Digireads.com Neeland Media LLC. Kindle Edition. Ch.5, p. 158.

acquisition of knowledge even today. But as Hume's contemporary Immanuel Kant showed, there is a third kind of knowledge that can be deduced logically without observed facts, but which nevertheless does not result in tautologies.

How is it possible to deduce real knowledge about the world, axiomatically, without making any observations of facts? The answer is one starts *not* with outer experience but rather with certain inner experiences, which are self-evident to every human being. These inner experiences are innate – the result of evolution's effect on the brain – and they include such intuitions as space and time, as well as the concept of causality. Kant did not know about evolution, but it is interesting to note that the latest developments in evolutionary biology and physics – particularly the general theory of relativity and quantum mechanical theory – appear to be compatible with Kant's ideas. What they show is that while the world as it appears to us in our everyday experience is very real, it is not the world as it really is in its entirety. There is more "out there" we can never experience or observe, even with the best scientific equipment, because as a rule the human mind is simply incapable of perceiving or conceiving it. However, from our inner experiences, it is possible to define the limits of our everyday experience and thereby realize there is an exception to the rule. Once we understand this, it is possible to see why we have free will.

Part II of this book (chapters five to seven) looks at how physiology and instinct influence our will. It is clear that our choices are guided, at least to some extent, by basic instincts to survive and reproduce. We do not make choices indiscriminately or act randomly, precisely because that would be antithetical to life. In this regard, we are similar to many animals. But because we have free will, we are able to choose how to go about accomplishing our desires and, in some cases, how to override them if we deem it necessary. This is something animals cannot do. Human beings *act*, which is to say we make free choices mediated by innate needs and other desires, whereas animals merely behave because they are motivated purely by instinctual feelings.

One of the most important instincts is the human tendency to cooperate. In this regard, we have something in common with a number of other social species. Since the 1960s, evolutionary biologists have recognized that much of our drive to engage in cooperation is mediated by so-called "selfish genes," which influence our thoughts and actions based on the genes' "desires" to be "immortal." Newer developments have challenged this thesis somewhat, but it remains the dominant explanation for social cooperation.

However, precisely because humans have free will, we are not always bound to cooperate. This is very clear, given that some individuals engage in action that is anti-social and sometimes violent. While the tendency to cooperate is innate, the question of why certain individuals initiate aggression against others is an essential one to consider, particularly in the context of studying interpersonal action. We cannot determine how best to organize society without looking at whether or not human aggression is innate behavior or malevolent action governed by thought and choice.

The most extreme forms of anti-social action are exhibited by psychopaths, who are responsible for the vast majority of serious crime. Psychopaths demonstrate an almost complete lack of empathy, so it is fortunate for the human race that empathy is a human emotion present in a majority of the population. Empathy, which many neuroscientists believe is an innate emotion, is probably a significant factor for why most people instinctively tend to cooperate. A number of other animal species also appear to be able to empathize, at least at a rudimentary level. However, because humans have reason, free will, and foresight, we are the only species that can understand the thoughts and actions of others and are therefore able to anticipate what other people need or are going to do. This understanding is nowhere near absolute, but it does give us a reasonable idea of the motivations of other human beings in many situations.

But it is essential to differentiate between this empathic, non-definitive, subjective understanding of human action from the kinds of actions we see in material objects governed by the laws of physics. Because the human will is not governed by any physical law, humans are only partially predictable, whereas the actions of material objects are, for the most part, strictly deterministic. The determinists would have us believe that because human beings are *somewhat* predictable, we are governed by the same physical laws, but this is false.

Part III (chapters 8-14) examines what free will and human nature means for the individual and for society in general. Two fundamental instincts of nearly all animate living things are, on the one hand, the preservation of bodily integrity and the avoidance of death, and on the other hand, sexual attraction and reproduction. From a purely physical perspective, the outcome of these innate tendencies is a reduction of entropy in both the individual and in the species as a whole. Entropy is the degree of disorder, randomness, and uncertainty within a particular system, and it is a pervasive feature of the universe. Countering this tendency is life itself; indeed, all living things are, in essence, biological engines that harness free energy locally to create material order out of chaos against the general tide of entropy.

But because human beings have free will and can engage in purposive action, we have the unique capacity to reduce the effects of entropy in the form of novel objects external to our bodies. We call these objects goods, which are then used either directly for consumption or for purposes of further production. Not everything we do is creative, of course, but on balance, reducing entropy is a fundamental aspect of civilization. We are able to create many such goods precisely because we understand cause and effect, are able to harness a variety of energy sources, and, most importantly, can exploit the physical laws of nature.

But we also employ two very different kinds of laws for reducing entropy in other areas of our lives in both the mental and social spheres. While material goods provide utility and can satisfy many immediate needs, non-material goods, such as a happy marriage and close friendships, can often lead to a longer lasting state of happiness. But human flourishing cannot be attained in the presence of personal chaos, random and intrusive events, or persistent uncertainty.

One of the ways these negative outcomes can be avoided is through self-discipline and virtuous conduct. In antiquity, virtue was highly regarded, not merely because it led to the esteem of the community, but more importantly because it was an end in itself for the individual who practiced it – a condition which the Greeks referred to as *eudaimonia* or human flourishing. It was a form of conduct that regarded excellence in all human endeavors as the highest good because it led to equanimity of the soul. While the basic concepts of virtue are universal, virtuous conduct is not necessarily enduring, and the circumstances under which it applies is often subjective. Not only does one have to maintain it in practice, but one also has to choose how it should be exercised, all of which requires a will to do it while other more primitive forces are pulling in the opposite direction.

The final area of life I shall consider, and the one to which I shall pay special attention, involves society as a whole. In this case, the laws should lead to an orderly society, low in social entropy. But given that human beings possess a will that is free, what kind of legal principles are required if we want to create a harmonious society in which everyone has the chance to lead a flourishing life to the maximum extent possible?

The answer given by the present author is to establish a legal code based strictly on the libertarian principle of nonaggression. This precept states that it is illegitimate to initiate physical force, or threat of force, against another human being or their property. It allows a person to exercise their will to the maximum extent possible but does not allow them to use physical force to prevent the exercising of anyone else's will, except in self-defense. The nonaggression principle is universal and objective, and, provided it is rigorously adhered to, renders all interpersonal exchanges voluntary. It is strictly negative in that it prohibits physically aggressive acts. As such, any law that mandates positive acts violates the principle.

But what is the justification for rigorously adhering to the nonaggression principle? Why should the law *not* allow for government intervention that violates the will of the individual under certain circumstances? Why should all exchanges be purely voluntary?

Libertarian philosophers have suggested a variety of reasons, but unfortunately, they are not particularly convincing. The deontological argument maintains that it is one's duty not to aggress against others under any circumstances. It asserts that this is especially true when it comes to government intervention. But what is duty if nothing other than a belief, akin to religious dogma? Faith is the cause of many ideas which might be good because they seem affirmative of life, but faith is not an argument.

Another contention, related to the first, is that all forms of aggression and violence are wrong on moral grounds. Maybe so, but many people, including those in positions of power, believe it is perfectly appropriate to threaten force in order to enact policies they deem necessary for the benefit of society. We need proof that the use of force is wrong in every situation, particularly when it is employed under color of law in a way that violates the principle.

The utilitarian argument maintains that if all exchanges are voluntary, then social utility – the supposed happiness of everyone – is maximized. But while it is true that every voluntary exchange increases utility for both actors' *ex ante*, the concept of social utility – or overall satisfaction – is a troublesome one. How do we know, for example, there are no involuntary exchanges that might produce superior results?

One final argument in support of the nonaggression principle is that it is the only ethical precept that can be applied universally in an objective manner. This is true. But why should any commandment be universal or objective? The authors of this argument simply assert it must be so, but moral relativists would maintain that all ethical principles are subjective, and certainly not universal, while nihilists would claim all moral statements are false. To each his own, they might say.

The position taken in this book is that the nonaggression principle is indeed fundamental to creating a society that allows for the maximum possible human flourishing. But in order to maintain this claim, we need a rational and axiomatic argument deduced *a priori* to justify it. Arguing on deontological, moral, or utilitarian grounds does not measure up, and claiming it is the only ethical principle that can be universally applied will not satisfy moral relativists.

I therefore present an argument which I hope provides its rational justification. For I believe it can be deduced axiomatically and done so from self-evident propositions based on inner experience, in much the same way the existence of free will can be proven. By employing this same methodology, I hope to demonstrate, logically, that the nonaggression principle is a commandment that should undergird all interpersonal relations in society. Most people intuitively know this principle is right. What is needed is clear and convincing proof that it should be followed.

PART I

Why We Have Free Will

1

The Conundrum

It goes without saying that most people feel they control their own will. There are times when we might not be able to *act* upon our wishes, and there are some occasions when our choices appear to be limited, but our decisions never seem to be controlled by some outside force. Only the unfortunate few who are afflicted with a severe mental disorder may feel they are not in control of their thoughts. For most of us, our thoughts and choices feel like our own. And yet, when we look at the world around us, we see that every event appears to have a definite cause. Why should the operation of the mind be any different? Our brain is composed of matter, and the functioning of the brain can be observed to be a physical process, so it would seem that the decisions we make ought to be controlled by the same process of physical cause and effect, which would mean they originate outside our ultimate control. This is the conundrum that has puzzled philosophers at least since the time of the Ancient Greeks.

Broadly speaking, there are four different opinions on this issue. They are (1) hard determinism, which posits free will is merely an illusion; (2) compatibilism, which asserts free will and determinism can coexist; (3) indeterminism, which argues there is no specific cause for what we do; and (4) libertarian free will. Libertarian, here, refers not to the political philosophy, but only to the idea that the will is free from being controlled or determined solely by outside

1

events or by mere chance. Each of these positions has its problems, and I shall consider them each in turn.

Hard Determinism

Hard determinism is the idea that all events, including human actions, have a definite, precise, and necessary outcome. It precludes *any* form of free will. There are two kinds of hard determinism: theological and causal.

Perhaps the most famous theological determinist was the Protestant reformer Martin Luther. Luther's position on the subject of free will and determinism was laid out in *On the Bondage of the Will,* a polemical work published in 1525 which was directed against Desiderius Erasmus, who, a year earlier, had published *Discourses on the Freedom of the Will.* In that work, Erasmus had maintained that despite the fall of Adam and Eve, human beings must have free will because if they did not, then God's commandments would be meaningless. In response, Luther argued that if people have absolute free will, then this would imply God is not omnipotent, which would be an insult to His glory. Moreover, since God is all-powerful, said Luther, there would be no point in creating man only to allow him to commit sin. Luther claimed that no one achieves salvation by his or her own choice; rather, only God can decide to change a person's heart, at which time they come under the influence of His will. Unredeemed human beings – those who commit sin – are simply dominated by Satan.

Another notable theologian, John Calvin, preached an even stricter form of determinism. For Calvin, God is omniscient, and all events are preordained. In *Institutes of the Christian Religion: Book III,* he wrote:

> All [people] are not created on equal terms, but some are preordained to eternal life, others to eternal damnation; and, accordingly, as each has been created for one or other of these ends, we say that he

has been predestinated to life or to death.[3]

Predestination of this kind is more accurately called fatalism; indeed, it is fatalism in the extreme.

Hard *causal* determinism, on the other hand, takes the position that all events are necessitated by prior events as a consequence of the physical laws of nature.[4] From the perspective of classical mechanics, the claim is that at any given moment of time, there exists a prevailing set of conditions consisting of a definite distribution of matter and energy that is the unique cause of everything that occurs at the next instant. As history unfolds, the process moves forward in time ineradicably and inevitably. It means that all events – including the growth, behaviors, and actions of all living things – are a necessary consequence of everything that has gone before.

It also implies that from the present, there is a causal chain of such states one could in principle trace back to any point in the past. In other words, if we could rewind the clock and begin again with exactly the same starting conditions, all of history would repeat in precisely the same way. Consider an argument first put forward by the French mathematician Pierre-Simon de Laplace, who proposed a thought experiment in which a "demon" knows the position and energy of every fundamental particle in the universe. Laplace argued that because all events must necessarily occur in accordance with the laws of classical mechanics, the demon would in principle be able to predict all future events, including all human thoughts and actions. This concept implies human beings have no free will, no motivation, no volition, no agency, and no possibility of purposive action. It reduces human beings to very complicated machines that respond to given stimuli.

---

[3] Calvin, John (1845) [1536] *Institutes of the Christian Religion III.* Translated by Henry Beveridge Christian Classics Ethereal Library Ch. 21, p. 2207.

[4] This lies in opposition to a number of doctrines concerning probabilistic determinism, soft determinism, and indeterminism, where multiple futures are considered possible.

But can this possibly be true? Does this make sense? Hard causal determinists might profess everyone's future is determined, but the truth is they do not act out their own lives that way. For if they really believed they had no free will and none of their thoughts mattered – that none of their choices and decisions were their own – then it would be impossible for them to act in any purposeful way. They would simply give up planning anything in their lives. A genuine belief like that would mean they could behave only like automata, responding to base instincts in the heat of the moment without reason or regard to the future. It would mean they could not engage in purposive action at all.

Certainly, it seems as though people do not behave in this way; rather, they do indeed act as though they have free will. But determinists have a response. They point to the latest neuroscience, which seems to show that via the process of natural selection, we have developed brains that provide us with the *illusion* of free will. This, it is argued, prevents us from falling into a fatalistic mindset and a nihilistic outlook. Social psychologist Jonathan Haidt argues that research demonstrates our brains actually make decisions a split-second before we are even aware of it, after which we rationalize the decisions and, in effect, make them our own. He makes the claim that the mind is therefore divided into two parts: an automatic part which he compares to an elephant, and a rationalizing element which he likens to a rider on top of the elephant who *thinks* he is in control. In reality, however, the elephant does whatever it wants to do, and the rider is simply along for the ride.[5]

A pioneering experiment in this regard was conducted by Benjamin Libet in 1983.[6] In the original test, each subject was asked

---

[5] Haidt, Jonathan (2012) *The Righteous Mind*. Ch. 3 pp. 61-83 Knopf Doubleday Publishing Group. Kindle Edition.

[6] Libet, B., C. A. Gleason, E. W. Wright, and D. K. Pearl (1983) "Time of Conscious Intention to Act in Relation to Onset of Cerebral Activity (Readiness-Potential). The Unconscious Initiation of a Freely Voluntary

to move his or her hand and report the exact time they felt the intention to move it while observing a clock. Brain scans of the volunteers seemed to show that unconscious brain activity preceded the conscious (felt) decision to move the hand by up to half a second, indicating that volition is something the brain invents after the fact.

However, the research was controversial and fraught with difficulties, not the least of which involved the problem of coordinating the observation of the time noted by the subject with the felt decision. Measurement of brain activity by the machine was instantaneous, but the felt decision had to be coordinated by the subject with the observation of a clock, and this takes time for the brain to process. By the time the subject had looked at the clock, registered the time, and, most significantly, coordinated his conscious decision with the time he subsequently observed, there was a delay. Thus, while it might seem the brain scan demonstrated some kind of preceding unconscious activity, this was likely false. There was no illusion concerning the subject's free will. On the contrary, illusion lay in the experiment.[7]

It is perfectly possible for us to have free will and yet not be aware of how we make decisions. For even if the process by which our thoughts arise might be hidden, this is not sufficient to prove they are not *our* thoughts. It is not necessary for us to know how we arrive at our decisions or even when. Indeed, it is certainly possible for us to make real choices ourselves and yet only come up with good reasons for them afterwards. Our brain might flash the signal of desire without us immediately rationalizing it, but that does not mean it is not *our* desire. None of this research necessarily implies hard determinism is true. Without hard scientific proof, it remains a philosophical position and is in essence no less a faith than that of

---

Act." *Brain*, September 1983, Pt. 3, pp. 623-642.

[7] Taylor, Steve (2017) "Benjamin Libet and the Denial of Free Will: How Did a Flawed Experiment Become So Influential?" *Psychology Today* Sept. 5, 2017. https://www.psychologytoday.com/us/blog/out-the-darkness/201709/benjamin-libet-and-the-denial-free-will

theological determinism. Its adherents simply believe it to be true. Or do they?

A fundamental principle of epistemology – the study of how we know what we know – is that all knowledge must be grounded in belief.[8] In order to know something, you have to believe it. But if, in their day-to-day lives, determinists have to suspend a belief in determinism in order to operate as though they have free will, then they cannot claim their theory to be knowledge. A theory cannot be something you believe in only when it is convenient. But if, on the other hand, they genuinely believed in determinism, not as a detached philosophical exercise or a form of mind-play, but as a consistent mode of thought, and if they were to live their lives accordingly, then both life and the theory would become meaningless. Under normal circumstances, knowledge is beneficial inasmuch as it improves our understanding. This is a necessary prerequisite of human action directed toward the future in an uncertain world. But the theory of hard determinism is a dead end because anyone who *genuinely* believed his life was governed in this way would find that the knowledge the theory supposedly conveys ceases to be of any use. It implies no possibility of understanding.

There is a clear performative contradiction here, and it is this: Human beings do not come into this world with a knowledge of determinism. All knowledge that is not instinctive has to be acquired in some way, and this requires an action. But all human action is purposeful behavior, which necessarily implies free will. Thus, in order to acquire knowledge of a theory that says we have no free will, we have to have free will in the first place. Determinists might counter there is no such thing as action, because to say human beings *act* is to assume the very thing that does not exist – namely, free will. But this can only mean we learn about the theory, not through our own volition, and not because anyone willed that we

---

[8] There are three elements upon which knowledge rests: (1) belief, (2) truth, and (3) justification (internalism) or reliability (externalism).

learn it, but rather as an effect necessitated by the inevitability of a physical law. In which case, what is this theory telling us exactly? And why do hard determinists even bother to tell us about it? It cannot serve a purpose, because there is no purpose in a deterministic world. Therefore, quite literally, it means nothing. There would be no benefit in possessing this kind of knowledge.

Now, one might say there is a lot of knowledge that is not beneficial and yet it is still knowledge. For example, knowing there are rocks on the moon is probably of no benefit to me, but that does not preclude my knowledge of them. But if I claim there is no free will, then this is in an entirely different category. For if I truly believe it – which is only possible if I behave without regard to the future – then not only does that knowledge serve no purpose, *all* knowledge serves no purpose.

The moral implications of a true belief in hard causal determinism are dire, for if we have no free will, then we have no moral responsibility either. It permits the justification of any crime imaginable on the grounds that the perpetrator is "forced" to do it because of past circumstance. In effect, the criminal is just unlucky to have engaged in bad behavior. Perhaps, we should even feel sorry for him. In response, many determinists argue that even though choice is impossible and moral responsibility moot, it is nevertheless profitable to punish transgressors of society's rules in order to create a deterrent.

But this raises another issue. If the world is deterministic, all laws and punishments, like everything else, are destined to exist. If for some reason a particular law does not exist, then it was never going to do so, at least not now. Of course, before laws and punishments can be implemented, a decision has to made, but the decision-making process itself is determined, and nothing can affect the outcome one way or the other. Indeed, *everything* that happens is determined, regardless of what one *thinks* is necessary, because what one thinks is necessary is itself determined.

Ultimately, a belief in hard determinism involves a logical

contradiction. Those who push the doctrine are disingenuous because it is simply not possible to live a life as if it were true. On the other hand, hard determinists might simply be suffering from cognitive dissonance, so even though they act as though they have free will, this does not prove definitively that free will exists.

Quantum Indeterminism

Hard causal determinism is generally advocated by physicalists who subscribe to reductionist theories typical of classical mechanics. However, some physicalists contend that the brain comes under the effect of quantum mechanics. Their claim is that we are still biological machines, but quantum mechanics introduces randomness and indeterminacy into our thoughts among an array of possible outcomes that are probabilistically determined. Stephen Hawking takes this position in his 2010 book *The Grand Design*.[9] Hawking contends that everything, including the mind, is governed by the laws of nature, but quantum mechanics makes our thoughts and actions unpredictable, albeit within limits defined by probability. This gives us the illusion of free will.[10] But is this any more credible than causal determinism?

Quantum mechanics is a theory which describes the behavior of the very small at the atomic and sub-atomic level. It differs from classical mechanics, which deals with matter and energy on the scale of everyday experience. At the quantum scale, a fundamental particle – whether it is radiation or matter – can act like a particle

---

[9] Hawking, Stephen and Leonard Mlodinow (2010) *The Grand Design*. Bantam Books, New York.

[10] For example, Hawking says, "It is hard to imagine how free will can operate if our behavior is determined by physical law, so it seems that we are no more than biological machines and that free will is just an illusion." (Ibid, pp. 31-32) And later he says, "Quantum physics might seem to undermine the idea that nature is governed by laws, but that is not the case. Instead, it leads us to accept a new form of determinism: Given the state of a system at some time, the laws of nature determine the probabilities of various futures and pasts rather than determining the future and past with certainty." (Ibid, p. 63).

or a wave. This behavior is described by a wave function defined by the Schrodinger equation, which can be used to compute probabilities concerning the particle's position, momentum, and energy. The wave function itself and the associated probabilities it defines are strictly deterministic and dependent on the properties of the particle, but the values it yields for the particle's position are indeterminate and unpredictable; they cannot be defined except as a probability. In other words, the probability is determined, but the actual outcome is undetermined.

Many physicists assume these undetermined outcomes are truly random (within the bounds of the determined probability distribution).[11] And certainly, in nature, there are physical processes that appear to be so. Examples include radioactive decay, photon emission and photon absorption. In addition, a number of quantum mechanical devices, such as hardware random number generators and quantum computers, rely on randomness for their operation. However, among physicists, there is some debate as to whether or not quantum mechanical effects exhibit *true* randomness. While the early view of quantum mechanics, known as the Copenhagen interpretation, assumed this to be so, a later hypothesis, the Bohm interpretation, posits an underlying variable that creates merely the appearance of randomness.[12]

---

[11] Randomness does not necessarily imply equal randomness. There can be "unequal" randomness. For example, if I throw two dice, and add the numbers together, and do this many times, the combined numbers that come up are random, but some are more likely than others. For example, the probability of throwing 2 is 1/36, 3 is 1/18, 4 is 1/12, etc.

[12] The original Copenhagen interpretation posits that as soon as observation takes place, the wave function collapses, whereupon the outcome is considered to be probabilistic only, and therefore indeterminate. It might seem we live in an indeterminate universe, in which multiple realities are possible and a single reality is randomly selected. However, on a macro scale, this is not the end of the story. According to Einstein's special theory of relativity, when one observer is moving relative to another, time moves more quickly in the observer's frame of reference than that of the observed, especially near the speed of light. As a consequence, there is no way to

Suppose, however, certain processes in the brain are truly random. In other words, let us assume that the brain's inner workings operate according to the laws of quantum physics and the outcome is indeterminate, not because we have free will, but rather because there is a truly random quantum effect present. Let us call this effect *quantum indeterminism* to contrast it with the kind of indeterminism associated with genuine free will.

Now, it is clear the brain's operation cannot be entirely random. If that were the case, our lives would be completely chaotic. For example, at any given time, there exist an infinitude of possible choices I could make. I could decide to eat a sandwich, work on this book, or go for a walk. These might seem fairly agreeable to me right now, but one is more appealing than the others, namely, working on this book. On the other hand, I could also stand on my head, swim with sharks, or rob a bank, but I am not going to do any of these things; not now and not ever. Even though I *could*, I would never consider them. So, clearly the random element, if it exists, only operates to some degree. Some other process must narrow the field by assigning probabilities to the various options.

But here lies the problem. This other process cannot be random. The *ultimate decision-making process* might involve randomness, so if eating a sandwich and going for a walk each have a probability of say 20% and working on this book 40%, then quantum effects might decide which one I opt for – in this case, with the odds favoring the latter. But the process of *assigning the odds* cannot be random. Whatever it is that makes working on this book more desirable than eating a sandwich or going for a walk cannot be indeterminate, otherwise none of them would be consistently more probable than

_____

define a single present in the universe. One person's present will be someone else's past, and vice versa, even though the difference might be very small. The implication for this under the Copenhagen interpretation is that with multiple people in the universe, the wave function will have already collapsed before any particular observer reaches a specific point in time in his own frame of reference.

standing on my head, swimming with sharks, or robbing a bank.

The question is, what creates this non-randomness among the various options that lie before me? And here there are only two possibilities. Either they are causally determined – that is, by laws of strict cause and effect. Or they are not determined by the law of causality at all, in which case they are decided by me – as a consequence of my free will. But since the quantum indeterminists reject the concept of free will, they have to accept some degree of strict causal determinism operating in the brain, even if they invoke quantum mechanics, probability, and unpredictability as a foil. Indeed, this is consistent with the fact that according to quantum mechanics, the wave function and its associated probabilities are strictly deterministic.

For these physicalists, quantum mechanics cannot be used as a means to escape the logical difficulties associated with hard determinism. If you advocate quantum effects, then at some level you must still accept that the brain operates in a strictly determined way. I call this idea hard probabilistic determinism. The fact that there may be some randomness involved in the brain's operation still means the individual is along for the ride because it implies decisions are being made, not by the individual himself, but rather by a physical process, albeit a quantum mechanical one. It is outside of his control and analogous to the toss of a coin. Indeterminists can claim such randomness equates to free will, but in subscribing to this idea, life still becomes fatalistic, nihilistic, and meaningless.

Compatibilism

There is a long tradition of philosophers who attempt to explain that determinism and free will are compatible. However, compatibilists often employ different definitions of free will or determinism or both, and in doing so, their arguments are often filled with obfuscations and riddled with contradictions that cannot be overcome.

One of the most notable such theorists was Thomas Hobbes. In his most famous work *Leviathan* (1651), Hobbes states:

> Liberty and Necessity are Consistent . . . yet because
> every act of man's will, and every desire, and
> inclination proceedeth from some cause, which
> causes in a continual chain (whose first link in the
> hand of God the first of all causes) proceed from
> Necessity. [13]

For Hobbes, God is the first cause of everything, which proceeds in
a causal chain to the actions of man. But the only way Hobbes can
make this determinist view compatible with free will is by redefining
the term "free will." According to that philosopher: "A Free-Man, is
he, that in those things, which by his strength and wit he is able to
do, is not hindered to do what he has a will to." [14]

According to Hobbes, as long as one is not restrained in some
way from taking the action, then there is free will. But this is not
what most people would view as genuine freedom of the will. The
freedom not to be "hindered" is merely the freedom to take an
action without restraint, which is hardly the same as the freedom to
think and act. Hobbes' definition of free will evades the ultimate
cause of the action, which for Hobbes is God.

If defined in this way, free will is indeed compatible with
determinism because, from Hobbes' perspective, the difference
between a free and unfree will is the difference between an act which
is unconstrained and one which is constrained by force or
circumstance. But this is very different from viewing free will as
being the *thought* behind an act as unconstrained. In the latter case,
one can have the will to take an action and be prevented from taking
it, and yet the will remains free precisely because the thought cannot
be taken away. Additionally, one can have the will *not* to do
something and be coerced to do it, but in this case also, the will

---

[13] Hobbes, Thomas (2014) [1651] *Leviathan*, Digireads.com Neeland Media
    LLC. Kindle Edition. Ch. 21, p. 91.
[14] Ibid, p. 91.

cannot forcibly be subverted and is therefore free. In the context of genuine free will, even a slave has free will, even though he is not physically free, because he still has freedom of thought.

Perhaps the most famous compatibilist was David Hume. Hume's view was expressed in *A Treatise of Human Nature* (1740) and later in *Enquiry concerning Human Understanding* (1748). In *Enquiry,* Hume contends that as regards "matters of fact" – that is to say, empirical observations – we understand how things operate by the principle of cause and effect. But, according to Hume, this principle is understood only because we observe "constant conjunctions" from which we make "necessary connections" as a result of "custom or habit."[15] In other words, there is no rational foundation for the principle of causality itself. Nevertheless, he says, all action in the physical world very much appears to have a cause, and there does not seem to be any such thing as chance. This seems to imply a fairly strict determinism, but it is qualified by his view that causality can never be proved conclusively.

Hume also maintains a deterministic position when it comes to the connection between mind and matter. Therefore, he notes, we frequently observe a certain regularity in human events, and we can often predict what human beings are going to do based on circumstance and previous experience. Even though he acknowledges that the regularities in human action are obviously less clear than those we see in the motion of physical objects, his claim is that they both belong to the same category of constant conjunctions and necessary connections.[16]

---

[15] Hume, David (2018) [1748] *An Enquiry Concerning Human Understanding.* Digireads.com Neeland Media LLC. Kindle Edition. Ch.5, p. 40.

[16] In some parts of the text, Hume claims causality in human action is often irregular because we cannot find the underlying necessary connection. For example, "I grant it possible to find some actions, which seem to have no regular connexion with any known motives and are exceptions to all the measures of conduct which have ever been established for the government of men. But if we would willingly know what judgment should be formed of such irregular and extraordinary actions, we may consider the sentiments

The problem with Hume's argument is that he conflates his quasi-physicalist notion of determinism, seen in the material world, with a less stringent interpretation applicable to human action, and justifies them as being in the same category by invoking his qualified view of causality. Hume's claim amounts to the proposition that because the principle of causality cannot be demonstrated rationally and can only be known empirically – whether it be with regard to the motion of physical bodies *or* human action – the difference in necessity (determinism) we observe between the two is only a matter of degree. But in essence, he has redefined the word "necessity" to have two different meanings: on the one hand, a strict determinism applicable to physical objects where cause and effect is obvious, and on the other hand, a more permissive determinism observed in human action where it is less obvious or not present. He then fuses them into a single elastic definition.

On the question of the will, nowhere in *Enquiry* does Hume examine free will as such.[17] Rather, he regards the important aspect here to be "liberty," which he defines as follows:

---

commonly entertained with regard to those irregular events which appear in the course of nature, and the operations of external objects. All causes are not conjoined to their usual effects with like uniformity." (Ibid, p. 80) Also, "The internal principles and motives may operate in a uniform manner, notwithstanding these seeming irregularities; in the same manner as the winds, rain, cloud, and other variations of the weather are supposed to be governed by steady principles; though not easily discoverable by human sagacity and enquiry." (Ibid, p. 82) On the other hand, in other areas Hume claims that causality in human action is precisely the same as that seen in physical objects – e.g., "Thus it appears, not only that the conjunction between motives and voluntary actions is as regular and uniform as that between the cause and effect in any part of nature; but also that this regular conjunction has been universally acknowledged among mankind, and has never been the subject of dispute, either in philosophy or common life." (Ibid, p. 83).

[17] Indeed, he says, "It would seem, indeed, that men begin at the wrong end of this question concerning liberty and necessity, when they enter upon it by examining the faculties of the soul, the influence of the understanding, and the operations of the will." (Ibid, p. 87).

> By liberty, then, we can only mean a power of acting
> or not acting, according to the determinations of the
> will; this is, if we choose to remain at rest, we may;
> if we choose to move, we also may. Now this
> hypothetical liberty is universally allowed to belong
> to everyone who is not a prisoner and in chains.
> Here, then, is no subject of dispute. [18]

But this obscures the question of whether or not the *will* is free.
Like Hobbes, Hume takes the position that liberty is the freedom to
act, or not act, according to one's will. This is true as far as it goes,
but it has no bearing on whether or not the action or inaction is
governed by the law of causality and necessity. Conflating this
definition of liberty with freedom of the will makes it *seem* as though
liberty is compatible with necessity, but it is not.

Another notable compatibilist is present-day philosopher Daniel
Dennett, who outlines his position in his 1984 book *Elbow Room: The
Varieties of Free Will Worth Wanting*.[19] Dennett begins his exposition
with the example of a wasp, busily going about its business
preparing a nest. When the wasp is interrupted by a researcher
blocking its path, it blindly repeats the same behavior over and over
again in a fruitless and futile exercise. Because the wasp's
performance is pre-programmed, evolved over the course of many
generations through the process of natural selection, it lacks the
ability to adapt to unfamiliar conditions. Unlike the wasp, however,
human beings have the power to alter their actions according to the
particular environment they encounter by making rational choices
that produce desirable results. But in the end, Dennett's argument
is that humans are just a more complicated version of the wasp. As
with other compatibilists, Dennett claims free will amounts to the
freedom to act upon choices and decisions that are guided by

---

[18] Ibid, p. 89.
[19] Dennett, Daniel C. (2015) [1984] *Elbow Room: The Varieties of Free Will Worth
Wanting*, The MIT Press, Cambridge, Massachusetts.

physical processes.

The notion that our decisions are controlled by prior events is not a problem for Dennett, who claims the essential requirement is that we have enough "elbow room" to act upon the kinds of choices that produce good results. As long as we are not constrained in any significant way, then we have free will. At bottom, this argument is the same as all other compatibilists: free will is equivalent to having enough freedom to act. But should we not be concerned this makes us little better than robots? No, says Dennett; after all, what more could we do in our daily lives with a will that is free than we can with physical freedom? We have all the freedom and choice "worth wanting."

The distinction between something "worth wanting" as opposed to "worth having" is an interesting one. Dennett maintains that because genuine free will is impossible, it is a waste of time to want it. According to Dennett, the intuition that we need free will to be morally responsible is mistaken. In other words, even though we want free will because we think we need it, in reality this is wrong. Much like Hume, Dennett argues that we hold each other responsible for choices and behaviors, not because they are the product of a good or bad will, but rather because they serve us well from the point of view of greater social utility, and we are driven toward it as a consequence of our genetic programming that has evolved over the eons – or as Hume would say, our nature.

There is one other philosopher I wish to consider – namely, the medieval scholastic Thomas Aquinas – who is sometimes labeled a compatibilist because he appears to adopt a theologically deterministic position that allows for free will. According to Aquinas, God is the prime mover, but human beings are still able to engage in voluntary acts. In his magnum opus *Summa Theologica* (1265-1274), he states:

> Free-will is the cause of its own movement, because
> by his free-will man moves himself to act. But it does

not of necessity belong to liberty that what is free should be the first cause of itself, as neither for one thing to be cause of another need it be the first cause. God, therefore, is the first cause, who moves causes both natural and voluntary. And just as by moving natural causes He does not prevent their acts being natural, so by moving voluntary causes He does not deprive their actions of being voluntary: but rather is He the cause of this very thing in them; for He operates in each thing according to its own nature. [20]

Aquinas claims "man moves himself to act" by virtue of his free will. This certainly has a non-determinist ring about it. On the other hand, by claiming God is the first cause, this implies determinism. Aquinas circumvents this problem by saying God is the cause of man's voluntary action. Here the word "cause" appears to have two meanings. God "causes" voluntary action in general, but the cause of the action itself seems to be left up to man. I think in the end Aquinas is *not* a compatibilist, and he does generally subscribe to the idea of free will with respect to individual choice, but God is still seen as the prime mover, the giver of choice, but not the chooser.

Libertarian Free Will (Metaphysical Libertarianism)

It is obvious that not everything we do involves a choice. Human beings frequently engage in behaviors that are instinctive or reflexive. To this extent, we are much like other animals. Newborn babies instinctively go toward their mother's breast. If you touch a very hot surface, you are likely to remove your hand instantly. In addition, some actions are reactive and fairly predictable. If you extend an open hand in a friendly manner to someone you meet, they will probably react positively and shake it.

Exogenous events do influence our thoughts. If your house is on

---

[20] Aquinas, Thomas (1265-1274) *Summa Theologica*, First Part, Question 83, Article 1, Reply to Objection 3.

fire, you are almost certainly going to have different thoughts, make different choices, and act in a different way than if it is not. However, this is not to say the choices we make when we act are made for us. In contrast to all the forms of determinism and compatibilism mentioned above, metaphysical libertarianism takes the position that even when the options appear limited, human beings do indeed make choices that are truly their own, and these decisions are never determined.[21] Certainly, if your house is on fire, then staying inside might not be an option, and calling the fire brigade is probably a very compelling one. But to the extent there are other opportunities – like staying inside to fight the fire yourself – then that action is the result of a choice that originates with the will. If there really is no choice involved or choice is not exercised – for example, if you were to jump out of the window in a blind panic without even thinking about it because you were about to burn to death – then it ceases to be an action and becomes merely an instinctive or reflexive behavior. In this case, the will is not operating. But to the extent there is prior thought behind what is done (or not done), then that is an action motivated by a will that is free.

Metaphysical libertarianism means that while our thoughts and choices can certainly be influenced by outside events, they are not determined by them. It assumes our choices and decisions are *not* generated by a unique causal chain of events originating with a particular set of conditions, either outside our bodies or within. They are not operating solely according to the laws of physics. Nor does it assume the decisions we make involve randomness. We are not automatons or zombies. The thoughts behind our actions are not strictly the result of a physical, biochemical, or electrochemical process at either a macro or micro scale. If it were possible to rewind the clock of time, our decisions and actions would *not* necessarily be the same.

---

[21] The term "libertarian" in this context indicates only freedom for the will and is not suggestive of libertarianism as a political philosophy, although a belief in metaphysical libertarianism may indeed lead to that point of view.

However, there is a possible problem with this position. For if our thoughts are not determined, what does it mean to say that *I* am the originator of my thoughts? We live in a world of causality, where every event seems to have a prior cause. If my thoughts and decisions are not made for me, but rather originate with me, then how can I make them if there is no prior cause? This is an extremely important question which must be answered if the case for genuine free will is to be made.

I believe we do indeed have genuine free will, and it can be demonstrated conclusively. However, before getting to the heart of the issue, it is necessary to examine the most significant philosophical and scientific ideas concerning the operation of the mind and the nature of consciousness. The question that needs to be addressed is this: How does consciousness arise from matter? For if consciousness exists not as a separate substance, but rather as something indistinct from matter as we know it, and which therefore operates according to physical laws and the law of causality, then it would seem there can be no such thing as a will that is free. If free will truly exists, then human consciousness, or perhaps matter itself, must be made of different stuff. So, what exactly constitutes the mind and human consciousness, and how does it relate to the physical body?

2

The Mind-Body Problem

Classical and Early Modern Views

Philosophers have long considered the nature of matter and its relation to the mind. Early pre-Socratic thinkers[22] believed all matter was composed of four elements, namely, water, air, fire, and earth. But it was not until Parmenides (c. 515 BC) that philosophers began to make any real attempt at trying to understand the connection between the physical and the mental. Parmenides' claim was that all physical objects are mentally constituted and therefore have no separate or independent existence outside the mind. For Parmenides, mind and body are ontologically indistinguishable, meaning physical and mental substances are essentially the same.[23] Democritus (460-370 BC) also subscribed to a form of mind-body monism, but he believed matter – not the mind – is the fundamental substance of nature. Democritus believed matter is reducible to

---

[22] For example, Thales (624-546 BC), Anaximander (610-546 BC) and Anaximenes (585-528 BC). See Copleston Frederick S. J. (1993) *A History of Philosophy Volume I: Greece and Rome*. Doubleday, New York. pp. 22-28.

[23] Parmenides' monist views on the nature of reality are revealed in a poem, Way of Truth, "[Everything] is now, all at once, one and continuous . . . Nor is it divisible, since it is all alike; nor is there any more or less of it in one place which might prevent it from holding together, but all is full of what is." According to W. K. C. Guthrie, ". . . the poem deduces the nature of reality from premises asserted to be wholly true, and leads among other things to the conclusion that the world as perceived by the senses is unreal." Guthrie, W. K. C. (1969) [1965] *A History of Greek Philosophy: Volume II*. Cambridge University Press

ever-smaller constituent parts, or atoms, and everything, including mental states, are the result of forces operating on such matter.[24]

Plato (428-328 BC), on the other hand, took the view that the mind (or soul) is distinct from the body. For Plato, all physical things have a true, ideal, and non-material form more real than the physical object ordinarily experienced. Material objects are mere imitations or shadows of real things[25] which exist as immaterial Forms or perfect examples. Unlike physical objects, however, the soul exists among the Forms only; it has no material "shadow." And the soul, which is immortal, resides in a "heaven" of Forms and enters the body only during life.[26] Therefore, in contrast to Parmenides and Democritus, Plato was the first to adopt a view of the mind and body that leaned toward dualism.

The first Western thinker[27] to take a strictly dualist view of the

---

[24] Guthrie, W. K. C. (1969) [1965] *A History of Greek Philosophy: Volume II.* Cambridge University Press. pp. 389-396.

[25] For example, Plato's dialogue *Republic Book VII*, between Socrates and Glaucon, Allegory of the Cave.

[26] Later, in The Phaedrus, Plato elaborates his notion of the mind with an analogy of a charioteer, whose chariot has two horses, one of which is obedient and the other unruly. The charioteer represents the rational part of the mind, the obedient horse is the spirited component, and the unruly equine is the appetitive element of the soul. The mind is thus controlled by three separate forces, an idea adopted much later in Freud's concepts of the superego, ego and id, and by Marx in his tripartite theory of the socially evolving mind in the natural, alienated, and species self.

[27] The mind-body problem has long been debated in Eastern philosophy, particularly within the Indian philosophical traditions. For example, in the Astika, an ancient philosophy that adheres to the religious texts of the Vedas, representing some of the oldest scriptures of Hinduism, there are several schools of thought which adopt either a monist or dualist position. One such school is the Samkhya, which posits two realities – namely, Puruṣa, which represents pure consciousness, and Prakṛti, from which all unconscious forces and physical bodies are derived. In the Vedanta system, the Dvaita Vedanta sub-school also subscribes to a dualist notion in which God (Vishnu) and individual souls are quite distinct from material bodies. This contrasts with the non-dualist (monist) position of the Advaita Vedanta, in which the highest reality (Brahman) is oneness that includes the human soul. Another non-dualist sub-school is Vishishtadvaita, which subscribes to a qualified

mind-body issue was Rene Descartes. Descartes lived during a period of increasing skepticism in which philosophers began to demand rigorous proofs regarding all aspects of knowledge. In *Meditations on First Philosophy* (1641), Descartes asked, if everything seems so questionable, is there really anything at all of which I can be certain? It seems I cannot even rule out that I am living in a dream or being deluded by a demon. However, because I think, I can at least be certain I am a thinking thing. As Descartes famously stated in his earlier *Discourse on Method* (1637), "I think, therefore I am." To Descartes, it was clear that the world outside the mind (*res extensa*) must be separate from that within (*res cogitans*), and thus while the mind and body are closely linked and the human being is a composite of both, the two substances are distinct.[28]

Contemporary Views: Physicalism

Most scientists and philosophers today are physicalists. Physicalism is a thesis which views everything in the universe, including mental states, as being physical or arising out of the material. This is an idea that has its origins with Democritus. With some exceptions, it generally implies a deterministic world without free will. One view, called the *reductionist hypothesis,* contends that the mind (and all mental states emanating from it) are reducible to physical processes.[29] In this interpretation, all mental activities can

---

form of monism. In this case, human souls and all matter are believed to be a substance that is the body of God, but the soul, being conscious, is considered to be a higher form of matter. See "Hindu Philosophy," *Internet Encyclopedia of Philosophy*. https://iep.utm.edu/hindu-ph/

[28] Descartes states, "From that I knew that I was a substance the whole essence or nature of which is to think, and that for its existence there is no need of any place, nor does it depend on any material thing; so that this "me," that is to say, the soul by which I am what I am, is entirely distinct from body, and is even more easy to know than is the latter; and even if body were not, the soul would not cease to be what it is." Descartes, Rene 2009 [1637, 1641] *Discourse on Method and Meditations on First Philosophy*. Digireads.com Neeland Media LLC. Kindle Edition. p. 16.

[29] Reductive physicalism is sometimes called materialism, but materialism is an

be explained in terms of the brain's biological systems, which are in essence reducible to biochemical and electrochemical mechanisms, and these in turn are reducible to physical processes. Therefore, everything within the brain, including thoughts, can in theory be explained in terms of the prevailing matter and energy state. In this view, the explanation for the existence of every substance, from the motion of inanimate objects to the behavior and growth of plants and animals to the thoughts, choices and actions of human beings, are reducible to basic physical states. This would imply a strictly deterministic universe in which there is no free will.

Most present-day physicalists, however, subscribe to the notion that mental states *supervene* on various material states. Supervenience implies that thoughts are an *emergent* property of matter and energy, and they represent a higher-order physical state but not an entirely different substance. Consider the analogy of a dot matrix printer, where each picture produced by the printer is composed of hundreds or thousands of tiny dots. A given picture depicts a scene which is dependent on the particular configuration of dots, but the scene itself contains an idea that is greater than mere dot configuration. In other words, the scene *supervenes* the dots and is an emergent property of them. However, since the scene is entirely governed by the position of the dots and cannot change unless the dots themselves change in some way, the relation is strictly one-to-one and therefore deterministic. Therefore, like reductionists, supervenience physicalists contend that thoughts are not *ex nihilo* – in other words, they do not spring out of thin air. Rather, they are causally determined.

In terms of physicalism, emergentism of this kind (or "supervenience physicalism" as it is sometimes called) implies the underlying property of everything in the universe is physical, but from a particular configuration of certain physical elements, a

---

older term more often used to describe the idea that everything is the property of matter rather than that which is physical.

mental state emerges. Because of the one-to-one relationship, this implies that no physical configuration can give rise to two different mental states. Or, more generally, a given underlying physical structure must always yield a world with unique mental, biological, or social properties. Simply put, supervenience physicalism implies there is a direct emergent relationship between the physical and the mental, and therefore free will is impossible.[30]

There are a number of arguments against physicalism, but perhaps the most notable is the "Mary argument" first proposed by Frank Jackson in 1982.[31] In this thought experiment, we are asked to imagine a woman named Mary, a scientist, who knows everything there is to know about color and how it affects the brain objectively. She knows how variations in the visible part of the electromagnetic spectrum are responsible for the different colors, how these different wavelengths of light affect the eye, and how that information is sent to the brain. She also knows how the brain's neural correlates of consciousness correspond to the different colors and how they distinguish between different hues. However, Mary is completely colorblind herself and has only ever seen the world in black and white.[32]

Then, one day, she has an operation on her eyes and her colorblindness is gone. She looks at a rose, and now she sees it as red. She has a brand-new experience of the rose which she did not have before.[33] In seeing color for the first time, she has acquired new knowledge. However, it is not the kind of knowledge she could have gained from any of her previous scientific studies of the objective

---

[30] Davidson, Donald (1970) "Mental Events" In L. Foster, & J. W. Swanson (eds.), *Experience and Theory*. University of Massachusetts Press. pp. 79-101.

[31] Jackson, Frank (1986) "What Mary Didn't Know". *The Journal of Philosophy*. Vol. 83 (5), pp. 291–295.

[32] In Jackson's original exposition, Mary is confined to a black and white room, and has only ever been allowed to see the outside world via a black and white television. Jackson, Frank (1982) "Epiphenomenal Qualia". *Philosophical Quarterly*. Vol. 32 (127), pp. 127–136.

[33] This kind of experience is sometimes referred "qualia."

aspects of color, no matter how extensive those studies might have been. The conclusion one draws is that not all knowledge of the world can be explained in physical terms, and therefore there is something beyond the physical that lies solely in experience.

Strong Emergentism

The emergent process described above by supervenience is sometimes referred to as *weak emergence.* Familiar examples of this kind of emergentism exist in nature. They include ocean waves generated by the dynamics of water molecules, fractal patterns in snowflakes, and social groups formed by collections of individuals. In all these cases, the emergence of the new object does not produce a new substance; rather, it creates a different manifestation of the same underlying substance. This means that the new object – whether it be pictures, waves, snowflakes, or social groups – can in principle be predicted by the dynamics of its fundamental components. As applied to the mind-body issue, the weak emergence theory is ontologically monist because the mind *is* physical and not something other than physical. It implies the world is deterministic.

Australian philosopher David Chalmers, a critic of the weak emergence theory, contrasts this idea with *strong emergence*, which claims a dualist view.[34] For Chalmers, the mind's conscious experience arises as something special and unpredictable. By putting the neurons of the brain together in a certain configuration, something totally new and unpredictable emerges. In the weak emergence theory described by supervenience, Laplace's demon would be able to predict all future physical and mental states, including all conscious experience from the Big Bang to eternity. However, under Chalmers' strong theory, the demon would be

---

[34] Chalmers, David J. (2006) "Strong and Weak Emergence" In P. Davies & P. Clayton (eds.), *The Re-Emergence of Emergence: The Emergentist Hypothesis from Science to Religion.* Oxford University Press.

incapable of doing so in any world where consciousness exists because the thoughts of those beings would be completely unforeseeable.

It is tempting to think of consciousness as something which science will eventually solve strictly in terms of physical processes. Indeed, many scientists today assume this will be the case. They point to the fact that a hundred years ago, the theory of vitalism posited that all living things were animated by a unique life-force that was seen as something entirely different from the physical forces then known to operate in the universe; but today, with modern biochemistry and the discovery of DNA, the biological processes of life can be explained in terms of those forces. However, Chalmers argues against this view. He maintains that in the case of vitalism, the issue to be solved was itself physical, and it was therefore not unreasonable to conclude that the solution might lie in that ambit. But conscious experience, says Chalmers, really does appear to lie outside any physical realm.[35]

From Chalmers' perspective, consciousness arises *not* from the physical properties of the underlying matter, *per se*, but rather from its organizational structure. The matter is important only in the sense that it must be capable of conveying data, but what is crucial is the *organization* of the matter.[36] This implies that if it were possible to replace a person's carbon-based biological brain piece by piece with, say, silicon, while retaining the exact same neural network, then that person's conscious experience would continue unabated. What this means is that if one creates a substrate with enough neural cells or silicon chips or other information-carrying material, and arrange it in the right kind of *pattern*, then a mind spontaneously emerges.

---

[35] Chalmers, David J. (2003) "Consciousness and its Place in Nature" in S. Stich & T. Warfield, (eds.), *Blackwell Guide to Philosophy of Mind*. Blackwell.
[36] Chalmers, David J. (1995). "Facing Up to the Problem of Consciousness". *Journal of Consciousness Studies*. Vol. 2 (3), pp. 200–219.

The Views of Panpsychists

Panpsychism is a form of monism and one of the oldest ways of addressing the mind-body problem. At its core, it views the mental state as a fundamental feature of the universe, whereby *everything* has a mind-like quality, at least to some degree. Perhaps one of the earliest panpsychists was Thales, who after observing the motion of magnets, concluded they possessed a self-moving property which indicated a kind of mental property. Anaxagoras believed that to create any kind of mental substance from simple matter was impossible. He thus rejected a reductionist and materialist view of the mind and concluded that all the properties possessed by every object, including the most complicated of them all – the human brain – must be an intrinsic property of everything else.[37]

While Enlightenment philosophers such as Galileo and Newton adopted materialism,[38] a notable exception during that era was Baruch Spinoza, who embraced the more unified approach offered by panpsychism. Spinoza reasoned that all matter could be viewed as an attribute of either extension or thought, which for Spinoza was all one and the same kind of substance. The peak popularity of panpsychism was reached in the nineteenth century, notably among the philosophers William James and Arthur Schopenhauer. James adopted a neutral form of monism in which reality and matter are composed of a third underlying substance that is neither mental nor physical, but which nevertheless has mind-like *and* material qualities.[39]

Schopenhauer, on the other hand, believed that "Will" is a

---

[37] For a more detailed explanation of the views of Thales and Anaxagoras see Copleston, Frederick S. J. (1993) *A History of Philosophy Volume I: Greece and Rome*. Doubleday, New York. pp. 22-24 and pp. 66-71.

[38] Even though they viewed the world in mechanistic terms, they resisted the more radical materialism of, say, a Democritus, or the physicalist approach seen today, and thus resorted to dualism.

[39] James, William (1904) "Does Consciousness Exist?" *Journal of Philosophy, Psychology and Scientific Methods*, Vol. 1 (18).

fundamental property of all matter. Like his mentor Immanuel Kant, Schopenhauer believed that material objects exist outside of space and time in a so-called noumenal realm, but he contended that the *sine qua non* of this realm is what he called Will.[40] For Schopenhauer, Will is the basis of all cause and effect we observe in the material world of reality, and it is manifested in the physical forces of nature. It is also present in the biological processes of plants and animals, in animal instinct and behavior, and in human thought and action. This is expressed as a blind striving, in which all the forces in the phenomenal world of experience are in conflict with one another, in a constant preoccupation to survive; a "will to live."[41]

While panpsychism fell into decline in the twentieth century, it has nevertheless seen a recent revival due to physicalism's inability to provide a cogent explanation for how unconscious material processes can give rise to the subjective properties of individual conscious experiences – or qualia – an issue which David Chalmers calls "the hard problem of consciousness."[42] The most common panpsychist school regards consciousness as a fundamental property of all nature. In this view, all material things, from the most complex to the most mundane, have conscious properties of varying amounts, depending on their complexity and organization. At the high end lie human beings. Consciousness diminishes as one proceeds down the consciousness ladder to animals, microorganisms, plants, and finally, to inorganic matter. But even the most basic fundamental particles possess at least a minimal level. This means that man-made objects like computers, particularly if they involve advanced forms of artificial intelligence, might possess

---

[40] This is a single Will because in the noumenal realm there is no multiplicity or causality since space and time are absent.

[41] Schopenhauer, Arthur (2012) [1859] *The World as Will and Representation Vol III*. Digireads.com. Kindle Edition. Ch. 23, Loc 521.

[42] Chalmers, David J. (1995). "Facing up to the problem of consciousness." *Journal of Consciousness Studies*, Vol. 2 (3), pp. 200–219.

significant levels of consciousness.

Panpsychists see the different levels of awareness as arising in one of two ways. The first is by the addition of micro levels of consciousness possessed by the constituent matter, which when combined form a greater level of experience. In this view, the brain's awareness arises from the combination of its smaller parts. The second idea is that consciousness arises by the interaction of micro amounts of conscious-containing matter to produce an *emergent* higher-level of consciousness. Different orders of awareness can emerge if sufficient levels of complexity in the underlying structure are reached. However, whereas the emergentism of the physicalists sees consciousness as arising from complex structures of *un*conscious matter, panpsychist emergentism views the underlying parts of matter as already possessing at least a minimal level of consciousness. The latter is therefore a less radical form of emergentism because it does not require supervenience.

The American philosopher Thomas Nagel argues that because no one has provided a precise explanation as to how or why the conversion from the unconscious to the conscious domain takes place, the radical emergent property claimed by the physicalists is untenable. Therefore, for Nagel, panpsychism is a possible answer.[43] In response, some physicalists claim that the changeover is similar to the phase transitions seen in thermodynamics; for example, when a liquid changes to gas, or a liquid to solid. However, in the case of phase transitions, we can easily understand the process as a result of a distinct change in the atomic or molecular binding forces from one phase to another. The transition is therefore characterized by a single underlying concept – namely, the forces change with alterations in temperature and pressure. But as philosopher Galen Strawson explains, there is no such analogous concept to explain the transition from unconscious to conscious matter. Like Nagel, he

---

[43] Nagel, Thomas (1979) *Mortal questions.* Cambridge University Press. Ch. 13, pp. 181–195.

concludes it is possible that consciousness is the primary element of all matter.[44]

The idea that inanimate matter, even the smallest particle, can be conscious does seem very strange to most people. Should it be taken seriously? Panpsychists respond that many ideas we now take for granted, like the universal law of gravitation, electromagnetism, or relativity, would have seemed profoundly counterintuitive at one time or another. Intuition is not always the best guide to that which is true, they say.

Determinism versus Free Will

Solving the hard problem of consciousness would probably provide the answer as to whether or not human beings possess free will. If reductive physicalism or weak emergentism is true, then the human mind is almost certainly entirely determined by exogenous physical forces. If on the other hand, strong emergentism or panpsychism is the case, then free will is possible. But because there is little empirical evidence for any of these positions, they are clearly conjectural. Having strong convictions one way or the other does not prove one is correct.

If solving the mind-body problem appears to be intractable for lack of empirical evidence, then perhaps evolution can tell us something about free will. There is if course a fundamental difference between humans and animals because even our closest relatives – chimpanzees and bonobos – do not seem to have a will, at least not like ours. Given that our brains evolved from earlier species that did not have full agency, how did the change come about, and what made the difference?

---

[44] Galen Strawson (2006) "Realistic Monism: Why Physicalism Entails Panpsychism." *Journal of Consciousness Studies*, Vol. 13 (10–11), pp. 3–31.

3

The Evolution of Consciousness

First Steps Toward Perception.

It is clear that human beings are not the only animals to possess consciousness. It is also evident there are different levels of awareness. Consciousness is not merely the ability to register an input, which is something a computer can do. Rather, at its most basic level, it involves a sensation associated with that input which is called perception. It is likely that many animals can perceive things, but we cannot know for sure the degree to which any particular species has this ability. A worm is probably not conscious, at least not in the sense we understand it. For example, it probably does not feel pain. A fly, if it is conscious, is only barely so. Certainly, its eyes can register a flyswatter coming in its direction, but we do not know what it feels, if anything. On the other hand, a frog probably has a greater level of awareness, in that it can perceive objects fairly well and likely feels pain.

In higher-order animals and human beings, consciousness involves more than mere perception. It involves an ability to understand outside events in terms of cause and effect. Determining which animals can think in these terms is difficult, and a true understanding of causality is probably limited only to *homo sapiens,* but who can deny that a dog does not have at least some understanding in this regard? But human beings are unique because we have the additional capacity to think in abstract terms, and to be aware not just of our surroundings but to be *self*-aware. This is the

33

highest level of consciousness that we know of. How did this remarkable ability evolve?

The first evidence of self-replicating life is found in stromatolite fossils from about 3.7 billion years ago, which indicate the presence of cyanobacteria. Multicellular organisms arrived on the scene about 1.7 billion years ago, during a geologic eon known as the Proterozoic. Up to this point, no life on earth possessed a nervous system, although the components of an electrochemical mechanism were beginning to develop in organisms known as choanoflagellates. It was not until the beginning of the Cambrian period, approximately 540 million years ago, that the first neural arrangement appeared in a worm-like sea creature called a urbilaterian, and then in primitive mollusks and jellyfish, which possessed simple nerve nets that could respond to external stimuli.

The next level of complexity to evolve was a small brain mostly connected to the mouth and eyes, which had the capacity to respond to different degrees of stimulation. It is likely that the first animal to possess this arrangement was the trilobite, a marine arthropod somewhat similar to the present-day horseshoe crab. The crab's brain is merely a clump of neurons in the head, about the size of a pencil point, but what distinguishes it from more primitive species is that its neurons can amplify certain incoming signals, such as light hitting the eye. Where light is brighter, a stronger signal is sent to its brain which creates a rudimentary form of vision. However, it is doubtful the crab is truly aware of its surroundings. More likely, it simply responds instinctively.

Brain evolution continued in early forms of fish and is found in amphibians, such as frogs, today. The frog not only processes visual information, but it can also handle auditory and tactile signals. It is believed to do this by creating a three-dimensional representation of its surroundings that correspond in a one-to one relationship with specific locations on the surface of its brain, such that the animal can focus its attention on specific objects and respond to them.[45] For example, the frog can precisely pinpoint the location of a moving insect, and react to it, because the insect's location is tracked by a kind of map in the frog's brain. The ability of the frog to track a moving object in this way is called overt attention. Overt orienting allows the animal to respond to objects but only to those that directly stimulate the senses. If at any moment the frog loses sight of the insect, the only way it can be tracked again is if it accidentally ventures back into the frog's visual field. The frog probably has no memory of the insect even if it disappears for just a second. Obviously, there is still a long way to go before we see the kind of consciousness present in human beings.

Overt and Covert Attention

Mammals, which first appeared 300 million years ago, incorporate in their brains a similar structure to that of the frog, which directs behavioral attention towards specific points in space based on an inner representation or map of visual and auditory stimuli. However, this aspect of brain function is only one component in the mammalian toolbox. Like earlier neural networks, a mammal's brain prioritizes incoming sensory data by amplifying the strongest signals and dampening the weaker ones, but it does so in a massively more complex way. In comparison to the frog's brain, the mammalian cerebral cortex acts like a huge processor that creates multiple hierarchies of sensory information. Psychologist and neuroscientist Michael Graziano likens it to a spotlight that allows the animal to point its attention internally, not just at the incoming data, but on the data that has previously been received. This faculty is called covert attention.[46]

With covert orienting, mammals not only have the ability to

---

[45] Graziano, Michael S. A. (2019) *Rethinking Consciousness: A Scientific Theory of Subjective Experience*. W. W. Norton & Company. Kindle Edition, pp. 17-20.
[46] Ibid., pp. 35-36.

fixate on objects directly stimulating their senses, but they can also focus inwardly onto the workings of the brain itself. However, the cerebral cortex has billions of neurons firing at any given time, which is simply too much to spotlight all at once, so in a manner similar to the way in which overt orienting prioritizes sensory signals, the covert mechanism focuses on the internal data which are strongest. In doing this, a simplified account of the neuronal operations in the brain is created, which results in a low-resolution and somewhat fictionalized world model. This model is a dynamic and constantly shifting picture representing the animal's perceptions, and it is completely transparent. In other words, it is not recognized as a model as such; it just feels real. Graziano proposes that this covert attention schema is what allows the animal to have an experience, to remember, to concentrate on certain objects, and to respond. And this, he claims, is also the kind of consciousness and perception that we experience as human beings.

Consciousness in Space and Time

The philosopher Thomas Metzinger takes this idea one step further and suggests that this advanced model of perception and awareness is like a collection of shadows projected onto the walls of what he calls a "consciousness tunnel."[47] He compares this idea to the cave in Plato's famous allegory. In the Allegory of the Cave, Plato describes a group of people who have been chained to the floor of a cavern all their lives, so that all they can see is the wall opposite them. Behind them is a fire, constantly burning, which projects shadows onto the wall. The shadows are of people and objects moving in front of the fire that the prisoners cannot see directly.

Metzinger argues that the wall of the consciousness tunnel is like the wall in Plato's cave. We never sense objects as they really are, as

---

[47] Metzinger, Thomas (2009) *The Ego Tunnel: The Science of the Mind and the Myth of the Self*. Basic Books. Kindle Edition. p. 21.

things-in-themselves, because our sensory organs and our brains are too limited for that. Rather, our brains construct a three-dimensional shadowy image of the real objects "out there." We are like captives watching the shadows dancing on the walls. (Shadows are normally two-dimensional of course, so the analogy should not be taken too literally!). These are our perceptions, and the fire, says Metzinger, "is the incessant, self-regulating flow of neural information-processing, constantly perturbed and modulated by sensory input and cognition . . ."[48] Unlike Plato's cave, this process occurs in a tunnel because the shadows are generated as we move forward through the tunnel in time. Glancing back, we see our memories. Looking ahead, we imagine our future.

Somehow, this fabricated world seems coherent to us in three-dimensional space. Under normal circumstances, our brain allows for just the right degree of internal correlation, bringing our perceptions together so that a unified phenomenon emerges from a multitude of stimuli. If the neurons in the brain were to fire simultaneously, then our world model would not be synchronized. For some unfortunate people, this is precisely what happens in an epileptic seizure. The mind is completely overwhelmed. On the other hand, if every input were maximally differentiated, then all our perceptions would be a jumble of disconnected sensations. We would not be able to make sense of anything.

Our brain also unifies our perceptions in time. Our brains create the present – the Now – so that every event we experience as perception can be differentiated from memories of events that have happened in the past, and from circumstances we anticipate might happen in the future. Says Metzinger:

> The sense of presence is an internal phenomenon, created by the human brain . . . For certain physical organisms, such as us, it has proved viable to represent the path through reality *as if* there were an

---

[48] Ibid., pp. 22-23.

> extended present, a chain of individual moments
> through which we live our lives. [49]

Indeed, if we had no sense of the Now, then memories and anticipations would flow into present perceptions, and we would be immersed in a kind of hallucinogenic state.

This world model we create in space and time is completely transparent to us. We do not realize that it is only mere sketch of reality, because it is not necessary for us to do so. If evolution had somehow given us a brain that attempted to analyze every aspect of the billions of neuronal firings in our head, it is doubtful we would have a conscious experience at all. Instead of a unified experience, we would endure a mass of endlessly looping streams of data that would overwhelm us. It would be like staring right into the fire in Plato's cave and being blinded by it. This is why we turn away, so to speak, and look at the shadows on the wall. To be sure, the shadows are not an accurate rendition of things as they really are, but it is enough for us to get by on, such that we can navigate our world.

But this raises the question: if objects appear to us in space and time as we move through the consciousness tunnel, and yet the tunnel is the mental scaffolding onto which we project our reality, does this mean that space and time are themselves constructs? It would seem that they are. If that is the case, then they exist not "out there" as objective phenomena – as things-in-themselves – but rather as faculties of our minds with which we frame our perceptions and without which we would have no sensations. The issue of whether space and time could be internal phenomena, rather than a part of objective reality, is a very important one which I shall return to in a later chapter.

Animal Self-Awareness

When a cat stares at a mouse, it almost certainly has a perception of the animal within space in much the same way we do. But its

---

[49] Ibid., pp. 37-38.

perception of objects with respect to time is likely more limited. Therefore, while it probably has a consciousness tunnel built along the same lines as our own, the length of the tunnel is likely shorter and more truncated. Perhaps, it has the capacity to remember toying with the mouse from a short time ago, and maybe it can anticipate pouncing on it in the immediate future, but beyond that, much is driven by instinct. The cat does not frame objects within time to the same extent we do. Its brain, however, is clearly more advanced than that of the frog, which merely reacts to stimuli and probably has no memory or forward-looking ability at all. But while the cat's larger brain allows it to behave in such a way as to satisfy basic desires and accomplish forward-looking tasks, it is probably not aware it is doing these things. This is because it is not fully self-aware. It can focus on other objects like the mouse, which it perceives directly, but it cannot focus on its own mind; it does not see itself as having a consciousness that is separate from the world it perceives. In other words, it has no ego. And it does not have the faculty of ratiocination. It cannot think or act as humans do.

No doubt many animals like cats, dogs, horses, etc. have the beginnings of self-consciousness. Animals like this are aware of their own bodies as being separate from the bodies of others. But this sense of selfhood is limited. For example, animals cannot pass the "false belief" task, which most children can accomplish around the age of four to six, and which demonstrates an understanding of the existence of another mind separate from their own.[50] In the task, two boxes are placed in front of a child, and the child is shown a marble being placed in one of them. An observer, who witnesses this, leaves, and then in full view of the child the marble is transferred to the other box. The observer returns, and the child is asked which box the observer will look in first to find the hidden

---

[50] The classic experiment was conducted in the 1980s. See Wimmer, H and J. Perner (1983) "Beliefs about beliefs: Representation and constraining function of wrong beliefs in young children's understanding of deception." *Cognition*, Vol. 13 (1), pp. 103-128.

marble. The child passes the test if she says the first one. Variations on this task have been given to animals, and only apes show possible recognition that the observer has a separate mind.

In most animals, it seems, the internal spotlight in their brains cannot readily be controlled; it merely points to wherever the neuronal activity is greatest. Therefore, there is little or no regulation over thoughts, feelings, and desires. And while some animals almost certainly have memories and anticipations – take, for example, the excitement of a dog about to be taken for a walk – their bodily self-awareness does not include the awareness of a mind of their own that can alter the future, even though the anticipation of a future event might elicit certain strong emotions. Thus, they have no free will.[51] And because of this, and their inability to control their thoughts, they have no capacity to prioritize future goals or to choose means to achieve goals – except for those in the immediate present. Hence, they have no real agency.

Some animals, particularly primates, do seem to show the beginnings of agency. Chimpanzees are well known for using elementary tools – such as sticks for fishing termites out of a mound, and stones for cracking nuts – which might indicate a basic understanding of means and ends. However, whether or not these practices are evidence of true agency or merely copycat behavior passed down through the generations is not clear. Crows, which have

---

[51] A will is not required for a sense of bodily self, and this is the case even in humans. In the famous rubber-hand illusion, a volunteer is shown a dummy hand which appears to be connected to his body while his real hand is hidden from view. If both the real and the dummy hand are stroked simultaneously, the rubber hand starts to feel real, even though the volunteer has no control over it. (Metzinger, Thomas (2009) *The Ego Tunnel: The Science of the Mind and the Myth of the Self*. Basic Books. Kindle Edition. p. 3) Another experiment creates a whole-body illusion in which a subject wearing virtual reality goggles sees an image of himself from behind. This creates an of out-of-body experience in which the image of his body seen through the goggles seems, for the subject, to be his actual body. What this demonstrates is that bodily self and seeing self can be separated in human subjects, and free will or agency is not required for the bodily self. (Ibid., pp. 98-101).

particularly large brains compared to other birds, are able to fashion tools in novel ways in order to achieve specific goals. In one test, a team at Oxford University observed a New Caledonian crow bending a straight piece of wire which it then used to extract a food bucket out of a glass tube.[52] At first, researchers thought the bird had spontaneously come up with its own unique solution to a fairly complex problem. However, according to lead scientist Christian Rutz, it was later discovered that this seemingly innovative action was probably a combination of genetically controlled instinctual behavior and observation-based learning. To Rutz and his team it was clear there is much we simply do not understand about animal behavior.

The Human ego

Obviously, the human brain gives us additional capabilities that no other animals possess. In addition to language and the ability to think in abstract terms, we have an image of ourselves as having a separate mind, a self-aware model that includes the ego, which is firmly anchored in our bodily sensations and feelings. This self-model is just as transparent to us as our world model. Thus, we are not aware at the neuronal level of the mechanism by which we possess an ego, any more than we recognize the process that creates the perception of the world around us. It just exists.[53]

---

[52] https://www.theguardian.com/science/2016/aug/10/crow-that-bent-wire-to-retrieve-food-was-acting-naturally-scientists-discover

[53] There are certain neuropsychiatric conditions that can cause a separation between the will and body. For example, in alien hand syndrome, the afflicted individual has one hand that works normally, while the other "alien" hand seems to have a life of its own and moves without any voluntary control over its operation. This disorder is caused by a brain injury in which it is theorized there is a disconnect between the primary motor cortex that controls the wayward hand's movement, which remains fully operational, and regions of the brain concerned with agency. Thus, the alien hand does not move randomly; rather it appears to accomplish specific tasks, but it does so against the controlled thought or will of the individual. Biran, Iftah and Tania Giovannetti, Laurel Buxbaum, Anjan Chatterjee (2006)

The ego makes us markedly different from other animals. Nevertheless, human beings incorporate in their bodies many of the more basic features that have appeared along the evolutionary road to a fully self-aware mind. This is not surprising, because evolution rarely invents something new from scratch. Thus, humans have an autonomic nervous system, which controls operations like breathing, heart rate, digestive system, etc.; we have an overt attention schema, which allows us to follow something that catches our eye; we have covert attention and a consciousness tunnel, which allows us to perceive, think, feel, and remember; and we have an ego and a will.[54]

In the ontogeny of a human being – i.e., the physical and mental

---

"The alien hand syndrome: What makes the alien hand alien?" *Cognitive Neuropsychology*. Vol. 23(4), pp. 563–582.

[54] One popular model is the triune brain first proposed by Paul Maclean in 1970, which divides the human brain into three distinct functional areas that have emerged successively over evolutionary time. The oldest and most primitive part – the reptilian brain – includes the brainstem and cerebellum. The functional aspect of the reptilian brain includes the regulation of autonomic responses and other vital bodily functions, many of which operate reflexively. These include breathing, body balance, and heart rate, and many others. A more recent development along the evolutionary ladder is the limbic brain, which appeared in the first mammals. The limbic system includes the amygdala, hypothalamus, and hippocampus and is responsible for a wide variety of lower-order emotions, behaviors, and motivations. These include the fight-or-flight response, sexual arousal, and long-term memory of events that result in pleasant or unpleasant experiences. Much of the operation of the limbic brain is unconscious, but it nevertheless exerts great influence on emotions and behavior. The most recent development of the brain is the neocortex, found first in primates and reaching its culmination in human beings. The neocortex is responsible for all higher-order brain functions such as cognition and learning, and, uniquely in human beings, for language and a sense of self; the ego. While the triune model divides the brain into three distinct areas to emphasize its evolutionary development, all of these structures in human beings are interconnected and work in conjunction with one another. This is particularly true of the connection between the limbic and neocortical systems. Maclean, Paul D. (1990) *The Triune Brain in Evolution: Role in Paleocerebral Functions*. Springer Publishing.

development of an individual person from conception to adulthood – many of these features first emerge at various points before birth in the fetus as it grows in the womb. But the ego arises only after birth. 19th century philosopher William James wrote that infants are born in a state of "blooming, buzzing confusion."[55] Perhaps James was overstating the case, but it is certainly true that children are not born with an awareness of their own mind.

Emory University's Philippe Rochat has outlined five stages in the development of the self that occurs in early childhood.[56] Stage one is at birth, when babies already have a sense of their own body. A newborn who is touched on the cheek will immediately turn toward the stimulation, and often bring its hand to the area that is touched. At stage two, at about two months, infants begin to recognize themselves as a differentiated entity from the world around them. In one study,[57] two-month-olds were able to copy the tongue position of an adult – either left or right – with their own tongue, indicating they realized they had a body of their own which they could manipulate separately from that of the adult.

Stage three occurs at 18 months. This is when babies can first pass the mirror test by reaching for a painted mark on their body that is observable only in their reflection. With the exception of the great apes, dolphins, orcas, and some birds, this is something no other animals can do. It is also the point at which language starts to develop, perhaps not coincidentally, since language requires at least a minimal sense of self. At two to three years old – stage four – toddlers begin to realize the image in the mirror is "me," but there is still some confusion because they do not necessarily realize the "me" that *they* see is in fact the same person that everyone else sees.

---

[55] James, William (1890) *The Principles of Psychology Vol. 1*. Henry Holt & Co. New York (p. 488).

[56] Rochat, Phillipe (2003) "Five levels of self-awareness as they unfold early in life." *Consciousness and Cognition*, Vol. 12 (4), pp. 717–731.

[57] Meltzoff, A. N. and M. K. Moore (1992). "Early imitation within a functional framework: The importance of person identity, movement, and development." *Infant Behavior and Development*, Vol. 15 (4), pp. 479–505.

However, this confusion disappears during the final stage at around age four when a fuller self-awareness is reached. Children at this age become *self*-conscious and often respond to their reflection with shyness because, for the first time, they realize the "me" in the mirror is how everyone else perceives them.

Consciousness and self-awareness are found only in the uppermost branches of the phylogenetic tree of life. However, the evolutionary origin of these faculties can be traced back to the autonomic responses of simple organisms lying at the base of the tree. Simple organisms later evolved into more advanced creatures with overt attention, then to mammals with perception and consciousness, and finally to human beings with a full sense of self. The pinnacle of consciousness is a being that is fully self-aware with an ego, a being that appears to have a will of its own and can engage in purposive action, and a being that has language and the ability to think in abstract terms. But throughout this journey, at each stage of the process, the more advanced animal retains much of the more primitive mechanisms inherited from its evolutionary past.

Evolution has no goal, no telos, and it is never perfect. It proceeds haphazardly in whatever way works, in a manner that allows the individual to grow and reproduce. Through billions of years of evolution, our brains have developed to give us a particular human view of reality that allows us to navigate the world in ways that are beneficial to us as human beings, in keeping with the physical characteristics and functional attributes of our bodies. But since our bodies are not radically different from other animals, we still possess much of the autonomic, instinctual, and attentive mechanisms of other animal species.

Throughout geological time, there have been many ways that organisms have negotiated their surroundings, but in general, very few have developed something entirely new. Indeed, many of the more primitive species today still function extremely well by employing only very ancient mechanisms. This is because a simpler brain is not necessarily inefficient from an evolutionary perspective.

One only has to consider the incredible number of insects on this planet to recognize that fact. Indeed, a large brain with human self-awareness is not necessarily better. Rather, it is simply the adaptive mechanism that evolution has "chosen" for us in order that we may flourish and reproduce, given how the rest of our body has developed and given the environment in which we find ourselves.

We Are All Individuals

So, what can evolution tell us about the relationship between mind and body? The mind is defined by a property – namely, consciousness – which seems to emerge from matter. At a minimum, consciousness involves perception. The most advanced form of consciousness includes abstract thought, ratiocination, self-awareness, and the ego, which is fully developed only in mature human beings. In the course of evolution, many animals have developed perception, but the separation between those animals which possess it, and those which do not, is fuzzy. This is also true with regard to the development of consciousness in the human fetus. Babies are born with perception, but no one can say with precision at what point prior to birth this phenomenon first appears. The same might be said regarding the development of the ego after birth. The line between mere perception and full human consciousness is not clear-cut.

A mind that is self-aware possesses a will, but the degree of agency possessed by an individual continues to increase into adulthood. This is why we generally do not punish children for wrongdoing to the same extent as adults. Full agency is attained at about twenty-five years, at which point the capacity to control thoughts, emotions, and desires reaches a plateau. Babies are not born with a will or any degree of agency; they have only reflexes and instinct. But even in a mature individual, there are many functions of the brain and nervous system over which there is little or no control. These include instincts, reflexes, and in some cases, morbid desires and addictions. The ability to dominate and control these forces using "will power" varies with the individual and the circumstances. Some people have a stronger will than others, but there are moments in every person's life when it is hard not to give in to certain influences and temptations, some of which ultimately may prove harmful.

There is a distinction to be made, however, between desires and social pressures on the one hand, and reflexes and instincts on the other. The former is often dependent on the kinds of interactions one has during the course of one's life, and these influences vary according to time and place. Nurture as well as nature plays a role. The latter are strictly the consequence of evolutionary processes that have evolved precisely because they are almost always beneficial to the individual. Examples of reflexes include the cough and sneeze reflexes, the withdrawal reflex (e.g., from a hot stove), and the startle reflex (in response to a threat). Important human instincts include sexuality, the infant cry, maternal instinct, disgust (to avoid disease), fight or flight response, and so on.

It is clear from a study of the evolution of consciousness that in many situations the human will is tempered to a great degree by ancient mechanisms over which we have limited control. Nevertheless, while the will is not absolute in everything we do, there are many things where the will predominates, and this is what makes us markedly different from animals. Human action, which by definition involves *only* the will, is qualitatively different from mere animalistic behavior that is instinctual, autonomic, or reflexive. Unfortunately, what the investigation of evolution does *not* tell us is whether or not the will is genuinely free in the libertarian sense. The question that still needs to be addressed is this: Do human beings have real agency, or is free will merely an illusion implanted in our minds by evolution?

There is a way out of this quandary, involving a different methodology, and it shows that the will is indeed free. Just as importantly, it demonstrates that it is possible for the will *not* to be governed by strictly physical processes. Explaining how this is so has traditionally been a big stumbling block for those who argue against determinism, but this problem can be overcome. The methodology involves neither science nor philosophy nor religion – in other words, neither empiricism nor conjecture nor faith. Nevertheless, it reveals objective truths about the world, including the nature of our will.

In order to do this, it is necessary to examine the nature of reality and how we come to perceive and understand it. In particular, it is critical to challenge the notion, so prevalent today, that everything we know about reality can be explained empirically by employing the scientific method. For, as we shall see, science is not as cut-and-dried as many think it to be. There are some things that science can never know. There are boundaries, beyond which there exists a reality that is not phenomenal and which cannot be experienced; except in one very unique case. That exclusive circumstance provides the key to answering the question of why we have a will that is free and how we can have thoughts and choices with no prior cause. In the next chapter, I will try to make good on these statements.

4

Why We Have Free Will

Understanding the Nature of Reality

What is the nature of reality? This is a question that has puzzled philosophers for millennia. After the scientific revolution, classical physics assumed the world operated mechanistically within three-dimensional Euclidean space, and time was a separate entity that moved forward inexorably from the past through the present to the future. The world was a stage in which events played out in space and time. Classical mechanics suggested that matter was subject to certain forces that obey definite laws. And particles were constrained by continuity and locality – that is, they were continuous in their motion and could not interact with one another except under the influence of a force.

Einstein's special theory of relativity changed the concept of space and time. Einstein recognized that if two observers are moving relative to each other, they will differ in their measurement of how much time passes between two specific events. They will also disagree on the distance between the events and even on the order in which they take place. At the level of everyday experience, these differences are extremely small, but they are not zero, and they become much greater at very large scales. Therefore, the question arises: is there a variable upon which all observers can agree? More importantly, how must our concept of the universe change in order to accommodate it? The answer, according to Einstein, is the spacetime interval,[58] and it forms the basis of a four-dimensional non-Euclidean manifold called Minkowski space. Minkowski space implies that we live not in space or time, *per se*, but rather in a continuum called spacetime, in which every event corresponds to a coordinate within four dimensions. In spacetime, your birth corresponds to one point, your death another, and a sinuous line connecting the two points represents all the events in your lifetime. In spacetime, there is no past, present and future as we think of it. Rather, all events occur within a four-dimensional spatiotemporal continuum.[59]

Einstein's subsequent *general* theory of relativity greatly modified the concept of spacetime to take account of the effects of gravity. According to the general theory, we do not live in Minkowski space, which is static, but rather in a continuum called a pseudo-Riemannian manifold that curves from the effects of gravity.[60] Gravitational waves cause it to shake or ripple, and in the interior of black holes it even melts away, such that all that is left is a kind of spaceless "space." We cannot readily conceptualize this world, because the geometry which describes it is literally impossible to visualize other than by means of a three-dimensional translation. We do not possess the necessary mental apparatus.

If the world at very large scales seems strange, it becomes even weirder when quantum mechanics – physics at the level of atoms and below – is taken into account. Consider the issue of quantum non-locality – Einstein called it "spooky action at a distance" – in which two or more particles sharing the same wave function act together in a coordinated way, no matter how far apart they may be. The equations of so-called quantum entanglement appear to demonstrate that this correlation occurs instantaneously – i.e., faster

---

[58] The spacetime interval is described by the formula $\Delta d^2 - (c.\Delta t)^2$, where Δd and Δt are the differences in the distances and times between events, as recorded by the observers, and c is the speed of light.

[59] https://en.wikipedia.org/wiki/Spacetime

[60] https://en.wikipedia.org/wiki/General_relativity

than the speed of light – and that the particles can act together, even at immense distances from each other. Non-locality is a violation of the principles of classical physics and clearly defies our intuitive sense of nature, and yet the phenomenon has been verified by numerous experiments. Various theories have been put forward to explain the circumstance, perhaps the most prominent of which is the many-worlds theory, which maintains that different universes are created every time the particle adopts a different property from among the various alternatives. However, none of the proposals are overwhelmingly convincing.

Quantum mechanics seems very bizarre and beyond the realm of our everyday experience, and yet on a practical level, many of its behaviors have been verified by experimentation. The bigger problem is trying to integrate it with our other notions of the universe, particularly that of general relativity. While it is relatively easy to explain quantum theory in terms of flat Minkowski space, it becomes exceedingly difficult to resolve it with the gravitational effects of curved space. Of the four known forces in the universe, electromagnetism and the strong and weak nuclear forces are compatible with quantum mechanics, but gravity is not. Some physicists have tried to explain quantum gravity in terms of string theory. Others have adopted theories with exotic-sounding names like loop quantum gravity, spin foam theory, and causal dynamical triangulation.[61] Yet others have abandoned the search altogether and suggested that gravity is not real.

What seems clear is that the deeper physicists dig into the mysteries of the universe, the more complicated it becomes. Of course, each theorist is convinced he has the correct answer, and yet it seems that in each particular case the theory only serves to raise

---

[61] https://en.wikipedia.org/wiki/Loop_quantum_gravity
https://en.wikipedia.org/wiki/Spin_foam
https://en.wikipedia.org/wiki/Causal_dynamical_triangulation
https://physics.stackexchange.com/questions/545776/difference-between-loop-quantum-gravity-lqg-and-causal-dynamical-triangulation

as many questions as it answers. Increasingly, it appears there is a deeper level of reality that underlies space, time, and matter as we know it, and that our perceptions of reality, whether it be at the quantum level, the scale of relativity, or at the level of everyday experience, is an illusion.[62] Perhaps a paradigm shift – a term first introduced by the philosopher and historian of science Thomas Kuhn – is necessary in our thinking in order to herald in an entirely fresh approach.

For centuries, scientists have tended to think in reductionist terms. Epistemologically, reductionism holds that complex mechanisms can be understood in terms of more fundamental processes; for example, biological mechanisms can be explained in terms of chemical interactions, which in turn are reduced to physical processes. From an ontological perspective, reductionism involves the quest to explain all of reality in terms of a single fundamental substance or idea. Increasingly, however, philosophers and scientists are beginning to ask if this is the right approach, and some are considering its precise opposite, namely antireductionism or holism. This is the idea that the only way to fully understand a process is to consider it as a whole unit, because even if it is possible to break it down to its ultimate constituent elements, we simply would not be able to grasp its meaning.[63] From the ontological perspective, antireductionism claims that reality cannot be explained in terms of elementary particles, and it asks whether other principles such as strong emergentism are at play.

We may never know the true nature of reality; it might be that the human faculties are simply incapable of comprehending that

---

[62] This is the view of theoretical physicist Alexander Unzicker who argues that it ought to be possible to describe nature entirely in terms of mathematics without considering problematical constants, like the speed of light or Planck's constant. See Unzicker, Alexander (2020) *The Mathematical Reality: Why Space and Time are an Illusion.* Independently Published. See Ch. 10: "Alternatives to Space and Time" pp. 137-155.

[63] Nagel, Thomas (1998) "Reductionism and Antireductionism" *Novartis Foundation Symposium.*

which we are not equipped to discover. Perhaps, without a superintelligent mind and a more advanced sensory mechanism, we are trapped within a particular paradigm, the limits of which we have not yet reached, but beyond which we can never go. Even if artificial intelligence attains general superintelligence, which in turn develops novel means to detect hitherto unknown realities, we can never be sure we will ever comprehend the meaning of such discoveries. And even if we make our own minds superintelligent, at what point can we say we know the *true* nature and meaning of everything?

Evolution has equipped us to perceive reality and to conceptualize phenomena in a way that is suitable for negotiating our everyday surroundings as human beings. This is why at relativistic scales we can neither perceive nor conceptualize four-dimensional pseudo-Riemannian manifolds, and why at the quantum level, the behavior of particles is so bizarre that it contradicts all our notions of causality. We can describe these worlds in mathematical terms and employ specific models to predict real-world outcomes with remarkable success, but these results still have to be described in terms constrained by the perceptual, conceptual, and logical structure of our limited minds. What seems certain is that our phenomenal reality – the world we experience – is fundamentally different from the true reality that is "out there," whatever that might be.

In our everyday existence and in our interactions with other people, we are not aware of the quantum world, nor do we experience the effects of relativity. Our conscious experience is not the *true* reality "out there," but rather the reality framed by our limited perceptual and conceptual apparatus, which we cannot fundamentally change. It is reasonable to ask, therefore, what is the nature of that apparatus, and how does it affect our understanding of the world? And knowing this, is there anything it can tell us, not of the world outside of our mind, but rather of our thoughts in the world within?

Space and Time

The notion that phenomenal reality is not the true reality, but rather reality shaped by the mind, is not new. Perhaps, its most famous exponent was Immanuel Kant, one of the greatest philosophers of the Enlightenment. In Kant's great treatise on the limits and scope of human cognition, *Critique of Pure Reason* (1781), Kant set out to determine what we can and cannot know about reality using reason as a guide. It is without doubt brilliant and original. However, due to Kant's turgid prose, its difficult subject matter, and his inconsistent use of terms, it is often misunderstood and misinterpreted. Because of its difficulty, Kant published *Prolegomena to Any Future Metaphysics* (1783) in an attempt to clear up some of thc confusion. This much shorter work provides the key to his magnum opus and contains the main ideas in a way that is more accessible to the general reader.

Kant's argument is that all human beings are born into this world with what he calls "pure intuitions," through which we experience our phenomenal reality. The pure intuitions are *space* and *time*, and these are the means by which we perceive objects empirically. Space and time are not "out there," but rather exist only in the mind. And they are innate. Because we do not acquire these intuitions from sensory experience, they are *a priori*.[64] (I use the term "out there" to mean the reality outside of perception, as it really is, sometimes referred to as the world of "things-in themselves," or the "noumenal realm." This is in contrast to the world we perceive, the "experiential world," or the "phenomenal world.")

Now Kant has been criticized for this position because, ostensibly, it represents a type of *idealism* – a view that reality is in some way indistinguishable from the content of consciousness. There is a long tradition of philosophers who have subscribed to

---

[64] In The Critique of Pure Reason, Kant refers to the process of perception by superimposing the pure forms of intuition on sensation as the transcendental aesthetic.

various forms of idealism. Plato claimed that the true and essential nature of a thing is to be found not in the material object, but rather in an ideal Form that exists only in the mind. For example, chairs come in all shapes and sizes, but the ideal Form of a chair, according to Plato, is the *idea* of that object by which we recognize particular chairs in the physical world despite their many variations. In the early modern era, the idealist philosopher George Berkeley proposed a theory called "immaterialism," or what is now referred to as "subjective idealism." Berkeley claimed there is no existence at all independent of perception. For Berkeley, God produces all the ideas we sense, and all the regularities we perceive in Nature as described by classical mechanics are simply impressions implanted in our minds by Him.

However, Kantian idealism is of a very different kind.[65] Kant's view is *not* that our mind creates or alters reality, or that reality exists only in the mind. On the contrary, the world exists in a very real and objective sense, and our mind cannot change that in any way. Rather, Kant's position is that because of the limitations of our mind and the way in which we perceive and think, we can never know reality as it really is. More specifically, because the human mind is not infinite, all material objects in the world around us, as well as the physical laws applicable to those objects, are perceived and understood by us not as they are in themselves, but in a way that is uniquely human. An alien being with a different structure to its mind might perceive and understand the very same reality in an entirely different way. However, the basic common structure of the human mind makes us perceive the world in *our* particular way. The mechanism by which this occurs involves what Kant calls pure intuitions – i.e., innate properties of the mind – that include space and time.[66] Space and time do not exist "out there," but rather *only*

---

[65] Kant's ontological position is known as transcendental idealism.

[66] Kant, Immanuel (2016) [1783] *Prolegomena To Any Future Metaphysics*. Palala Press §10.

in the mind. We are born with these intuitions already in place, and they are the lens through which we perceive our material reality. Indeed, they provide the structure to our reality, without which we would perceive nothing.

Why did Kant believe space and time exist only in the mind? Consider an object, say a house, given to us empirically in space. (By space, I do not mean outer space, but rather the space in which objects appear extended.) We can easily imagine the absence of the object, no matter what it is. But we cannot imagine the absence of space. Consider also that empirically given objects can exist only in space. But if space lies in the noumenal realm – i.e., "out there" – then it can exist only in *more* space, and *that* space must exist in space, and so on, *ad infinitum*, which is an absurdity. Moreover, we can easily imagine the existence of many instances of any particular object. But we cannot conceive of multiple instances of space. This again seems to imply that space cannot be a thing-in-itself. Additionally, we think of space as being infinite because beyond space, there is only more space when we conceive of it. However, while we could in principle think of an infinite number of houses, no house can be infinite in its conception, as is the case with space. Taking all this into consideration, space cannot be empirically given; it cannot come into the mind from outside. Rather, it must already exist in the mind, and only in the mind, *a priori*. To claim otherwise involves multiple contradictions.

Similar kinds of argument can be made for the pure intuition of time. Any object given to us empirically always exists in time. We cannot conceive of it in any other way. But if time is given to us empirically, then it must also exist in time, and that time must exist in more time, and so on, which is an absurdity. Moreover, while we can imagine the existence of an object in time, we can only imagine its absence when it is *not* in time. However, we cannot imagine the absence of time. Therefore, time must exist only in our mind *a priori.*[67]

Recall the consciousness tunnel discussed in the previous chapter. The representations we witness in the three-dimensional "shadow" on the wall as we move through the tunnel is the image of reality that our brain creates in space and time. (I am alluding here to visual representations, but it could equally well apply to tactile or auditory sensations, which we also experience in space and time.) Our *phenomenal* reality – i.e., the reality that is experienced in our perceptions – is a low-resolution image of objects that are "out there" in the *noumenal* realm – i.e., the world of things-in-themselves.

Space and time do not exist in the noumenal realm; rather, they are intuitions which originate within the mind itself and which provide the framework – the walls of the tunnel, so to speak – onto which we project our perceptions from the sensory inputs flooding into the brain. Put simply, the tunnel is created by the mind from the intuitions of space and time, without which our minds would be filled with a jumble of disconnected sensations and our perceptions would be non-existent. Perhaps, in principle, it is possible that alternative perception mechanisms could exist, but the intuition of space and time is the machinery that evolution has created in us, as well as in many other animals.

Now suppose the physicists are right, and reality truly consists of four-dimensional spacetime, and our intuition of three-dimensional space and one-dimensional time is simply a poor man's version of the real thing. This does not alter the notion that space and time are purely in the mind. Even if the model of spacetime is accurate, it cannot change the concept we hold in our minds of space and time, nor alter the way in which we perceive reality. More likely, spacetime is not the compete answer, but merely an arbitrary way of conceptualizing the noumenal realm in a way that is translatable to a being that thinks the way we do. It might lie closer

---

[67] For a more detailed exposition on why Kant believes space and time are pure intuitions, see Ibid. §10-§13.

to the truth than mere human intuition, but in all likelihood, there is a deeper level of reality of which we are completely unaware and which we may never come to understand.

If space and time are intuitions that originate within us and are indispensable for perception, this raises the interesting question of whether anything can interfere with this mechanism. And indeed, there are various psychedelic drugs that can do precisely that. Take the drug dimethyltryptamine (DMT), which is found in many plants and is an active ingredient in the psychoactive brew known as ayahuasca made by several indigenous tribes in Amazonia. The effects of DMT when taken alone are fairly short-lived, but they are intense. They include a variety of visual, tactile, and auditory distortions, as well as severe time-dilation. There have been cases reported where subjects experienced hyperbolic geometry[68] and seeing impossible objects reminiscent of Escher drawings. In one study, conducted by psychiatry professor Rick Strassman, volunteers on high doses of DMT experienced bodily dissociation.[69] Neuroscientist Michele Ross describes her experience on DMT as though time and space were bending, as if falling into a black hole.[70]

Psilocybin, the active compound found in various "magic" mushrooms also creates spatiotemporal distortions, but it is particularly effective in inducing a state of time dilation.[71] Mescaline is another psychedelic that induces time dilation, and it is also associated with the visual flattening and geometricization of three-dimensional objects, such that they appear to have cubist-like properties. Indeed, cubist painters Georges Braque and Pablo

---

[68] https://qualiacomputing.com/2016/12/12/the-hyperbolic-geometry-of-dmt-experiences/

[69] Strassman, R. J. and C. R. Qualls, (1994) "Dose-response study of N,N-dimethyltryptamine in humans. I. Neuroendocrine, autonomic, and cardiovascular effects." *Archives of General Psychiatry*, Vol. 51 (2), pp. 85-97.

[70] https://www.youtube.com/watch?v=yqtvuzcL84M

[71] Wackermann, Jiri et al (2008) "Effects of Varied Doses of Psilocybin on Time Interval Reproduction in Human Subjects." *Neuroscience Letters*, 434, pp. 51-55.

Picasso, who were known to have taken mescaline, were probably influenced in their art by its psychedelic properties.[72]

Consider also the question of why something like geometry works. Why is it that all the truths of Euclidean geometry can be deduced from nothing other than intuition – *a priori* – without the backing of any kind of empirical information, and yet these truths are applicable to objects we experience? The answer seems to be that geometry involves constructions made in space, and space provides the structure – the scaffolding, if you will – that makes material objects appear extended. But precisely because space exists as an intuition in the mind, geometry is able to describe that scaffolding *a priori* within which these objects exist in perception. If space existed outside the mind, then geometry would not be able to do that; it would have no independent mind-connection to material objects.[73]

Even though the propositions of geometry are deduced axiomatically from first principles, they provide real knowledge about the world of experience – they are not tautologies. This is also the case for the propositions of arithmetic and pure mathematics. Kant maintained arithmetic works because the concept of number is based on the pure intuition of time, more specifically on the successive addition of units in time. And pure mathematics works because it involves both space and time. Like geometry, it has relevance to the phenomenal world, even though its truths are deduced *a priori*, precisely because space and time are pure intuitions

---

[72] Giannini, A. James (1997) *Drugs of Abuse*. Practice Management Corporation, University of Michigan pp. 137-141.

[73] It has been argued that since the development of non-Euclidean geometry, Kant's contention that geometry consists of the logical implications of the *a priori* intuition of space is erroneous. However, human beings do not perceive the world in anything other than Euclidean terms. We can certainly employ hyperbolic geometries as tools in various disciplines, but we do not normally experience everyday phenomena through hyperbolic spectacles. In attempting to comprehend non-Euclidean geometry, we still have to conceptualize it in our minds in Euclidean terms.

that exist only in the mind. This is why applied mathematics is able to describe the physical world of motion, even though it employs pure mathematical propositions that are deduced axiomatically without reference to the physical world.[74]

The Synthetic A Priori

Much of Kant's work was inspired by his older contemporary, the Scottish philosopher David Hume, who Kant famously declared had woken him from his "dogmatic slumber." However, Kant disagreed with Hume on many issues, and one of them was on how we come to have knowledge of the world. Hume maintained that only two kinds of proposition are possible: namely, those which are necessarily or axiomatically true, but do not increase our knowledge of the world, because they are true only by definition, which he termed "matters of relation;" and those which are empirically true, and therefore contingent, but which do indeed add to our knowledge, which he termed "matters of fact."

For example, a statement of the kind "all bachelors are unmarried men" is necessarily true, but it does not tell us anything we do not know already. This is because bachelors are unmarried men by definition, and the statement is a tautology. On the other hand, "the tree over there is an evergreen" tells us something new because the predicate "is an evergreen" is a fact not contained in the subject, "tree over there." We can only know the tree is an evergreen, empirically, from experience – i.e., by observing it, or from some other kind of evidence. But Kant's position was that these are not the only possible kinds of statements. Indeed, said Kant, there are some forms of knowledge that are *not* gained from ordinary experience that also add to our understanding of the outside world. And this gives rise to a completely different type of proposition.

---

[74] Kant, Immanuel (2016) [1783] *Prolegomena to Any Future Metaphysics*. Palala Press §10.

Now, in the Kantian terminology, statements which are tautologies are termed *analytic,* and those which say something new and relevant about the world are *synthetic.* In addition, knowledge which is axiomatic and *not* derived from experience is termed *"a priori,"* and that which *is* derived from experience – i.e., from evidence or by observation – is *"a posteriori."* Thus, "all bachelors are unmarried men" is *analytic a priori* (because it is a tautology not derived from experience) whereas "the tree over there is an evergreen" is *synthetic a posteriori* (because it tells us something new and it is derived from experience). Kant's position was that some forms of *a priori* knowledge do *not* lead to mere tautologies, but rather add to our knowledge of the world. This claim amounts to the fact that a third type of proposition exists – namely, propositions which are *synthetic a priori.*

But how is this possible? What kind of *a priori* knowledge – that is, knowledge which we neither experience nor observe from the world around us – could possibly expand our knowledge of that world? The answer is *inner* experience. And what is inner experience? It is knowledge we possess, innately; in effect, knowledge with which we are born and which we cannot deny, because to do so involves a contradiction. It is knowledge which everyone possesses, and which requires no experience of the world to obtain, and yet it informs us of the world. The two examples given above are the innate knowledge of space and time. We are born with these intuitions already instilled in our minds. Obviously, Kant could not have known anything about evolution, but it seems that evolution has given us – and presumably some other living things – a brain preprogrammed to conceptualize the world via these intuitions. And this is why, with nothing other than this inner experience and a process of logical deduction, these intuitions can give rise to the propositions of geometry and mathematics. These in turn have real relevance to the physical world. They involve no outer experience, and yet they are not tautologies. Rather, they are *synthetic a priori*.[75]

The methodology employed in geometry and mathematics employs neither empiricism nor conjecture nor faith, and yet it can reveal absolute truths with real world relevance. But geometrical and mathematical statements are not the only *synthetic a priori* propositions. As the great Austrian economist Ludwig von Mises showed almost two centuries later, similar kinds of statements can be made with respect to human action. All human beings are born with an intuition of what it means to act. Indeed, it is precisely because we involve ourselves in a contradiction if we attempt to deny that we act – because the very denial is itself an action – that the concept exists as inner experience. And from this axiom of action and a couple of minor empirical propositions, many of the laws in the social sciences can be deduced. Again, these laws, like those of geometry and mathematics are *synthetic a priori*, and yet they have real relevance to the world.[76]

We are now on the verge of discovering the process by which we can know whether or not the will is free. For it is this methodology – a methodology that bridges the gap between concepts contained in the mind and objects in the outer world – that can help us understand the nature of our thoughts and their meaning. Before getting to the crux of the matter, however, I need to examine the possibility of employing this process in the natural sciences, for only then can I hope to answer the fundamental question posited earlier; *viz.* how can the will be free?

Cause and Effect

David Hume concluded that even though it seems that physical objects adhere to a law of causal necessity, this law cannot be

---

[75] Kant, Immanuel (2016) [1783] *Prolegomena to Any Future Metaphysics*. Palala Press §2.

[76] Rothbard, Murray N. (1997), "Praxeology: The Methodology of Austrian Economics," in *The Logic of Action One: Method, Money, and the Austrian School*, by Murray N. Rothbard, Edward Elgar, pp. 58-77.

discovered empirically; it is only assumed from "custom or habit." However, Kant maintained that causality exists as an innate concept in the mind – a *"pure concept of the understanding"* – like the pure intuitions of space and time. Hume might have been right when he said we cannot *experience* cause and effect, but he was looking in the wrong place. From Kant's point of view, human beings are, in essence, preprogrammed to see causality in the natural world of phenomena, not because causality exists "out there" or because it can be experienced, but rather because it exists within us, as an innate concept like space and time.[77] Without it, we would have perceptions but not understand what they mean. For us as human beings and probably for some animals, it makes sense of the world.[78] It is how we understand nature. Why did Kant think causality was innate? Consider the following:

To know that an event is caused, we must somehow be able to distinguish between (1) a series of perceptions which change because our perspective changes (for example, looking at the door of a house, then the roof of the house, and then back to the door again) and (2) a series of perceptions which change because of an event having taken place (for example, seeing a star in one position followed by seeing the same star in another position). The question to ask is: how can we tell the difference? The answer is that the perceptions in (1) are reversible because they are subjectively ordered, but those in (2) are not, precisely because their order is objective. In other words, we can switch to a view of the roof and then back to the door any time we want, but we cannot reverse seeing the position of the star. The only way we can view the star in the original position is for another caused event to take place. But the irreversibility of such events cannot be known from the

---

[77] Kant, Immanuel (2016) [1783] *Prolegomena to Any Future Metaphysics.* Palala Press §27-32.
[78] These are derived from logical rules; axiomatic principles we can recognize, because they exist as a consequence of the logical structure of the mind. The law of causality is derived from the logical rule, "if A then B."

perceptions themselves. And if irreversibility cannot be known from perceptions, and yet this is a necessary condition to know an event has been caused, the concept of cause and effect must be innate or *a priori*.

While newborn children seem almost immediately to possess the intuitions of space and time, the concept of cause and effect takes a little longer to develop. Nevertheless, from a very young age, children are able to recognize causality in their daily lives. Consider a young child who grabs a cup and accidentally spills the drink over herself. The first time this happens, perhaps she does not make the connection between holding the cup upright and the disagreeable feeling of wet clothes. But after a few mishaps, she notices that if the cup is not held in the right position, then wet clothes will follow. Sometime after that, she understands that the cause of the wet clothes is the liquid spilling from the cup. This understanding is innate. And it is a principle that underlies all of natural science.

In the natural sciences, we unite various perceptions by employing the hypothetical, "if A then B." If B happens after A often enough, then a hypothesis can be made where we say "A causes B." Hume assumed we arrive at this process through induction – from "custom or habit" – but as the 20th century philosopher Karl Popper showed, we arrive at the conclusion that A causes B precisely because we expect to see it. We look for repetitions in nature and then find them. We do not wait for regularities to occur; rather, we "impose" them on the world because causality is innate. The laws of nature we discover in this way add to our knowledge and yet they rely on experience (empirical observations) – i.e., they are *synthetic a posteriori*. However, empirical observations are based on subjective judgments of perception, and these can be wrong, even ones that are seemingly certain. This means that laws of nature can never get to the absolute truth; they are always falsifiable, even something like the law of gravitation. And it is the very fact of falsifiability that makes them scientific.

Nevertheless, a few natural laws can be deduced logically

directly from pure concepts, *a priori*. (Kant outlined twelve pure concepts, of which the law of causality is probably the most important.) Laws deduced in this way are therefore *synthetic a priori* and analogous to the laws of geometry and mathematics. Examples include the conservation of matter, the law of inertia (Newton's first law), and the equality of action and reaction (Newton's third law). From the perspective of classical mechanics, these laws are absolutely true because it is logically impossible to deny their validity.

It is the case, however, that at the levels of the very small and the very large, these laws break down or have to be modified. For example, in order to comply with quantum mechanics and special relativity, the law regarding the conservation of mass has to include the concept of energy under the principle of mass-energy equivalence. Does this mean that our intuitions are wrong? Not at all. While quantum mechanics and relativity alter our understanding of the phenomenal world, the laws of classical mechanics are still absolutely valid in our everyday lives.[79] The pure concept of causality has been endowed in us by nature, *a priori*, in order that we may understand the world from the perspective of normal experience. Evolution does not require us to experience nature at the quantum level. The important point here is that we possess a mind that permits us to understand nature in a way in which cause follows effect, not because that is how nature in the noumenal realm operates, but rather because that is how *we* operate.[80] And it is precisely because we are neither equipped nor

---

[79] Some may ask, how can laws like these be absolutely valid, when quantum mechanics rules that out? However, this is looking at it from the wrong point of view. The question is not what is actual reality but what is our reality. If causality is *a priori*, then whatever is deduced axiomatically from that concept must be logically valid, whether or not it conforms to certain situations we would not normally encounter. What matters is that causality is an innate concept we are given by nature, and since this axiom is verified by the law of noncontradiction, its logical implications must be valid.

[80] As Kant states: ". . . we ourselves bring into the appearances that order and

required to handle objects at the level of the very small or the very large that our intuition breaks down when we observe certain quantum effects or when we try to visualize the world on the scale of relativity.[81]

Reason

As mentioned above, we *perceive* the world by applying the mind's *a priori* intuitions of space and time to sensations. Our perceptions form the basis of consciousness and give us an experience of the world. Most animals have at least some degree of spatiotemporal awareness. We form *judgements* by applying the mind's innate sense of cause and effect to these experiences. Higher-order animals such as mammals and birds have at least some degree of this kind of consciousness.

Reason, however, goes beyond perception and judgement. As far as we know, it is an ability possessed only by human beings. In contradistinction to every other living thing in the animal kingdom,

---

regularity that we call nature, and moreover we would not be able to find it there if we, or the nature of our mind, had not originally put it there . . . Although we learn many laws through experience, these are only particular determinations of yet higher laws, the highest of which (under which all others stand) come from the understanding itself *a priori*, and are not borrowed from experience, but rather must provide the appearances with their lawfulness and by that very means make experience possible. The understanding is thus not merely a faculty for making rules through the comparison of the appearances: it is itself the legislation for nature, i.e., without understanding there would not be any nature at all." Kant, Immanuel (1998) [1781] *Critique of Pure Reason*. Translated by Paul Guyer & Allen W. Wood, Cambridge University Press. (A125–126).

[81] Indeed, the terms "very small" and "very large" imply extension in space, but since space exists only in the mind, and allows us to perceive the world only at the level of everyday phenomena, it has little meaning beyond the boundaries of normal experience. Time also falls into this category, as does the concept of causality. Since we cannot have any knowledge of the underlying true reality – precisely because the noumenal realm is not accessible to us – and since our mental apparatus is designed to work only at the level of normal experience, our limited "everyday" intuitions and concepts fail at quantum or relativistic scales. The conclusions we reach are perplexing and contradictory.

it is the faculty of the mind that drives us to seek answers to problems that cannot otherwise be experienced or understood. Reason helps us to form *ideas* by thinking abstractly about concepts which cannot be provided by perception or judgement alone. The process of ratiocination involves deduction, which employs logical rules which are themselves intuitive. Reason can be used to deduce the logical implications of the intuitions of space and time, and this gives us the disciplines of geometry and pure mathematics. Reason can be used to deduce the logical implications of the concept of causality in the physical world, and this gives rise to the study of pure natural science. And reason can be employed to deduce the logical implications of human action – from the axiom of action – which gives rise to the study of praxeology.

Kant posited that reason also gives us the study of metaphysics.[82] But here it is limited. This is because, for the most part, reason can extend our understanding only of the phenomenal world in which we live – the world of experience – given the limitations of the human mind. It cannot help us in any great way with regard to the noumenal realm – the world of things-in-themselves. Once we go beyond the phenomenal into the realm of, say, quantum mechanics and relativity, it starts to seem *un*reasonable. We can certainly experience the *effects* of these worlds by, for example, observing the behavior of subatomic particles or measuring the effect of time dilation, and we can put some of these effects to good use, but we can neither experience nor fully comprehend these worlds themselves. We can only perceive and comprehend their effects, and only in terms of our own intuitions and concepts. We cannot really get to grips with what they are.

This is because reason is applied to intuitions and concepts of the mind – namely, space, time, and causality – which are *a priori*. They exist *only* in the mind. Reason assists in completing our

---

[82] Kant, Immanuel (2016) [1783] *Prolegomena to Any Future Metaphysics*. Palala Press §40-42.

understanding of phenomena because phenomena are presented to us in terms of our own intuitions and concepts, but it cannot help us truly understand the world that lies behind the phenomena, precisely because we have no possibility of experiencing it ourselves. And this is because things-in-themselves in the noumenal realm do not exist in terms of space, time, and causality, etc.; rather, they are *out* of space and *out* of time and *not* subject to cause and effect.

Attempting to use reason to deduce the logical implications of space, time, and causality, as though they exist as things-in-themselves, when in fact they are products of the mind, gives rise to puzzling paradoxes and contradictions. Consider these four examples:[83]

1. On the one hand, everything has a beginning and an end and is limited. On the other hand, time never began and will never end, and space extends forever.
2. On the one hand, everything is made up of fundamental particles. On the other hand, such particles must be made up of even more fundamental particles, and so on.
3. On the one hand, we feel as though we are the originator or first cause of our own thoughts. On the other hand, since every event has a cause, our thoughts must be determined.
4. On the one hand, since every effect has a cause, there must be a first cause of the universe called God. On the other hand, cause and effect is an infinite regress and there is no God.

It is the third paradox that provides the key to answering the fundamental questions posed earlier: Do we, or do we not, have free will? And it also reveals why the "hard question" of consciousness is so difficult to answer. Suppose we analyze the mind scientifically, not our own mind, but the mind-in-general as a phenomenal object, like any other object in the phenomenal realm, in order to explain the

---

[83] These are known as Kant's antimonies. (Cosmological Ideas) Kant, Immanuel (2016) [1783] *Prolegomena to Any Future Metaphysics*. Palala Press §51.

brain's operation. We observe the seat of the mind – the brain – exists in space and time, and this brain consists of billions of neurons connected by synapses and axons into networks. We then make judgements about how and where particular experiences and thoughts are generated, and we call these areas of the brain the neural correlates of consciousness. We reason that thoughts and consciousness must be the product of a physical process. In addition, since all physical processes are necessitated by prior events, we conclude that the brain's operation must be caused, and thoughts are therefore determined. This is the perspective of the physicalist.

However, when we think about our *own* mind, we can neither perceive nor judge it as a phenomenal object. Our sensory organs do not permit it, and even if they did, we could never apply the pure intuitions and concepts of the understanding – space, time, and causality – to themselves. While our own mind is not subject to phenomenal experience, I propose that it is nevertheless the one object in the universe we are in contact with as a thing-in-itself; the one thing in the noumenal realm that is not "out there" but rather "in here." As such, we are aware that our thoughts lie outside of space and time, and that therefore our consciousness is composed of a different substance to the tangible and extended objects we perceive through sensation. Moreover, since causality is also applicable only to the phenomenal realm – indeed, it is merely part of the overall framework onto which we hang our phenomenal reality – we realize that our thoughts are not subject to cause and effect either. We realize this precisely because the experience of our own minds lies outside of phenomenal reality in the noumenal realm, where there is no cause and effect. *In other words, our thoughts are self-caused. We thus realize our thoughts are free; we have free will.*[84]

This experience of our thoughts as being incorporeal and free is *not* an illusion, for we alone experience our mind as a thing-in-itself. If anything is an "illusion," it is the other objects of our world,

---

[84] This is not Kant's claim but rather my own.

including our own bodies, which we can only experience phenomenally. The conscious and free entity that is the human mind gives rise to the idea of self; "I think, therefore I am." Thus, by having reason, human beings not only have free will, but they also gain self-awareness and an ego.

We are not born with reason; rather, it develops slowly with time. This is why newborns have no sense of self. Even two-year-olds lack comprehensive self-awareness precisely because they have very little reason. Only by about the age of four do children develop reason to a level where the ego becomes apparent. The same is true for the will. Very young children are not free. Babies have no free will. In this respect, and this respect only, their consciousness is similar to that of non-human animals. However, as the ability to ratiocinate develops, so does the will along with the ego. This continues into young adulthood until the mature mind comes into being, a mind with the maximum power of reason and the greatest control over base instinct. This is why we do not impose the same standards of behavior and morality on children as we do on adults.

Rationality marks us as human. It is true that the very young or the very old or the incapacitated might be unable to think clearly or not be able to think at all, but as a species we possess reason, and it is this that distinguishes us from all other animals. Of course, among the human population of the planet, there are a wide variety of personality types, and there are large differences in intelligence, but these differences are relatively small compared to those between the average of our species and the average of others.

A few animal species might have very primitive forms of reasoning, a very rudimentary sense of self, and extremely limited forms of communication, but none come even close to the level of rationality, sense of self, and language ability that human beings possess. None can think or will or engage in purposive action like we do. All races and both sexes have the same logical structure of the mind. As regards *homo sapiens,* we are all sapiens. There is no such thing as polylogism. In this respect, a man in Mongolia is no different than a woman in Mexico. Different peoples might have very different customs, habits, traditions, and abilities, but basic human perception, understanding, and rationality is the same the world over. As a species, reason makes all human beings free, no matter where we come from or who we are.

Addendum

If the mind is the true reality, then it would seem that the fundamental essence of the universe is not matter and energy as such, but rather consciousness, and matter and energy are merely the phenomenal representations of this fundamental essence. It would imply that everything we witness in the phenomenal realm is really a form of consciousness or, more precisely, contains quanta of consciousness. In this view, the smallest unit of this substance does not possess perception or awareness, and certainly not self-awareness – at least not as we know it – and even large aggregations do not do so either unless arranged in a particular way. Thus, for example, a rock is certainly not aware, but if a collection of matter is arranged in the right kind of pattern or configuration, such as a neural net, then awareness – and even self-awareness and a will – can emerge. This is the so-called weak emergentist position of panpsychists mentioned in a previous chapter.

If this is the case, then matter, energy, and the physical laws are simply representations and interpretations of the underlying reality – namely consciousness – by a being that possesses the intuitions of space, time, and causality. Fully aware entities from another planet, with minds that possessed entirely different intuitions and concepts other than those that exist here on earth, would experience phenomena not as matter and energy, but rather as some other substance. And the laws which would apply to that substance would not be the physical laws that we witness, but rather laws that made sense to them. Their own phenomenal experience would be very different from ours, but the underlying property of consciousness would be the same.

Consider the following analogy. The electromagnetic spectrum consists of electromagnetic radiation of different wavelengths that range from very low frequency radio waves through microwaves, infrared, visible light, x-rays, and ultra-high frequency gamma rays. As humans, we cannot perceive most of the spectrum. We can only sense the part of it that comprises visible light. Moreover, we do not perceive light waves as such, nor the particles of light known as photons. Rather, we have an experience of light that is governed by our sensory apparatus, namely, the eye and the visual processing centers in the brain. We cannot perceive directly the rest of the spectrum at all, but we know it exists because we have instruments that can detect radio waves and gamma rays that present the information in a way we *can* perceive. For example, while radio waves are invisible to the human eye, they can be translated by an oscilloscope into a pattern we can see on a screen. Gamma radiation can be detected by a Geiger counter that translates the particles into clicks we can hear, and so on.

Continuing this analogy, consider the nature of reality as a spectrum of sorts, from very large relativistic scales at one end to very small quantum levels at the other. And instead of mere perception, include *conception* as a factor. We can neither perceive nor conceive four-dimensional spatiotemporal continuums or quantum non-locality. We cannot perceive them, because we do not have the sensory apparatus, and we cannot *conceive* them either, because we do not have the conceptual framework. Four dimensional manifolds and quantum non-locality violate all our intuitions and concepts of space, time, and causality.

However, we know these areas of reality exist because even though they violate our concepts, we can translate them into a form we can understand, not with physical instruments, but rather with mental instruments or mental translations. These mental translations do not enable us to conceptualize relativity or quantum mechanics directly, any more than physical instruments allow us to perceive radio waves or gamma rays directly, but they give us a mental understanding that lets us know what their properties are in terms of our own concepts.

What we experience directly is only a part of this spectrum, namely, the world at the human scale of everyday experience. But given the properties of the rest of the spectrum, we can conclude that our everyday conceptual understanding of this reality is not as it really is, any more than our perceptual experience of light is that of waves or particles. Matter and energy, as well as the concepts we hold of the physical laws and the law of causality, all exist as mere shadows in the noumenal realm of our own consciousness, presented to us as phenomena and framed by the particular perceptual and conceptual apparatus of the human brain.

PART II

How Human Nature Influences

Our Actions

5

Social Cooperation

Free Will is Guided by Instinct

There is one object in the universe, and one object only, which we can relate to as a thing-in-itself, and that is our own mind. As human beings with the power of reason, we realize our thoughts originate in us; they are *self*-caused precisely because we alone experience them in the noumenal realm. Because our mind is not assessed by the faculty of understanding but rather by the power of reason, it lies outside of cause and effect, and is thus free. Only when the mind is examined as a phenomenal object does it appear to be determined. But in the noumenal reality – the true reality – it is free. And it is genuine freedom; it is *not* an illusion.

While animals merely behave through reflex and instinct, reason and free will gives human beings the ability to make choices and engage in purposive action in ways that animals cannot. It gives us the foresight to imagine the consequences of our actions so that we can plan ahead. It allows us to build tools that enhance our productivity. Reason also permits us to realize that with the division of labor, we can greatly increase our output over and above that we could each achieve individually. For most animals, the resources consumed are almost entirely restricted to that found in nature, so that what one animal takes, another is deprived to an equal degree. But through specialization and the division of labor, human beings are able to increase the size of the pie, so to speak, so that the quantity and variety of goods produced are greater than they would otherwise be. Life ceases to be a zero-sum game.

Nevertheless, even though we have free will, it is important to realize there are many things that humans do that are instinctual, whether we know it or not. We cannot deny our evolutionary inheritance. Our free will does not have absolute dominion over all bodily functions. Moreover, it is guided and moderated to a great extent by various instinctual needs, the primary ones being the impulses to live and reproduce, which is something we have in common with all other living things. This drives a range of other needs necessary for our survival, including sexual desire. Another instinct is social cooperation. We are not the only living things to engage in some form of cooperative behavior. For example, dolphins, whales, and wolves, all cooperate in various ways. These animals probably understand cause and effect to some extent and may even have some very rudimentary ability to think rationally. But it is clear most of their impulse to behave socially is guided by instinct. Ants, termites, and bees also cooperate, and their social behavior is driven entirely by instinct or reflex. It is clear, therefore, that social cooperation is *not* a purely rational activity. Indeed, the propensity to cooperate in a basic form is a product of natural selection, and almost certainly evolved in early hominids before modern humans developed reason and volition. Natural selection has given most human beings a brain that *wants* to cooperate instinctively.

The instinct to cooperate is fundamental to all social species, but especially so for human beings, given how vulnerable we are by ourselves in a state of nature. Very few people could survive, naked and alone in the wild and without any kind of tools, even if they found themselves in a natural paradise full of resources. Most animals would be very comfortable with such plenty. But humans generally need other humans to divide the labor according to expertise, or to assist in creating goods too labor intensive for one person to accomplish, or to learn from, or simply to provide moral support and comfort.

However, as rational beings with a will that is free, we are the only species that can satisfy our basic needs in various ways of our choosing. We are not limited to mere behavior by yielding to an unthinking impulse. We can moderate the impulse and even act to deny our instincts completely. We can abstain from food, deliberately put ourselves in harm's way, abstain from sex, choose not to cooperate, and even choose to die. Moreover, we can formulate rules of conduct to impose on ourselves and on others. We can choose to act aggressively or not. The irony is that reason and free will also give humans the ability to act in ways that undermine our instinctive disposition to collaborate, even though it is fundamental to our existence.

How Instinct Evolved

Evolution rarely invents something radically new from scratch. Mutations in genes can cause large changes in an individual's offspring, but at the population level, the process of natural selection is usually – though not always – a gradual process.[85] Moreover, if we look at the morphology of plants and animals that exist today, many retain features inherited from their ancestral past. Even the most complex organisms – including humans – possess many similar components to those of more primitive species. Nature does not necessarily discard the simple, in favor of the complex, over evolutionary time. If simple mechanisms continue to serve a purpose, nature preserves them. If simple organisms remain adapted to their environment, natural selection does not discard them. Indeed, if all simple organisms were eliminated, then the food

---

[85] This concept was first explained in Fisher's 1930 book The Genetical Theory of Natural Selection and in Haldane's The Causes of Evolution in 1932. But the postmodern synthesis now claims that evolution can occur very rapidly due to a variety of epigenetic, cultural, ecological and behavioral factors. For an explanation on the difference between the modern and postmodern synthesis, see New Scientist (2017) *How Evolution Explains Everything About Life.* (Instant Expert) Quercus, Kindle Edition. Ch. 11, Loc. 2640-2658.

chain would cease to exist, and more advanced animal species could not survive.

Sometimes evolution even works in reverse. For example, eyeless cave fish are descended from fish that had eyes, and gutless tapeworms are descended from a species that had a digestive system.[86] And on a larger scale, sometimes whole classes of very complex organisms are condemned to the grave when they cease to be properly adapted to their environment. One need only think of the dinosaurs.

Nevertheless, over many millions of years, multi-cellular organisms have in general become more complex. One of the most prolonged and extended advancements, with the greatest increase in complexity, is the animal brain. The first step in the brain's long evolutionary development was a simple arrangement of neurons – as seen today in animals such as jellyfish, sponges, and earthworms – which allowed for reflexive bodily movement in response to certain external stimuli. This was followed by neurons clumping together into a brain-like bundle, which, when coupled with sensory organs such as eyes, allowed the animal to navigate its surroundings. The first species to do this was probably the trilobite, mentioned in an earlier chapter. In addition, gene mutations that gave rise to more complex neuronal arrangements, coupled with changes in body physiology, led to other reflexes and instincts, such as eating, defecating, and copulating. Many of these behaviors occurred in different branches of the phylogenetic tree at different times, which means that similar kinds of traits evolved among dissimilar classes of animals independently, a phenomenon known as convergent evolution.

As geological time proceeded, more sophisticated instincts of widely varying kinds developed. Consider spiders weaving webs, birds building nests, salmon returning to their spawning grounds, and humans learning to walk. These impulses represent a kind of

---

[86] Ibid, Ch. 6, Loc 1351.

genetic "knowledge" that has been passed down from generation to generation over millions of years; knowledge that has gradually broadened and expanded in concert with the changing brain function and morphology of the species and its adaptation to the environment. Instinct is a drive to engage in these behaviors precisely because it satisfies some kind of urge. We do not know if spiders or other insects feel anything. However, birds and mammals have pleasure and pain receptors in their brains, and the most recent research shows that fish do as well.[87] In these animals, some instincts are probably driven by an uneasy or unpleasant feeling when failing to undertake the behavior, or by pleasurable sensations when the opposite is the case.[88] Others seem to occur in response to neither pleasure nor pain and may be purely reflexive.

The development of the prefrontal cortex in mammals gave rise to ever more sophisticated brain functions, including short-term memory, predictive capacity, and elementary decision-making. Some species, notably *homo sapiens*, gained empathy and long-term memory. All of this contributed to the instinct that many mammals have of social cooperation. But it is clear that social cooperation is not restricted to animals with a large brain. Bees, ants, and termites all cooperate, and do so to a greater degree than mammals. In fact, their cooperation is so great that they will readily sacrifice themselves, even if it means death, in order that another of their number can live. So, what is the common denominator?

Group Selection, Behaviorism, or Selfish Genes?

Social cooperation within a group necessarily requires a degree of selflessness, which might appear to be antithetical to the animal's

---

[87] Douglas, Jamie M. et al, (2017) "Pain in Birds: The Anatomical and Physiological Basis." *The Veterinary Clinics of North America Exotic Animal Practice*, Vol. 21 (1), pp. 17-31.

[88] Halper, Phil, Kenneth Williford, David Rudrauf and Perry N. Fuchs (2021) "Against Neo-Cartesianism: Neurofunctional Resilience and Animal Pain." *Philosophical Psychology*, Vol. 34 (4), pp. 474-501.

survival. If natural selection implies survival of the fittest, it would seem that individuals who behave in a cooperative manner would easily be outcompeted by less altruistic members of the group who would eagerly accept their generosity without returning the favor. Charles Darwin's answer in the *Descent of Man* (1871) was that if a tribe happened to have a few individuals willing to make personal sacrifices, then their contribution would make the tribe more successful than other groups whose members were more self-interested. This would enable the altruistic group to grow, produce more cooperative descendants, and dominate the selfish tribes which would eventually disappear.[89] Among evolutionary biologists, this idea was still popular until the middle of the 20th century. The general belief was that natural selection of this sort – later known as naive group selection – could apply to animals as well as humans and was more important than individual-level selection.

In the early part of the 20th century, a new consensus was emerging among some scientists that genetics played no role at all, at least in human behavior. Social scientists of the era maintained that the human mind was a *tabula rasa*, a view that was originally held by John Locke over two centuries earlier. Emile Durkheim, whom many consider to be the father of modern sociology, claimed that human nature was "merely the indeterminate material that the social factor molds and transforms."[90] For Durkheim, people were surrounded by various cultural phenomena that had an independent existence – he termed them "social facts" – which

---

[89] According to Darwin, "There can be no doubt that a tribe including many members who, from possessing a high degree of the spirit of patriotism, fidelity, obedience, courage, and sympathy, were always ready to aid one another, and to sacrifice themselves for the common good, would be victorious over most other tribes, and this would be natural selection." Darwin, Charles (1871) *The Descent of Man and Selection in Relation to Sex.* Appleton & Co. New York, pp. 159-160.

[90] Durkheim, Emile (1966) [1895] *The Rules of the Sociological Method.* Transl. Sarah A. Solovay & John H. Mueller, George E. G. Catlin (Ed) Collier-Macmillan Canada, Ltd., Toronto, p. 106.

directly exerted a coercive influence on their personality and temperament. Echoing Durkheim, the anthropologist Franz Boas contended that human behavior was not innate, but rather learned, and driven by the cultural milieu in which the individual was immersed. Cultural anthropologist Margaret Mead, who based most of her ideas about the origins of personality on field work conducted in a number of Pacific islands, also concluded that character formation was almost exclusively driven by culture.[91]

In 1948, Harvard psychologist B.F. Skinner, another pioneer in this field, published the novel *Walden Two*, a fictional account about a supposedly utopian community that exemplified the possibilities of what he called "radical behaviorism." In the book, Skinner assumed that people have no free will, and that cooperative behavior can be controlled entirely by environmental factors which, if chosen correctly, can create a near-perfect society. A number of real-life communities have been modeled on ideas similar to Skinner's – examples include Brook Farm in the 1800s, kibbutzim, and hippy communes – but not surprisingly, not one has been utopian, and many of them ultimately failed.

In the 1960s, however, a revolution occurred in evolutionary biology, displacing the dogmatic opposition to human instinct espoused by the behaviorists, while reimagining a genetic basis for social cooperation. This rewrote the book on group selection. Evolutionary biologists William Hamilton, George Williams, John Maynard Smith, and Robert Trivers proposed a gene-centered view of evolution, in which natural selection at its most fundamental level takes place neither between groups nor between individuals, but rather at the level of the gene. This idea was later expanded upon and popularized by E.O. Wilson and Richard Dawkins. Taken together their work radically altered the understanding of the mechanisms behind personality traits and social cooperation.

---

[91] For some of the misconceptions promoted by Mead, see Freeman, Derek (1983) *Margaret Mead and Samoa: The Making and Unmaking of an Anthropological Myth*. Harvard University Press.

The traits of an animal, known collectively as its phenotype, describe its morphology, psychology, and biochemical properties. Williams showed that traits cannot be the basic unit of natural selection, because they are easily altered by meiosis, the process by which the creature obtains half its genes from each parent. With the exception of a few species that reproduce asexually, a phenotype cannot make identical copies of itself in the animal's offspring. Traits and phenotypes are therefore not immutable. While some characteristics might remain to a certain degree, no trait is preserved in its entirety from one generation to the next. Genes, on the other hand, can persist unchanged. Williams proposed that gene competition between different versions of the same gene – or allele – is the basic unit of evolution, and a successful allele is one that has the most beneficial effect on the trait it affects.[92] In doing this, it assists in the individual's survival and reproduction, and allows the allele to pass to the next generation.[93]

The survival of a particular allele is also dependent on genes for other traits that make up the phenotype because all the genes have to work together for the animal to survive and reproduce. For example, genes for teeth that are short and blunt would put in jeopardy genes for sharp claws in a lion because the lion would be unlikely to survive. Unlike a parasite, which survives entirely at the expense of the host, all the genes within an organism can only survive by ensuring that the host reproduces, and they do this by being present in the organism's eggs or sperm. In this way, they share a common "objective." Herbivore teeth in a lion would never get passed to the next generation of lions. Only those that "work together" with all the other genes can survive.[94]

---

[92] Williams, George C. (1966) *Adaptation and Natural Selection: A Critique of Some Current Evolutionary Thought.* Princeton University Press, p. 307.

[93] In reality, a particular trait can be affected by multiple genes, and a particular gene can have multiple effects on different traits. The explanation has been simplified here by assuming that each gene affects a single trait, but this does not change the overall concept.

[94] Dawkins, Richard (2016) [1976] *The Selfish Gene.* Oxford University Press, pp.

Genes also affect the function of an organism's brain, and hence its behavior. An animal with a complex morphology has to be able to react to widely different situations within its environment. This means that genes for brain function that survive have to give rise to behaviors that are complementary and appropriate to the physical characteristics of both the animal's body and its surroundings. A lion that had the behavioral genes of an anteater would neither have the ability to catch gazelles, nor be able to survive on ants.

Social Cooperation and Kin Selection

Aside from the cooperative nature of all the genes within a single individual, an allele for a particular gene will do better in terms of its future survival if it exists in multiple individuals within the population. Therefore, it is to the gene's advantage if it can somehow influence the behavior of the animal to cooperate rather than compete with other individuals where the same allele is present. If the gene can cause this altruistic behavior, either by itself, or in concert with other genes, then its presence in the population at large will be maximized and its future will be more assured. In contrast, alleles of the same gene that fail to do this will be eliminated from the pool. William Hamilton, who developed this idea called it "inclusive fitness."[95]   The issue, from the gene's perspective, is that the animal's altruism should *not* be directed toward individuals where the allele is non-existent, as this would be disadvantageous. Dawkins later called genes "selfish," not because they have any motive, but rather because they exist at the expense of others of the same type that are less successful.

Successful genes are those that can engender cooperation with another animal that is closely related because next of kin are more likely to carry the same allele. This process came to be known as

---

86-114.

[95] Hamilton, William D. (1964) "The Genetical Evolution of Social Behaviour: I & II." *Journal of Theoretical Biology*, Vol. 7 (1), pp. 1-52.

"kin selection." Since the potential cost of altruism is death of the animal and loss of the gene, Hamilton theorized that an animal will engage in very costly behaviors only toward closely-related kin, in whom the probability of the allele being present is high. It will exhibit less risky and less costly behaviors toward more distant kin, where the allele is less likely to exist.[96] For example, squirrels generally live together in very closely related groups. One squirrel will happily let out a warning sound to advise the rest of the troop of the threat of an approaching eagle, thus allowing its close relatives to escape, even though the individual raising the alarm will frequently be attacked and die in the process. However, a squirrel is much less likely to do this for another group, because its members are more distantly related and possess fewer genes in common.

A perfect example of kin selection occurs in some insects. Certain species of ants, as well as bees and wasps, are clones of one another and therefore share exactly the same genes. Since their relatedness is 1:1, they are perfectly willing to sacrifice themselves for the benefit of another member of the group. Indeed, they will readily die to ensure the survival of just one other individual. They do not compete with one another at all. In other words, they are perfectly cooperative.[97]

Social Cooperation and Reciprocal Altruism

Kin selection also explains why human beings are far more likely to show love, affection, and self-sacrifice toward other people who are close relatives. It is why love or altruism is generally greater between siblings than between cousins, and greater still between

---

[96] In Hamilton's model, altruism will occur if $r \times b > c$ where r is the degree of relatedness (i.e., the probability of having the gene in question), b is the benefit, and c is the cost of the altruistic behavior. See Hamilton, William D (1963) "The Evolution of Altruistic Behavior." *The American Naturalist*, Vol. 97 (896), pp. 354–356.

[97] In the human body, the individual cells making up the body are also related 1:1 and are thus completely "altruistic" and non-competitive.

cousins than among total strangers. However, even among strangers, genes for benevolence can be favored in a process termed *reciprocal altruism*. This theory was developed by biologist Robert Trivers in 1971 and is similar in concept to the prisoner's dilemma in game theory.[98] The idea is that if a person initiates a generous act towards someone else, and that individual returns the favor, then both people benefit. If the favor is not returned, then the recipient profits a great deal, but the donor loses. The question in terms of evolutionary biology is this: In a group of people with multiple interactions of various kinds, which strategy is likely to be the most successful in the long run for the gene that influences behavior? Benevolence, selfishness, or something in between?

The answer was suggested in a trial of computer simulations, conducted in 1980 by political scientist Robert Axelrod that modeled different strategies for group behavior. Many different models were tried, but the winning strategy was contained in a program devised by mathematical biologist Anatol Rapoport called "tit-for-tat."[99] The idea behind tit-for-tat was simple: To be successful, an individual needed to be generous on meeting someone else for the first time, and if the recipient returned the favor, then cooperation was continued. If, however, the recipient ended the reciprocation at any time, or failed to reciprocate at all, then all further dealings with that individual were terminated. In the simulation, shirkers always lost in the end, even if they were initially generous, while reciprocators – i.e., those who engaged in reciprocal altruism all the time – came out on top. However, treating *everyone* with generosity, including those who were mean and miserly, was no more of a winning strategy than being self-centered. In short, to be successful, benevolence was good, but the benevolent individual had to refuse to deal with the scrooges.

---

[98] Trivers, Robert (1971) "The Evolution of Reciprocal Altruism." *Quarterly Review of Biology*, Vol. 46 (1), pp. 35-56.
[99] Axelrod, Robert (2006) [1984] *The Evolution of Cooperation*. Basic Books, New York, pp. 27-55.

From the experiment, it would seem that genes of selfish people would tend to be eliminated, while the genes of those who cooperate should become universal. However, in real life, people who are tightfisted, egotistical, or greedy often attempt to veil their self-centered personality behind a cloak of deception, which may allow them to prosper. An example of this is virtue-signaling, which arises when a person wants to be seen as virtuous without actually being so. Another aberrant behavior is projection, in which a guilty person deflects unwanted attention by falsely accusing others of the very wrongdoing of which they are at fault. Self-righteousness and sanctimony are often part and parcel of these kinds of personality.

Personality traits that spur these behaviors[100], along with traits for mendacity, deviousness, and hypocrisy can endure, particularly in a large population where one's true personality is easier to conceal. However, while the genes for these traits will always exist in any society, the experiments in kin selection and reciprocal altruism suggest that most genes exert a positive influence on social cooperation, and it is profound. From a genetic perspective, a majority of human beings are inclined to treat other people with fairness most of the time, even though an iniquitous few will not.

Friendship

Two other forms of cooperation should be mentioned here: friendship and pair bonding. Friendship is a feature of all human societies, but it is not exclusively human. Chimpanzees, baboons, elephants, whales, dolphins, and orcas frequently exhibit enduring non-sexual one-on-one relationships with unrelated members of the

---

[100] I am using the word "behavior" here to describe a personality trait, because it is tied to a person's genetic profile. However, human beings are also able to "act," which implies volition and a free will. While animals can only behave, human beings can override behavior by exercising their will, which is something animals cannot do. This means that unlike an animal, a person is not mindlessly controlled by his genes, and hence compelled to "behave" in a mean or selfish way, but rather can overcome these traits and choose to "act" with generosity and kindness.

species that go beyond normal social cooperation. Many of these animals appear to express human-like emotions such as empathy, compassion, and altruism.

In humans, childhood friendships focus on shared experiences, while adult relationships are based on trust, loyalty, empathy, affection, and supporting one another in times of need. Most friendships are symmetric, in that the persons involved are of a similar age, background, and socioeconomic status, and are likely to share similar interests. If there is indeed a genetic basis for friendship, it is easy to see why the bonds are formed; cooperation is useful for the genes they probably have in common. On the other hand, asymmetric friendships are more difficult to explain, but it has been suggested that they are a way by which evolution solves the so-called "banker's paradox" in tit-for-tat accounting.[101] In a purely tit-for-tat world, a person with a lot of resources certainly has the capacity to be benevolent, but might be less inclined to actually be so, because many of the people he interacts with have fewer assets at their disposal and may be unable to reciprocate. But if a relatively poorer or younger person is assessed to be a good credit risk, then friendship is something that obviates the need for immediate reciprocation. It is a way of not worrying about the need to be repaid right away, and it increases the degree of cooperation within the group.

Phenotypically, it has been shown that friends often share many traits with respect to their neurology, and exhibit exceptionally similar brain responses to external stimuli. In one study,[102] MRI scans of pairs of friends were shown to have the same blood flow patterns in their brains as they watched movies of various genres, while non-friends had dissimilar blood flow. It appears that the

---

[101] See Christakis, Nicholas A. (2019) *Blueprint*. Little, Brown & Co. Kindle Edition, pp. 248-251, Loc. 3957-4005.

[102] Parkinson, Carolyn, Adam M. Kleinbaum, and Thalia Wheatley (2018) "Similar Neural Responses Predict Friendship." *Nature Communications*, Vol. 9 (1), p. 332.

brains of the friends were working in the same way, which perhaps suggests complementary genetic profiles. The sociologist Nicholas Christakis has shown that friendship patterns of identical twins are more similar structurally than those of fraternal twins. He also found that 46 percent of the variation in the number of friends a person has can be explained by their genes.[103] This could result from the fact that friends often come from the same place where people are fairly closely related anyway. But it is probably also due to the fact that people with similar interests, or preferring similar environments, have compatible psychological profiles that are conditioned by having complementary genes.

Pair Bonding

The differences that men and women feel for each other can be explained to a great degree by their physiology and reproductive roles. From a gene-centric perspective, a man should want to have sex with as many different women as possible, and have as many offspring as feasible, in order to maximize the number of his genes in the population. Men have therefore evolved to have a high sex drive – largely induced by testosterone – and to be fairly non-selective with whom they have sex, provided the woman has sufficient youth and attractiveness, which are indicative of female fertility. Women on the other hand are compelled to be more selective because a woman has far fewer eggs than a man has sperm and cannot afford to be wasteful given the investment required in bearing children. As a consequence, women tend to have a lower sex drive than men. From an evolutionary standpoint, a woman is likely to select a man who will provide protection and resources, as this is essential during pregnancy and child-nurturing when she is at her most vulnerable. Therefore, women generally look for wealth and status in a man, but just as importantly, someone who is willing

---

[103] Christakis, Nicholas A. (2019) *Blueprint*. Little, Brown & Co. Kindle Edition, p. 252, Loc. 4017.

to provide the necessary male parental investment in children. If she chooses a man who is reluctant to provide support, or incapable of giving it, her child might not survive, and her genes will not endure.[104]

Pair bonding is not restricted to humans. The emotions might differ, but the biological strategies are often quite similar. The choosiness of females implies a high degree of competition among males. Therefore, a number of animal species, including humans, have evolved male strategies to attract the opposite sex. An example of this in the animal kingdom is the colorful display of feathers in the male peacock, which is an advertisement of health, strength and vigor. But since males might falsely advertise their fitness, females have developed strategies to detect this. Among humans, since male parental investment for a woman is extremely important, men have evolved to be good at exaggerating their wealth, status, and devotion, but women are good at spotting their deception![105]

Empathy

An important component of all cooperative relations is the ability to identify psychologically with other people with whom one interacts; to put oneself in their shoes. The question is: Are people naturally empathic, or do they acquire it through nurture and social conditioning?

It is clear that some social animals, such as bonobos, chimpanzees, and elephants also exhibit empathic traits. In the 1990s, scientists studying the brains of primates noticed that when one of the monkeys was watching another perform a specific task like grasping a banana, both of their brains exhibited electrochemical activity in precisely the same place.[106] The

---

[104] See Wright, Robert (1994) *The Moral Animal.* Knopf Doubleday Publishing Group, Kindle Edition, Ch. 3, Loc. 886-1554.

[105] Ibid., Ch. 3, Loc 997.

[106] Gallese V., L. Fadiga, L. Fogassi, and G. Rizzolatti. (1996) "Action recognition in the premotor cortex." *Brain*, Vol. 119, pp. 593–609.

premotor cortex of the observing monkey appeared to mirror that of the individual displaying the behavior, and so it was speculated there were specific neurons within the brain that were responsible. Further research showed mirror neurons also exist in humans, probably on a much greater scale, and within other areas of the prefrontal cortex.

While monkeys mirror mostly physical behavior, mirror neurons in humans are responsible for the copying of many different kinds of emotions. Using functional magnetic resonance imaging and electroencephalography on test subjects, researchers demonstrated that when an observer watches another person laugh or wince in pain, the same neural networks are seen to activate in both subjects.[107]   This seems to suggest that mirror neurons are responsible for empathy, and that empathy is a biological phenomenon that was probably acquired at some point during our evolutionary development after early humans became self-aware. According to philosopher Thomas Metzinger, once hominids developed an ego, the neural circuitry in the brain responsible for the body model of the self, evolved to be able to simulate that of another person. This was then modified again to permit the simulation of emotion and the creation of empathy.[108]

For the most part, mirroring is subconscious. In all our social interactions, we constantly mirror one another in both our bodily movements and emotions. Thomas Metzinger suggests that the mirroring of bodily movements may have been the way in which early humans were able to understand each other, and it thus served as a form of gestural communication. By copying the brain activity of another person engaged in some kind of activity, it allowed an onlooker to understand the thought behind the observed behavior

[107] Botvinick M. et al. (2005). "Viewing facial expressions of pain engages cortical areas involved in the direct experience of pain." *NeuroImage*, Vol. 25 (1), pp. 312–319.

[108] Metzinger, Thomas (2009) *The Ego Tunnel: The Science of the Mind and the Myth of the Self.* Basic Books. Kindle Edition, pp. 163-165.

and hence comprehend the underlying intentions of the action. Indeed, the first kind of language might have involved facial expressions like smiling, grimacing, or scowling, etc., and only later did language involve sounds as substitutes for these signs.

It is a popular belief today that empathy is the foundation of morality.[109] It is claimed that this is supported by case studies of people who exhibit a change in their moral perspective after suffering some kind of injury to the part of the prefrontal cortex associated with empathy. In some cases, the injury is said to lead to psychopathic behavior. Defects in other areas of the brain, such as the amygdala, are linked to moral functioning, and have also been shown to be associated with psychopathy.

However, it would be wrong to claim that a deficit in empathy is the sole cause of immorality. As human beings, we have free will, and therefore the ability to make choices. The fact that immoral actions are linked to a deficit or malfunction of mirror neuron circuits does not mean humans cannot override malign feelings. It is interesting to note that the phrase often chosen to describe conduct indicative of immorality is "immoral behavior," as though the person in question is not responsible for what is essentially an action. Animals behave because they do not make choices, but to the extent human beings exercise their will, they act. When the American serial killer Ted Bundy kidnapped, raped, and murdered numerous young women, does anyone really believe he did not choose to do so; that he did so merely on instinct, and was exhibiting psychopathic *behavior*? No, he engaged in psychopathic action, and unless a person is truly not exercising his will, or his will is severely compromised in some way, as might occur if he is psychotic for example, then his action should not be labeled as a behavior.

Since a number of animal species seem to exhibit empathy and

---

[109] For example, the Dutch neurobiologist D. F. Swaab states: "Empathy – the capacity to recognize and share the feelings of others – provides the basis for all moral behavior." Swaab, D. F. (2014) *We Are Our Brains*. Random House Publishing Group, Kindle Edition, Loc 3812.

altruistic behavior, some psychobiologists have suggested that animals might have a moral sense. One often cited example is that of the lowland gorilla Binti Jua who in 1996 rescued a three-year old boy who had fallen into the enclosure at the Chicago Zoo. It appeared the ape was protecting the boy and preventing him from coming to further harm.[110] While this seems to be a clear example of animal empathy, it is problematic to claim it as truly moral conduct. Morality implies reason and choice, and while some animals might have some very rudimentary form of will, it is doubtful they can truly decide to act in a moral way. More likely, this is animal behavior governed by mirror neuron activity in the brain that is instinctual, but not moral action that is the result of conscious thought. Empathy is a natural and instinctual feeling that is present in some social species, including humans, and may be the precursor to moral action, but only human beings have true morality because they are the only species that has free will and can engage in purposive action.

However, while most human beings have at least some degree of empathy, a small percentage of the population possesses little or none. That is the subject of the next chapter.

---

[110] Ibid., Loc 3819.

6

Dominance, Aggression, and Control

Psychopathy

In the last chapter, it was shown that the desire to engage cooperatively with others is influenced to a considerable degree by a person's genes. Genetic inheritance also likely affects the degree to which an individual has feelings of empathy. But because every fully developed person has a will that is free, no one's personality is cast in stone. While it is true that some people might be naturally less predisposed to be cooperative or empathic, no one is compelled by the inevitability of a physical law to act in a manner that is antisocial, inhumane, or cruel.

A significant factor detrimental to effective social cooperation within the population at large is the presence of psychopathy. While popular imagination views the psychopath as a rare and extraordinarily violent individual, psychopaths are far more prevalent than most people realize, and only a few engage in overt acts of extreme violence. The Canadian psychologist Robert Hare, who spent many years studying these individuals, maintains that about two to three percent of the population exhibit psychopathic tendencies. They comprise 20 percent of the prison population but commit about 50 percent of serious crime.[111] Typical personality traits include a lack of empathy; very low levels of fear, remorse, or

---

[111] Hare, Robert D. (1993) *Without Conscience: The Disturbing World of the Psychopaths Among Us.* Guilford Publications, Kindle Edition, pp. 86-87, Loc. 1388-1396.

shame; a high degree of selfishness, aggression, glibness, grandiosity, and mendacity; promiscuous sexual activity; a failure to establish long-lasting relationships; and superficial charm.

A psychopath should be distinguished from someone who is merely anti-social. The latter engages in outwardly objectionable acts that are antithetical to cooperation, and often displays a lack of consideration for others, but does not necessarily exhibit some of the more subtle subjective traits associated with psychopathy. Psychopaths are antisocial, but are often able to hide it, given their manipulative, mendacious, and sometimes charismatic personalities. As a consequence, they are often able to evade criminal prosecution. As Robert Hare states: "Most criminals are *not* psychopaths, and many of the individuals who manage to operate on the shady side of the law and remain out of prison *are* psychopaths."[112] Indeed, psychopaths can be found in all walks of life. They include politicians, CEOs, lawyers, police officers, academics, and physicians. Many obtain their high rank through highly manipulative and coercive tactics, and by exhibiting a stunning lack of concern for those who get in their way. Those who work for them are often subjected to abuse, intimidation, and derision.

In the field of psychology, the question of whether psychopathy is "nature or nurture" is hotly debated. Some psychologists distinguish it from sociopathy, which they claim has environmental causes. Hare maintains no such distinction and says that the tendency to engage in psychopathic action is probably mostly genetic. He finds no evidence that it stems from early social or environmental factors.[113]

From an evolutionary perspective, some studies have suggested that psychopathy might be adaptive because psychopaths typically have a high number of sexual encounters, which would increase the

---

[112] Ibid., p. 24, Loc. 442.
[113] Ibid., p. 170, Loc. 2690.

number of potential offspring. In the ancestral environment, this might have been the case.[114] However, given the number of attributes that are extremely detrimental to social cooperation, and the highly antisocial behavior in general, it is likely that cultural constraints would have weakened any biological advantage that psychopaths might once have had. Therefore, to the extent there is a genetic component, it is possible that psychopathy might be an evolutionary leftover from a pre-rational past.

Narcissism

Another significant factor that prevents effective social cooperation is narcissism. No human being can be completely selfless, but destructive and pathological narcissists exhibit a far greater degree of self-centeredness than the average person. Psychologists have long disagreed on what constitutes a narcissistic personality, but typical traits include self-centeredness, arrogance, entitlement, illusions of self-importance and superiority, grandiosity, and lack of empathy, underlain with hidden feelings of vulnerability, defensiveness, inadequacy, and shame.[115] Unlike the psychopath who has no sense of shame or fear, narcissists often have deep feelings of vulnerability and fear. Thus, while psychopaths exhibit many narcissistic traits, their personalities are not the same.

Narcissism exists on a broad spectrum from "normal" levels in most people to more destructive forms in a significant fraction of the population, and extreme pathological narcissism in a few. Individual differences within the population as a whole follow a smooth and continuous curve from one extreme to the other, with large variations. Even at the low end, the degree of "normal"

---

[114] Pullman, Lesleigh E. et al (2021) "Is Psychopathy a Mental Disorder or an Adaptation? Evidence From a Meta-Analysis of the Association Between Psychopathy and Handedness." *Evolutionary Psychology*, Vol. 19 (4).

[115] Krizan, Zlatan and Anne D. Herlache (2017) "The Narcissism Spectrum Model: A Synthetic View of Narcissistic Personality." *Personality and Social Psychology Review*, Vol. 1(29).

narcissism varies greatly.[116]

There are three core manifestations of the narcissistic personality – namely, self-enhancement, the need for admiration, and an adversarial orientation toward others.[117] With respect to self-enhancement, narcissists tend to overrate their intelligence and physical attractiveness, often appearing to others as arrogant, boastful, and snobbish. The need for admiration and validation stems from their underlying insecurity. Narcissists tend to place themselves at the center of attention, seeking opportunities for glorification in order to gain as many compliments as possible so that their precarious feelings of superiority can be maintained. Narcissists are also condescending and exploitative, often quick to anger, and prone to manipulate others for their own self-serving needs. Because their need for admiration outweighs their desire for interpersonal closeness, and because they are perfectly willing to inflict collateral damage in order to achieve their goals, their relationships tend to be shallow and short-lived.[118]

Narcissism seems to have both biological and environmental causes. With respect to genetic factors, a number of studies have concluded that certain traits associated with narcissism might have conferred an evolutionary advantage in the ancestral environment.[119] For example, narcissistic individuals might have been more successful in terms of dominance, which would have allowed for multiple short-term sexual partners, thereby conferring reproductive success. In addition, certain physical features, such as

---

[116] Ibid.

[117] Thomaes, Sander, Eddie Brummelman, and Constantine Sedikides (2018) "Narcissism: A Social-Developmental Perspective" in V. Zeigler-Hill & T. K. Shackleford (eds.), *The Sage Handbook of Personality and Individual Differences*, Sage Publications, London.

[118] Ibid.

[119] See Holtzman, Nicholas S. and M. Brent Donnellan (2015) "The Roots of Narcissus: Old and New Models of the Evolution of Narcissism" in Ziegler Hill, Virgil et al. (eds.), *Evolutionary Perspectives on Social Psychology (Evolutionary Psychology)*, Springer.

larger body size and strength, might have tended to encourage behaviors associated with narcissism involving intimidation and force, which became an effective strategy to obtain resources.[120] Thus, narcissists might have been more likely to survive and pass on their genes.

From the present-day perspective, nurture almost certainly plays a role as well. One theory posits that the narcissist's self-inflated view is compensation for early childhood neglect and a lack of parental warmth, and that narcissists seek the positive affirmation from others because they fail to receive it from their parents. However, a large prospective longitudinal study concluded that the most likely environmental cause is overindulgent parenting.[121] If children are led to believe from a young age that they are special, unique, or entitled, then it is possible they will start to feel superior to other people. The study judged that parental coldness (or warmth) is *not* correlated with narcissism but is instead associated with low (or high) levels of self-esteem.

A widely cited study concludes there are two distinct types of narcissism – namely, grandiose and vulnerable.[122] With respect to the so-called five-factor model – which describes personality in terms of the degree of conscientiousness, agreeableness, neuroticism, openness, and extraversion – grandiose narcissism is said to be positively correlated with extraversion and negatively associated with neuroticism. In vulnerable narcissism, however, the correlation with these two factors is reversed. Grandiose narcissists

---

[120] Buss, D. M. (2009) "How can evolutionary psychology explain personality and individual differences?" *Perspectives on Psychological Science*, Vol. 4 (4), pp. 359-366.

[121] Brummelman, Eddie, Sander Thomaes, Stefanie A Nelemans, Geertjan Overbeek, and Brad J Bushman (2015) "Origins of Narcissism in Children." *Proceedings of the National Academy of Sciences USA*, Vol. 112 (12).

[122] Miller, Joshua D., Brian J Hoffman, Eric T Gaughan, Brittany Gentile, Jessica Maples, and W. Keith Campbell (2011) "Grandiose and Vulnerable Narcissism: A Nomological Network Analysis." *Journal of Personality*, Vol. 79 (5).

have been described as aggressive and immodest, whereas vulnerable narcissists tend to be more anxious and complaining. However, both are low on agreeableness and are noted to be "bossy, intolerant, cruel, argumentative, dishonest, opportunistic, conceited, arrogant, and demanding."[123] As will be discussed in a later chapter, when a significant portion of the population exhibits these kinds of traits, the consequences for society can be highly detrimental.

Dominance

Hierarchies exist in all cultures and in many animal species. In humans, hierarchies are found in corporations, universities, social clubs, governments, and many other settings. However, it is necessary to distinguish between hierarchies established on *dominance*, which occur in both animals and humans, and those based on *prestige*, which are uniquely human.[124] Animal hierarchies are exclusively dominance-based. The pecking order is generally determined by strength, age, physical size, male sex, and especially aggression, with the alpha male exhibiting more of these characteristics than anyone else in the group. In some apes – especially chimpanzees – coercion, intimidation, and manipulation are some of the tactics used. Deference to the alpha male is always demanded. Being at the top of the hierarchy is especially important to males because of the reproductive advantage. Powerful males are more likely to attract or coerce females.

George Williams in *Adaptation and Natural Selection* showed that in many animal species, dominance exists as a compromise made by each individual in a competition for resources and mates. The dominant males are more likely to obtain the greatest quantity of food and the greatest number of females, but they are also more

---

[123] Wink, P. (1991) "Two Faces of Narcissism." *Journal of Personality and Social Psychology*, Vol 61, pp. 590–597.

[124] Maner, Jon K. (2017) "Dominance and Prestige: A Tale of Two Hierarchies." *Current Directions in Psychological Science*, Vol. 26 (7).

likely to suffer injury or death from challengers.[125] Submissives, on the other hand, are more likely to survive, provided they stay out of the fray by remaining passive and deferential. Evolutionary biologist John Maynard Smith noted that in animal social groups, dominants and submissives come into a kind of balance. When there are too many dominants, there is too much violent competition for food and other resources which causes their numbers to fall. As a consequence, the submissives start to prosper. However, as the number of submissives increases, the dominants take over again, and the cycle repeats until an equilibrium is reached.[126]

There are many similarities between animals and humans with regard to dominance hierarchies, but there are also significant differences. As in many animal species, human dominance hierarchies are typically governed by individuals high in aggression who employ intimidation and coercion. Dominant human psychology is often associated with excessive hubristic pride, as well as the dark triad personality traits of narcissism, Machiavellianism, and psychopathy.[127] In humans, aggressive females can rank highly, but given the degree of aggression required and the lure of sexual opportunities for the alpha of the group, men are more likely to seek and obtain high rank through dominance than women. The sexual advantage may be a significant factor in polygamous cultures where competition to attain high social rank is intense, given that so few women are available for men of low-order status. This could be one reason why many historically polygamous societies have often been governed by highly violent individuals.[128]

---

[125] Williams, George C. (1966) *Adaptation and Natural Selection: A Critique of Some Current Evolutionary Thought*. Princeton University Press, p. 218.

[126] Maynard-Smith, John (1982) *Evolution and the Theory of Games*. Cambridge University Press, Chapter 2.

[127] For a list of differences between dominance and prestige hierarchies, see Table 1 in Maner, Jon K. (2017) "Dominance and Prestige: A Tale of Two Hierarchies." *Current Directions in Psychological Science*, Vol. 26 (7).

[128] According to Edward Dutton, the Moroccan Emperor and tyrant Moulay Ismael the Bloodthirsty (1634-1727) is reputed to have fathered 888 children.

Another difference between animal and human dominance is that, in the former, it is a dog-eat-dog world, where all resources have to be derived from a state of nature, and where one animal's gain is another's loss. Human beings, on the other hand, are able to produce tools (capital goods) which increase the number of resources above that found purely in nature. Moreover, humans engage in the division of labor, which means that success in production is often determined by skill and aptitude instead of brute strength. Therefore, while dominance hierarchies exist, there is no evolutionary pressure for a stable or consistent ratio between dominants and submissives. On the contrary, aggressive and violent cultures tend to be less productive, and therefore have fewer resources, which keeps the level of violence high. The most successful societies are those which engage in non-violent and non-coercive – i.e., voluntary – cooperation, where violence tends to remain low. Unlike animals, the prevalence of these kinds of hierarchies in humans, and the degree of violence and aggression involved, is often a function of culture.

While hierarchies based on dominance can be found in both animals and people, prestige hierarchies are limited entirely to the latter and are linked to factors such as wealth, intelligence, skill, natural talent, sociability, and beauty. Deference to those with high rank is never coerced but rather freely conferred and given on the basis of respect and admiration instead of aggression and coercion. While dominance hierarchies establish themselves over many levels of rank, those based on prestige tend to be relatively flat.

There is a clear adaptive advantage to prestige hierarchies. With the development of human psychology in the ancestral environment, it became increasingly important to transmit knowledge efficiently from person to person. This was beneficial because it saved people from having to learn by themselves through trial and error. The development of language was the first step, but

---

Dutton, Edward (2018) *At Our Wits' End*. Societas, Kindle Edition, Loc. 977.

cultural transmission became far more efficient when very knowledgeable, wise, and highly regarded persons could be identified easily. It is reasonable to conclude, therefore, that natural selection favored individuals who had the ability to identify, pay attention to, and imitate those with expertise and talent. But it would also have favored imitators and admirers who were willing to champion these persons voluntarily to others, precisely because this would have further increased transmission. It has been suggested that veneration, respect, and deference arose as a means of doing this. Not only do these sentiments reward the talented person with well-earned pride and fame, but more importantly they are a signal of expertise to potential followers. Naturally, some experts will attract more adherents than others and hence more prestige, and so a social order arises.[129]

In contrast to social orders based on prestige, there appears to have been no adaptive advantage to dominance hierarchies in humans. Since dominant individuals do not earn respect and deference, but rather demand these kinds of sentiments, they would have corrupted hierarchies based on prestige, which would have been antithetical to the transmission of knowledge and the success of the group. Given that prestige hierarchies succeeded, and the cooperative transmission of knowledge was effective, it is likely that dominance as an evolutionary strategy receded. This is not to say that the genetic determinants of violence and aggression disappeared.[130] On the contrary, they are still very much prevalent today. However, the level of violence in humans is affected to a significant extent by culture. And as a strategy for survival, violence seems to become less important as knowledge increases, and civil

---

[129] For an excellent article on this subject, see Henrich, Joseph and Francisco Gil-White (2001) "The Evolution of Prestige. Freely Conferred Deference as a Mechanism for Enhancing the Benefits of Cultural Transmission." *Evolution and Human Behavior*, Vol. 22 (3), pp. 165-196.

[130] Pavlov, Konstantin et al. (2012) "Genetic Determinants of Aggression and Impulsivity in Humans." *Journal of Applied Genetics*, Vol. 53 (1), pp. 61-82.

society becomes more enlightened.

In *The Better Angels of Our Nature,* cognitive psychologist Steven Pinker lists several cultural factors as the cause for what he claims is a significant decline of violence throughout much of the world over the past few millennia. Among these are the Agricultural Revolution, beginning around five thousand years ago, which caused a reduction in the raiding and feuding that characterized life for hunter-gatherers; the increase in commerce and prosperity during the late Middle Ages; and perhaps most significantly, the Enlightenment, which brought about the pursuit of knowledge through reason, elucidated and defended natural rights, implemented fairer judicial systems, abolished torture, and eventually ended slavery.[131]

There is much evidence to suggest that culture also affects our genes, and that the changing genetic profile then feeds back on to culture. This process has been called gene-culture coevolution, and it can happen over relatively short time scales.[132] For example, if brutality becomes a less effective strategy within the cultural milieu, then this can have a negative effect on the reproductive efficacy of violent individuals, and genes for aggression will fall within the society. Edward Dutton has shown that in Europe before the 11th century, people were generally expected to settle their own disputes, and murder and revenge killings were common. But beginning in the Middle Ages, executions of felons became far more prevalent because of a change in the attitudes of the church towards capital punishment. It has been estimated that as much as 1% of the population was sentenced to death at any given time.[133] While a large number of these persons were condemned for non-violent

---

[131] Pinker, Steven (2011) *The Better Angels of Our Nature: Why Violence Has Declined.* Penguin Group, New York, pp. 40-58, pp. 61-81, pp. 175-188.

[132] Richerson, Peter J. et al. (2010) "Gene-culture Coevolution in the Age of Genomics." *Proceedings of the National Academy of Sciences,* Vol. 107, Suppl. 2.

[133] See "Executing the Less Intelligent" in Dutton, Edward (2018) *At Our Wits' End.* Societas, Kindle Edition, Loc. 1148-1165.

crimes, it is not unreasonable to conclude that the figure also included a considerable number of violent individuals. If many of them were executed before their reproductive years, then genes for aggression within the community were likely reduced.

The economist Gregory Clark notes that in the early modern era, increases in living standards caused a significant rise in the average intelligence of the population. This was probably due to a number of cultural factors, but one reason was that intelligent people were generally wealthier, and more of their offspring survived early childhood. Clark calls this "survival of the richest."[134] Since intelligence is at least in part an inherited trait, and significantly negatively correlated with physical aggression, impulsivity, and antisocial behavior, it is possible this was a contributing factor to a reduction in violence.[135]

Therefore, while cultural factors have a direct influence in delegitimizing violence, and this causes aggressive and antisocial individuals to exhibit less violent behavior, the same cultural factors may exert a genetic influence on the population, such that the percentage of violent individuals falls. Both of these effects might have worked together synergistically to reduce violence over the past few centuries.

False Ideologies and Total Control

If, as Pinker maintains, violence has been on the decline, especially during the last few hundred years, how can we explain the tens of millions of violent deaths that have occurred in the 20th century due to war and genocide? The simple answer would seem to be that with improvements in the technologies of both war and oppression, a single charismatic and intelligent psychopath can

---

[134] Ibid., Loc 152.
[135] Lynam D., T. Moffitt, and M. Stouthamer-Loebe (1993) "Explaining the Relation Between IQ and Delinquency: Class, Race, Test Motivation, School Failure, or Self-Control?" *Journal of Abnormal Psychology*, Vol. 102 (2), pp.187-196.

control, oppress, and murder entire populations. The millions of deaths that occurred during the two world wars, the Soviet purges of the 1930s, the Cultural Revolution, and the Holocaust could never have happened without modern munitions, artillery, tanks, warships, and military aircraft. Additionally, it is doubtful that personality cults, propaganda, secret police forces, and concentration camps could have been sustained without 20th century mass communications and modern industrial processes. Without these instruments of repression and death, Stalin, Hitler, Mao, and others like them would not have been able to kill so many.

There is a clear distinction to be made, however, between dictators, on the one hand, and leaders of totalitarian regimes on the other. In pure dictatorships, the leader and his close associates are motivated by a lust for power or money, and they attain their dominant status through violence and intimidation. But once power has been attained, their goal is to retain their position with the minimum amount of force. If they become too oppressive, then the masses will rise up and overthrow them.

Totalitarian regimes on the other hand are rather different. As the political theorist and philosopher Hannah Arendt explained, the key difference is that all totalitarian systems involve an ideology and a movement with which the masses must be won over through psychological manipulation and indoctrination. Arendt maintained that mass movements of this sort – such as those that existed under Stalinism and Nazism – are possible only when people feel isolated and atomized, a state of affairs that exists when class distinctions have been reduced or eliminated.[136]

The totalitarian state can emerge when a sufficient number of people subscribe to the ideology and sacrifice their individuality and

---

[136] For example, in order to create an atomized and structureless mass, Stalin first had to liquidate the various property-owning classes, middle classes, peasantry, and workers groups that had persisted up until 1930. See Arendt, Hannah (1951) *Part III: The Origins of Totalitarianism*. Harcourt, Brace, & World, Inc., New York. pp. 17-18.

will to become part of the mass movement. The mass is therefore the precise opposite of a society that is integrated on the basis of free exchange in which people retain their individuality. In the later stages, constant terror imposed on the population by paramilitary groups and secret police, aimed particularly at the recalcitrant segments of society but also directed arbitrarily against the purely innocent, is used to remove all initiative and spontaneity, eliminate any possibility of protest, and enable complete control.

In contrast to a dictator, the totalitarian leader can remain in power only as long as the masses adhere to the ideology.[137] Thus, maintaining the ideology is a constant concern for the regime who must keep the movement invigorated by avoiding any kind of stability or normalcy and by constantly invoking new enemies and threats with which to stir the population. If the movement becomes stale, the regime is in danger of collapsing. However, as long as the ideology is maintained through constant indoctrination and terror, the masses are generally incapable of exercising any independent thought – and certainly not any resistance – and the totalitarian state remains.

Arendt noted that there are generally three characteristics of totalitarian ideologies.[138] First, they have a grand explanation for the events of the past and present while claiming a reliable prediction of the future. Second, they are based on certain premises independent of all experience. And third, they order all facts to conform with the ideology, proceeding in a manner that is internally consistent but entirely *in*consistent with reality. All freedom is crushed because people are viewed as merely tools of an inevitable historical process in which everyone must submit to the spurious logic of the ideology, and not doing so is seen as refractory. Spontaneous and free exchange is non-existent, and voluntary

---

[137] Arendt states, ". . . [The totalitarian leader] can be replaced at any time, and he depends just as much on the "will" of the masses he embodies as the masses depend on him." (Ibid., p. 23).

[138] Ibid., pp. 169-170.

cooperation is replaced with mindless co-participation in an inevitable deterministic process.

A particular characteristic of totalitarian systems is the individual's loneliness that arises from the dissolution of bonds that would otherwise exist in ordinary life, the overall sense of meaninglessness, and the notion that human beings are superfluous.[139] In dictatorships, human connections involving interpersonal exchange can still exist to some extent. Under totalitarianism, in contrast, the individual loses his identity and his autonomy, and is therefore incapable of independent reason and experience. As such, patently absurd assertions made by the regime are accepted as fact. Indeed, even though the same false statements might be used repeatedly to explain government actions that clearly do not call for the same answers – and which under normal circumstances would be recognized as pure propaganda – their continued use is likely to be accepted uncritically by the mass. This is because the false narrative is the one constant feature – and hence source of comfort and stability – in the lives of a people who have been psychologically unmoored from reality, have lost their individual identity, and inhabit an environment of great uncertainty and fear.[140]

The Crowd

Another view of mass psychology was first described in 1895 by the French author Gustave Le Bon in his famous book *The Crowd: A Study of the Popular Mind.* In the book, Le Bon describes how under certain very specific conditions, when people are part of a large

---

[139] Ibid., pp. 172-176.

[140] Arendt states, "Totalitarian propaganda thrives on this escape from reality into fiction, from coincidence into constancy . . . If, for instance, all the "confessions" of political opponents in the Soviet Union are phrased in the same language and admit the same motives, the consistency-hungry masses will accept the fiction as supreme proof of their truthfulness; whereas common sense tell us that it is precisely their consistency which is out of this world and proves that they are a fabrication." (Ibid., p.50).

group, they can undergo a kind of mass hypnosis. When this happens, their individual will can be subsumed by the crowd as whole, which appears to take on a collective will of its own, often with very dangerous consequences. A classic example of this occurred during the French Revolution when ordinary people lost all sense of morality and committed appalling acts of violence which, under normal circumstances, they would never have contemplated.[141]

The social psychologist Mattias Desmet has labeled a similar phenomenon "mass formation," and lists four key psychological factors which must exist among a large number of people for it to occur. First, individuals must feel lonely and a deep sense of isolation. Second, they have to feel life has no meaning. Third, there must be persistent free-floating anxiety; people feel anxious but cannot pinpoint exactly why. And finally, the anxiety is manifested as generalized non-specific frustration and anger. When enough people feel this way, and it should be noted they do not have to be gathered together in one place for the phenomenon to occur, all that is required is a trigger.[142]

The trigger is fear, generated by a specific outside threat or enemy of some kind, upon which the crowd now focuses all of its attention. As a result, their anxiety is no longer freely floating, because it is now squarely directed on the threat. At the same time, each individual becomes part of a common cause, their sense of isolation is lifted, and life takes on new meaning and a sense of purpose. Any action which seems like it could eliminate the threat, no matter how irrational, is taken up by the crowd, which is now in a state of deep hypnosis, a kind of collective trance. The 10 to 30 percent of the population that are typically resistant to the hypnosis become an object of hatred – as they now stand outside the group

---

[141] Le Bon, Gustave (2005) [1895] *The Crowd: A Study of the Popular Mind.* Filiquarian Publishing.

[142] Desmet, Mattias (2022) *The Psychology of Totalitarianism.* Translated by Els Vanbrabant, Chelsea Green Publishing, Kindle Edition, Chapter 6.

– and so the generalized aggression, which had hitherto been suppressed by each member of the crowd, is now unleashed collectively against the outsiders.

The crowd's aggression need not necessarily be manifested as physical violence that its members employ themselves, but rather as calls for force to be used by those in positions of power. This delegates the responsibility of punishing the outsiders to the government. In situations like this, the crowd actively promotes the elevation of power-hungry fanatics, often unaware that it is these very same leaders who are the instigators and originators of the threat, and who are cynically whipping up the crowd's fear and animosity for their own purposes.

According to Desmet, this situation can be the genesis of a totalitarian system, where the leadership takes on ever more absurd measures in order to secure the fear-induced backing of the crowd, and the latter, deeply under the influence of the trance, readily goes along. Paradoxically, the more irrational the policies are, the more the crowd is likely to endorse them. The leaders will lie, cheat, manipulate, and murder, but their objective is not merely to hold onto power for power's sake. Rather, their goal is usually some utopian outcome, and the immoral acts they commit are self-justified by a fanatical belief in the ideology. Eventually, however, the measures become so absurd that the crowd turns on itself and its leaders, but it may take a considerable amount of time for this to occur, and not before incalculable harm has been caused.[143]

While systems of this kind eventually self-destruct, they can be ended early or prevented if people who do not succumb readily to the groupthink make their voices heard. This is especially important wherever and whenever an alleged outside threat is being used to galvanize the more impressionable elements of society into a crowd. As Desmet explains, when mass formation occurs, only about 30 percent of the population is ever truly in the grip of the hypnosis,

---

[143] Ibid., Chapter 7.

while 40-60 percent simply go along without being fully committed. Provided the remaining 10-30 percent speak out, and do so firmly and calmly, then it is possible to persuade the ambivalent center to reject the ideology, and the hypnosis can be broken before it causes too much damage. Simply removing those in positions of power is to no avail as there is always another fanatic waiting in the wings, ready to take over.[144]

Desmet maintains that the psychological makeup of the totalitarian leader is narcissistic rather than psychopathic; he has a messianic belief in his own greatness to lead. Be that as it may, it is certainly likely that among the Nazis, the Stalinists, the Red Guard, and leaders of other totalitarian systems of the past 100 years, there were a disproportionate number of psychopaths who were attracted to the violence these regimes meted out.

Finally, it should always be remembered that while ordinary people are quite capable of extraordinary evil – Arendt called it the "banality of evil" – the people who join the mass formation are generally not the true oppressors. Indeed, in many respects, they are as much victims as those who stand outside. Even though the mass is a precondition for the regime to exist, the ultimate responsibility for the evil of totalitarianism rests not with the hypnotized members of the movement, but rather with those who seek power, who manufacture the threat, and who manipulate the population precisely so they can order the world as they see fit in accordance with their twisted ideology. It is the leaders and the organizers, who cynically exploit the fear and isolation of ordinary people, who are the true villains.

Scientism

A significant element that seems to be required for a totalitarian state to emerge is a fervent belief that society can be organized mechanistically. This idea, known as scientism, results from a

---

[144] Ibid., pp.172-175, Loc. 2511-2562.

distorted interpretation of the scientific method. It sees the entire world in deterministic terms in which human action can be explained and controlled along scientific lines according to physical laws. But it is a tragic error which if unleashed upon society in its strictest implementation – in conjunction with the other factors mentioned above – leads to a form of totalitarianism called "technocracy."

Scientism is not science applied to material objects, which is science's true *raison d'être*. Rather, it is the scientific method applied to the human mind, which is utterly inadmissible. It assumes that human beings can be organized like the working parts of a complicated machine in which so-called experts "shape the future" by rearranging the components, or, if necessary, discarding some components and installing new more efficient ones. People become disposable units who are told where they can go, what they can do, and even whether they must die, all in the pursuit of a utopian technocratic vision that the leaders, and not coincidentally the masses, believe is for the betterment of mankind or the planet.[145] Obviously, the will of the individual is completely overridden in such a system, but a significant percentage of the population goes along in the belief that it is doing its part to serve the cause. The ultimate utopian goal adopted by the leaders of the movement could be eugenicist or Malthusian or transhumanist, but in the end, this is not the important issue. The ideology eventually crumbles, but not before many millions have suffered unnecessarily.

Throughout history, the most malevolent acts have been committed by a few individuals who have held sway over large

---

[145] Patrick M. Wood, who has studied the global elite for many years, explains that the "threat" circulating today is "climate change," which is being used to promote the ideology of "sustainable development." The real threat is that this ideology is leading the world towards the implementation of a technocratic totalitarian system in which people will be constantly monitored and controlled in every facet of their lives with the goal of drastically limiting their "carbon footprint." Wood, Patrick M. (2018) *Technocracy: The Hard Road to World Order*. Coherent Publishing, Mesa, AZ.

numbers of people, and who, for whatever reason, have been able to seduce, control, manipulate, or indoctrinate the masses, and in the process have committed heinous and wicked acts of violence. Very often, these murderous individuals have convinced themselves – and in some cases many others – that the means they employ are warranted in the pursuit of some lofty goal. But in every case, without exception, neither the goal nor the means are justified. For many of these narcissists and psychopaths, power is the ultimate good, and the more of it, the better. For others, it is a fanatical belief in an ideology, and a messianic conviction that it is their right to supplant the will of millions in the pursuit of their utopia.

Animals do not go to war or commit genocide, because unlike humans they do not engage in purposive action. Human beings, on the other hand, have free will, which can be used for good or for evil. Most people, most of the time, do not wish to dominate others. But there are always a few who seem to have an insatiable desire to be in control. Small-time politicians and petty government bureaucrats might not kill millions, but many are driven by the same kind of lust for power or false ideology as their more powerful and dangerous associates. They justify their desire to impose their will by claiming to "serve" the public – and might sincerely believe they do so – but often their mentality is that of the tyrant. It is this desire to override the free will of ordinary people by force in the political arena that is the cause of so much evil.

The sociologist Franz Oppenheimer noted that there are two ways to live one's life in this world. The first is to interact with people cooperatively in voluntary association. For example, if Alice has something Bob wants, and Bob has something Alice wants, and their valuations are such that they agree to exchange, then they both profit. Oppenheimer called this the "economic means." The second way to interact is *in*voluntary; for example, Bob puts a gun to Alice's head and takes what she has by force. This, Oppenheimer said, is the "political means." And all politics is like that.[146]

---

[146] In Oppenheimer's original exposition he said, "There are two fundamentally opposed means whereby man, requiring sustenance, is impelled to obtain the necessary means for satisfying his desires. These are work and robbery, one's own labor and the forcible appropriation of the labor of others. Robbery! Forcible appropriation! I propose in the following discussion to call one's own labor and the equivalent exchange of one's own labor for the labor of others, the "economic means" for the satisfaction of needs, while the unrequited appropriation of the labor of others will be called the "political means." Oppenheimer, Franz (1975) [1908] *The State*. Free Life Editions, New York, pp. 24-25.

7

How We Understand Human Action

Anticipating the Thoughts and Actions of Others

The ability to experience vicariously the thoughts and emotions of others is clearly important in all interpersonal exchanges. Empathy engenders beneficence, generosity, and kindness, all of which are positive for social cooperation. But being able to *anticipate* the actions, desires, and feelings of others in response to one's own actions is also essential. Cooperation does not merely consist in mirroring what someone else is doing or feeling. It also involves predicting what he or she is going to do, or going to feel, in the future. It would seem that free will ought to make this task impossible. If we are all truly able to make independent choices, then forecasting another person's thoughts and choices should prove very difficult. And yet despite this, it is clearly the case we often have an inkling as to how other people are likely to act under a given set of circumstances. We do not merely empathize with their thoughts in the moment; we also experience vicariously their will and their choices, at least to a certain degree, based on our own past experiences and empathic ability. Free will does not make humans completely unpredictable.

For example, if you give someone a birthday gift, it is likely the person in question will smile and thank you. This response is not absolutely certain, but you expect it in most situations. If you sign a contract to remodel your kitchen having been supplied with some excellent references, it is probable that the contractor will adhere to the terms of the deal, give you what you want, and not disappear with your money. Again, this is not a foregone conclusion, but you can reasonably expect this will be the case. These kinds of assessment are obviously rather different from the predictions made in the physical world, precisely because material objects behave in a more predictable manner. But clearly human action is not radically unpredictable, especially when dealing with people you know in a familiar setting. The Austrian School of economics refers to this empathic ability to predict the thoughts and actions of others as "understanding" (or *verstehen* in German).[147] However, *verstehen* must be distinguished from the kind of understanding associated with scientific theories and laws, which while not absolutely certain (because scientific laws can always be disproved by newly acquired empirical evidence) are nevertheless far more assured.[148]

It should be noted that *verstehen* applies only to human action as governed by the will. It does not apply to reflexes and behaviors which are autonomic, instinctual, or unthinking, precisely because they do not constitute human action.[149] They are not dictated by the will; rather, they are controlled by biology, and their predictability is not determined by any empathic ability. For example, it is easy to predict a person will reflexively withdraw his hand if it accidentally touches a very hot surface. If you do not eat for a week, it is not necessary to assess your state of mind to determine you will be hungry. And in most cases, it is not required to empathize with people to know they prefer life over death. This is basic human biology, and *verstehen* is not needed to predict these things. However,

---

[147] For a complete description of verstehen, see Mises, Ludwig von (1998) [1949] *Human Action: A Treatise on Human Action*. Ludwig von Mises Institute, Auburn, AL, pp. 49-50.

[148] For a discussion on certainty and uncertainty, see Hoppe, Hans-Hermann (1997) "On Certainty and Uncertainty, or: How Rational Can Our Expectations Be?" *Review of Austrian Economics*, Vol. 10 (1), pp. 49-78.

[149] See "On the Serviceableness of Instincts" in Mises, Ludwig von (1998) [1949] *Human Action: A Treatise on Human Action*. Ludwig von Mises Institute, Auburn, AL, pp. 26-28.

verstehen is required to understand the multitude of possible actions a person might take to pursue instincts such as life or hunger. It is also required where people choose to override an instinct. For example, if an individual is deeply unhappy, it might be that person's will to attempt suicide and thereby act against the normal instinct to live. And we might comprehend this, not on the basis of biology, but rather because given the circumstances, we understand the particular human emotions and feelings behind the decision.

The Objective Study of Human Action

Verstehen is a subjective individually held assessment of another human being's thoughts, desires, and possible future actions under a given set of circumstances. It is never objective. In analyzing the action of human beings, firm predictions are difficult given the existence of free will. Therefore, if we wish to make a study of the logical consequences of human action and do so objectively, we cannot employ empiricism and the methodology of the physical sciences.[150] Humans do not behave like rocks or rockets. They do not obey objective physical laws that are discoverable from empirical evidence. Indeed, any attempt to predict human action by analyzing reams of statistical data and then applying rules described by mathematical equations, is bound to fail. Lamentably, however, this is precisely the methodology of mainstream economics today, which attempts to make predictions concerning human beings in the manner of physics or chemistry.[151] Thus, from an examination of past data, the economist will contrive a law, usually described in mathematical terms, and then apply that law to the current data in order to predict what is going to happen in the future. Invariably,

---

[150] See Rothbard, Murray N. (1973) "Praxeology as the Method of the Social Sciences" in *Economic Controversies*. Ludwig von Mises Institute, Auburn AL, (2011), p. 29-58.

[151] See Davidson, Laura and Walter E. Block (2016) "A Critique of Definitions in Economics from an Austrian Perspective: Macroeconomics." *Journal of Economic and Administrative Sciences*, Vol. 32 (1), pp. 2-19.

the predictions are wrong precisely because no two human beings have the same needs and desires, and no individual is preprogrammed to act in the same manner every time.

Economics is the study of human action with respect to means and ends, and I mention it here because adopting the correct method is important if we want to research human action in other fields such as morality and justice. The error of the social sciences today is based on the falsehood, first promulgated by Hume and later by the logical positivists, that all synthetic (non-tautological) propositions about the world, including generalized statements concerning the action of human beings, must originate with some kind of *a posteriori* evidence.[152]

While this erroneous belief leads to the wrong conclusions in economics, it also leads to the belief that any objective study of morality is impossible. Why? Because clearly there can be no empirical evidence for what *ought* to be the case. One can indeed say what a person *did* or did not do on the basis of observed facts; but it is indisputable that one cannot determine objectively what a person *ought* or ought not to do on the basis of such facts. Even the logical positivists agree with that. And so it is the standard belief today that the worth of any moral action is subjective; there is no objective morality. But this is false. As I hope to show in a later chapter, it is possible to deduce axiomatically true objective moral statements by using the correct methodology.

So how should we approach the study of the logic of action? The correct method is to arrive at propositions from first principles by employing the same approach Kant used in deducing statements *a priori* that are applicable to the real world. The study of human action using this process is called praxeology, and its application in the field of economics – which is praxeology's hitherto best developed branch – was first fully elucidated in the 20th century by

---

[152] See "The Fallacies of Positivism" in Mises, Ludwig von (1962) *The Ultimate Foundation of Economic Science: An Essay on Method.* D. Van Nostrand Co., New York, pp. 122-124.

Ludwig von Mises, a leader of the Austrian School. Its method starts with a self-evident truth, and it proceeds using nothing other than formal logic. And because this initial truth – known as the "axiom of action" – is *not* dependent on a mere definition, but rather on innate evidence – or inner experience – the propositions derived from it are *not* tautological; rather, they also tell us something objectively and absolutely true about the external world. To use the Kantian terminology, they are synthetic *a priori*. They are synthetic because they tell us something non-trivial about the world, and *a priori* because they are deduced without external empirical evidence.[153]

What is the nature of this self-evident inner experience? All human beings know what it means to act precisely because any attempt to deny this truth is itself an action; it is a performative contradiction. But in comprehending this idea, we also intuitively understand the various categories of action. As Mises explains:

> As thinking and acting men, we grasp the concept of action. In grasping this concept, we simultaneously grasp the closely correlated concepts of value, wealth, exchange, price, and cost. They are all necessarily implied in the concept of action, and together with them the concepts of valuing, scale of value and importance, scarcity and abundance, advantage and disadvantage, success, profit, and loss.[154]

To illustrate this point, suppose Robinson Crusoe wakes up one morning and is faced with a choice of fishing or lazing under a palm tree. Let us say he considers fish for breakfast his highest priority

---

[153] See Rothbard, Murray N. (1976) "Praxeology: The Methodology of Austrian Economics" in *The Logic of Action One: Method, Money, and the Austrian School.* Edward Elgar, Cheltenham, UK (1997), pp. 58-77.

[154] Mises, Ludwig von (2003) [1933] *Epistemological Problems of Economics.* Translated by George Reisman, Ludwig von Mises Institute, Auburn, AL, pp. 24-25.

and taking a rest under the shadow of the palm the next best alternative. At that particular moment, he prefers fish to lying under the tree, and this preference is demonstrated in the very action he takes. In choosing the former, he intuitively understands the meaning of value, preference, and choice. He also comprehends that catching fish has a specific end (the consumption of fish) which involves means (the labor involved in catching them), and this action has a cost (the opportunity cost associated with the loss of pleasure of lying under the tree). He instinctively realizes this is a form of exchange (catching and eating fish in exchange for foregone leisure), and it results in an anticipated profit (the marginal utility of eating fish over that derived from leisure). He therefore knows what profit is, and that this profit exists in his mind; it is a psychic profit, and it is *ex ante;* that is, it is anticipated. However, Crusoe might find he is unable to spear any fish that day or the fish he catches are inedible, in which case he might regret his choice and realize he has suffered a psychic loss, *ex post.* And this is because nothing is certain in this world. There is always an element of uncertainty in everything we do. He knows this too.

Because the basic concepts contained in the action axiom are intuitive and *a priori*, it is possible to extend these ideas into a complete set of propositions concerning human action using nothing other than formal logic. Indeed, with the addition of two minor empirical statements,[155] all the laws of economics can be deduced. The fact that economic laws can be deduced from first principles in this manner is the core idea behind the Austrian School, a school of thought which lies in direct opposition to the neoclassical ideology taught today.[156] Austrian economics is a

---

[155] The two minor propositions are that leisure is a good, and resources are not uniform in their distribution. See Rothbard, Murray N. (1976) "Praxeology: The Methodology of Austrian Economics" in *The Logic of Action One: Method, Money, and the Austrian School.* Edward Elgar, Cheltenham, UK (1997), pp. 58-59.

[156] The most famous exponents of Austrian economics were Carl Menger, Eugen von Bohm Bawerk, Ludwig von Mises, Friedrich Hayek, and Murray

division of praxeology, and its laws are absolutely true precisely because they are derived *a priori* from true premises. This makes them markedly different from the laws of the natural sciences that are objective but empirically derived, which makes them falsifiable.

Natural science laws are of the form, if A then B. For example, Boyle's law says: "If you raise the pressure of a gas, then the volume it occupies will fall in proportion." In this example, the relationship between the pressure and the volume of a gas can be shown to be inversely related in an experiment in which temperature is held constant. This is easy to do because there are no other variables that govern the outcome.[157]

The laws of praxeology, on the other hand, take the form; if A then B, *all other things being equal (ceteris paribus)*. The *"ceteris paribus"* is crucially important because in analyzing the logic of action, it is not possible to control for a multitude of independent variables. But we can hold the variables constant *mentally* and then analyze the consequences *logically*. Unlike the physical sciences, this means praxeological statements, including economic laws, cannot be used to make firm predictions, but they can make absolutely true claims.[158]

Rothbard.

[157] The problem with mainstream economics is that it uses the same methodology, but in human action the variables are too numerous, which means they cannot be held constant experimentally to prove the case. For example, mainstream economics says: "If consumer demand is insufficient, then a productive crisis will ensue, and unemployment will rise." This relation is inferred from historical trends and various assumptions using mathematical modeling. But using statistics and mathematical equations to infer the result is a fatuous exercise because people have free will and the variables governing their psychology are impossible to determine. We cannot know for sure that a reduction in consumer demand will indeed cause the stated effect. See Rothbard, Murray N. (1976) "Praxeology: The Methodology of Austrian Economics" in *The Logic of Action One: Method, Money, and the Austrian School*. Edward Elgar, Cheltenham, UK (1997), pp. 58-77.

[158] Rothbard, Murray N. (1973) "Praxeology as the Method of the Social Sciences" in *Economic Controversies*. Ludwig von Mises Institute, Auburn AL.

For example, it is an economic law that if the minimum wage is raised, the number of people employed will fall, *ceteris paribus.* This is not to say it will always fall in practice, because other variables – such as a sudden increase in the demand for goods and services – might intervene to make it rise. However, employment will always be lower than it would have been had the minimum wage not been raised above its equilibrium point in the first place. And this is axiomatically true. Austrian economics can therefore say, for example, that a specific government policy will definitely not achieve its stated aims. It cannot say precisely what the future will hold, but unlike mainstream economics, it can say with absolute certainty that the goals sought would have been better achieved by not introducing the policy in the first place.

It is beyond the scope of this book to examine all the implications of this subject. Rather, the point I wish to make here is that it is possible to make absolutely true non-tautological statements about human action and to do so on the basis of self-evident axioms. Empiricism is not the only method for acquiring knowledge of the world. A great number of insights can be discovered in the form of *synthetic a priori* propositions that start with certain self-evident truths, and this includes the category of human action. But while the knowledge gained is absolutely true, it cannot take the form of firm predictions, precisely because humans are always free to think in a manner not constrained by physical laws.[159] In this regard, these insights differ markedly from those of physics.

In summary, praxeology gives rise to generalized laws that are objective and absolutely true regarding the logical outcome of human action but makes no specific predictions. Firm predictions of human action are impossible because human beings have free will. In contrast, scientific laws, while objective, are empirically derived and therefore falsifiable. They allow for predictions

---

(2011), p. 36.

[159] And this includes even a prisoner in chains, who might be constrained physically but not in thought.

regarding the behavior of physical objects and are true unless proved otherwise by countervailing facts. *Verstehen*, on the other hand, is an individual, subjectively held assessment of a particular situation with respect to the future. It involves predicting the thoughts and future actions of others, but the prognostications are far from assured. There are no hard and fast laws to describe *verstehen*. But *verstehen* should not be confused with the understanding of basic biological or physical functions which control instinctual drives, reflexes, and behaviors.

The Rule-Based Society

Prior to the Enlightenment, human thought and learning was dominated by religious dogma. While ordinary people understood the cause of many natural occurrences and used reason to search for specific solutions to practical problems, there was little need or desire by the average person to employ universal scientific laws or to explain the world in rational terms. As long as they had sufficient knowledge to cope with the challenges they faced in their everyday lives, basic rules of thumb were good enough. If an unanticipated event was not explicable with the knowledge at hand, it was deemed the will of God. The Enlightenment changed all that. For the first time in human history, people were told they could think for themselves, universal physical laws could be discovered, and no problem was too big to solve. Science had all the answers.

But science does not have all the answers when it comes to the output of the human mind. While psychology can provide descriptions of certain personality types, it is incapable of providing a precise answer as to why people think the way they do. Psychology cannot make an exact prediction concerning a person's future action, because such an answer is beyond the reach of rational or scientific explanation. In this limited sense, human psychology is irrational. No one's value scale, choices, or motivations can be measured or predicted. Even the individual himself cannot fully predict what choices he will make in the future. *A fortiori*, it is impossible for anyone, especially those who claim power or authority over others, to organize society along scientific principles with the objective of attaining some lofty goal. Science can predict the motion of physical bodies, and it can explain how to organize matter to attain certain ends, but it cannot do the same for human beings.

Nevertheless, there are those who contend, erroneously, that the human mind operates according to a predictable algorithm, and that in the near future silicon-based algorithms employed in artificial intelligence will be able to predict with perfect reliability all human thoughts and desires. People will be connected to various devices that will constantly monitor their shopping habits, internet viewing, leisure activities, and so on, as well as their biological data, and the computer's algorithm will be able to tell them what to do with consistently better results than if they made their decisions themselves. They predict a future society where artificial intelligence will know people's thoughts and needs better than they do themselves, and computers will be able to advise them on how they should act in almost every imaginable situation.[160]

Clearly if such a system were implemented, there would be no room for human thought and volition. Taken to the extreme, it would lead to a totalitarian dystopia where people would not be entirely human, but rather human-computer hybrids who could be manipulated and controlled by those in positions of power. It would of course represent the ultimate in technocracy, a system of government based on the pseudo-science known as scientism, the fallacious idea that human thoughts, emotions, and actions can be monitored, predicted, and controlled for the betterment of mankind by employing the scientific method.[161]

---

[160] See Harari, Yuval Noah (2018) *Homo Deus: A Brief History of Tomorrow.* Harper Perennial, pp. 160-163.

[161] As Rothbard states, "Scientism is the profoundly unscientific attempt to transfer uncritically the methodology of the physical sciences to the study of human action." Rothbard, Murray N. (1960) "The Mantle of Science" in

A technocratic society is totalitarian and a product of deterministic thinking. But according to social psychologist Mattias Desmet, in order for a technocracy to be fully implemented, there must exist a high degree of narcissism within the population at large, where many people clamor for rules and those in positions of power are happy to oblige.[162] Narcissists demand laws governing every aspect of life, either because they have an insatiable desire to be in control, or because to live without rules is to face fear and doubt in their lives, particularly in their interpersonal relations. We see this today in the proliferation of regulations governing work, the environment, social systems, health, and many other areas of life, where discretion is taken away from the individual and regularized according to supposedly scientific formulae. In addition, an increasing number of social rules governing speech, "microaggressions," and improper thoughts have resulted in a suffocating and oppressive new kind of morality, epitomized by cancel culture and "wokism."

Precisely because the results of organizing society in this manner cannot be predicted and are almost always counterproductive, a hue and cry go out for more rules to fix the problems, which the government, the media, or their enablers and supporters are all too eager to promote and enforce. The consequence of not allowing ordinary people to make choices according to their will, particularly in cases were doing so would harm no one, has stripped much of the spontaneity and joy out of life, and dissolved social bonds

---

Economic Controversies. Ludwig von Mises Institute, Auburn AL. (2011), p. 3. For a full explanation, see pp. 3-23.

[162] As Desmet explains, "Society is – it's hard to ignore – increasingly bogged down in an endless proliferation of rules. On the one hand, such rules are imposed by the government, but on the other hand, there is also a call for more rules – a hyper-strict morality – from the population itself. Like narcissism, this is a frantic attempt to contain the surge of fear and insecurity in human relationships." Desmet, Mattias (2022) *The Psychology of Totalitarianism*. Translated by Els Vanbrabant, Chelsea Green Publishing, Kindle Edition, pp. 94-95, Loc. 1368-1376.

because people no longer have to think for themselves or take the initiative. Life has been condensed into a rule-bound box.

But I want to be clear here. Laws, *per se*, are not the problem. Laws are a fundamental and very necessary aspect of life. Nor is logic or science detrimental to society. The solution is certainly not to abandon science and return to a pre-Enlightenment mode of thought. Rather, the problem lies in the fact that there are far *too many* rules and laws, meaning that the vast majority are formulated in an entirely illogical or unscientific or immoral manner, even though their authors frequently invoke logic or science or morality to justify them. Finding the right laws is therefore paramount.

Broadly speaking, human beings employ three very different kinds of laws, all of which are essential for life. I shall consider them each in turn.

First, are the universal and objective physical laws of nature, which broaden our knowledge of the universe and are essential in the field of technological innovation. They apply to material objects only, and *not* to the thoughts and actions of human beings. Physical laws are discovered using the scientific method, which involves formulating a hypothesis from empirical observations via induction, using the hypothesis to make deductions, and then testing the latter with experiments. If the experiments yield positive results, then a theory is the outcome. If the theory proves durable, it is said to be a scientific law. Not everyone is a scientist of course, but everyone employs a similar, albeit less rigorous process when observing cause and effect in their everyday lives. It is an essential element of human action.

The second set of laws essential for life is embodied in the concept self-discipline. Self-discipline consists of a set of rules we choose to impose on ourselves in order to lead a harmonious, orderly, and meaningful life. Each individual must personally decide the number and kind of rules to apply. The best-selling self-help book *12 Rules for Life: An Antidote to Chaos*, by the Canadian clinical psychologist Jordan Peterson, provides some basic examples of valuable things to know in developing one's character.[163] According to Peterson, this kind of advice is necessary because many people are simply not familiar with the kind of rules that are required to avoid chaos in their lives. The fact that so many are not is perhaps a reflection of the narcissistic society, and the seemingly widely held view that controlling others is more important than regulating oneself. But it is also clear that many people are crying out for help in this regard because they realize there is an essential component missing in their lives.

Third, are the laws we impose on society itself, and this is where most of the problems alluded to earlier arise. No society can live without basic laws, but formulating laws on the basis of preferred outcomes deemed good for society or good for certain classes of people is bound to fail, especially if attempted scientifically or on subjectively held moral grounds. It will fail precisely because it is impossible to evaluate quantitatively the overall utility of any policy for any individual or group, let alone make interpersonal comparisons of utility for society as a whole. Therefore, not only can no one predict whether the outcome will be good *ex ante*, they cannot even evaluate whether it *was* good after the fact. Even more importantly, as I shall discuss in greater detail in later chapters, many laws involve interventions against innocent people that violate their will.

But while we should assuredly reject any scientific rationale for the law, we should not throw out the rationalist baby with the bathwater. Logical arguments – not scientific ones – do have a very important place in determining the kind of laws that are necessary for a society. However, the proper application of ratiocination lies not in attempting to determine the consequences of the law, but rather in its deduction from fundamental underlying principles. And

---

[163] Examples include "stand up straight," "set your house in order," "tell the truth," "compare yourself to who you were yesterday, not to who someone else is today," etc. Peterson, Jordan B. (2018) *12 Rules for Life: An Antidote to Chaos*. Random House, Canada.

in the latter case, it is perfectly valid because the law is deduced *a priori*, with no attempt at psychologizing or moralizing or seeking a utopian outcome on a pseudo-scientific basis. As I shall show, it is possible to deduce a code of justice that is fair, objective, universal, and above all, in keeping with our humanity.

The final section of this book will examine these three different sets of laws and demonstrate why they are fundamental to human existence and happiness.

PART III

The Case for a Genuinely

Free World

8

Countering Entropy in the Material World

Finding Regularities

What does possessing a free will mean in our daily lives? By definition, human action involves prior thought. This differs from reflexive or instinctual behavior. Since animals do not possess reason, but engage the world only reflexively and instinctively, they merely *behave*. To a certain extent human beings do this also. As mentioned in previous chapters, there are some functions of the brain and nervous system retained from our evolutionary past that are autonomic. In addition, humans, like other animals, are subject to various instincts, many of which are necessary for life. We are also susceptible to a variety of external forces and appetites, such as customs, social pressures, advertising, propaganda, compulsions, addictions etc., all of which can exert an influence on our thoughts and choices. But because humans have reason and free will, we are also able to *act*, and in doing so we are often able to override these impulsive and instinctive feelings, for good or for bad, at least to some degree.

It is true that the will's ability to dominate some of the brain's more primitive reflexes is very limited or non-existent, and its control over many instincts and influences is sometimes difficult. But in carrying out any action, which by definition is premeditated, the decision always originates with the will. When I say, "this is the *reason* I did so and so," I imply there was a choice in the matter, and I took deliberative and purposive action to carry it out. In stating there is a reason for my action, I do not mean that it was caused by some external event. Quite the contrary. I mean just the opposite; that *I* caused the action by freely exercising my will with a motive that originates within me. My motive and my will are self-caused.

But why do we act? Action is the process of replacing an existing state of affairs with a new condition which is anticipated to produce greater satisfaction or happiness.[164] In the broadest sense, action is directed towards the attainment of any goal that is expected to produce a psychic profit. Happiness, or the removal of felt uneasiness, is an emotion that has been endowed in us by evolution to let us know that the action pursued and the consequences anticipated are positive for our lives. This is not to say that the ends sought always increase happiness, or that actors always pick the correct means to achieve a specific goal. All of us can err in our prognostications. But to the extent that an actor's forecasts are correct, the goals pursued increase satisfaction, at least in the short run.

All action is directed toward the future. But it is precisely because the future is somewhat uncertain that human beings find it necessary to find areas of certainty in order to predict the likely outcome of action in the world around them. Without the cognition of regularities involving cause and effect, actions would have little chance of success. Indeed, there would be no action at all.[165]

---

[164] Mises, Ludwig von (1998) [1949] *Human Action: A Treatise on Human Action.* Ludwig von Mises Institute, Auburn, AL, p. 13.

[165] As Mises states, "No thinking and no acting would be possible to man if the universe were chaotic, i.e., if there were no regularity whatever in the succession and concatenation of events. In such a world of unlimited contingency nothing could be perceived but ceaseless kaleidoscopic change. There would be no possibility for man to expect anything. All experience would be merely historical, the record of what has happened in the past. No inference from past events to what might happen in the future would be permissible. Therefore, man could not act. He could at best be a passive spectator and would not be able to make any arrangements for the future, be it only for the future of the impending instant. The first and basic achievement of thinking is the awareness of constant relations among the

In the physical world, we recognize such regularities exist, and together with the power of reason, we can exploit them for purposes of acting. This ability to understand and apply physical laws is not just confined to the natural scientist. It is innate in every person. All cognizant human beings possess an inborn disposition to seek regularity and discern cause and effect, at least at a basic level. Indeed, we employ it all the time, for without it, we would be unable to act and to live. It is part of the logical structure of the human mind and a natural inclination.

Reducing Physical Entropy

Two fundamental instincts of nearly all animate living things are, on the one hand, the preservation of bodily integrity and the avoidance of death, and on the other hand, sexual attraction and reproduction. From a purely physical perspective, the outcome of these innate tendencies is a reduction of entropy in both the individual and in the species as a whole. Entropy is the degree of *disorder, randomness, and uncertainty* within a particular system, and while it is a pervasive feature of the universe, living things are able to create material order out of chaos against the general tide of entropy.

But human beings have the unique ability to discover and employ regularities for the purpose of reducing entropy in other areas of life. We do so because low entropy is good. Animals have no need to find laws because they are able to maintain bodily integrity and order – and hence life – purely by instinct. They

---

external phenomena that affect our senses. A bundle of events that are regularly related in a definite way to other events is called a specific thing and as such distinguished from other specific things…. Whatever philosophers may say about causality, the fact remains that no action could be performed by men not guided by it. Neither can we imagine a mind not aware of the nexus of cause and effect. In this sense we may speak of causality as a category or an *a priori* of thinking and acting." Mises, Ludwig von (1962) *The Ultimate Foundation of Economic Science: An Essay on Method.* D. Van Nostrand Co., New York, pp. 19-20.

naturally search for food, and they need little else to sustain themselves. In addition, like humans, they create order in the form of their offspring through their natural instinct for sexual intercourse. But humans can create life-benefitting low entropy conditions in additional ways. For example, we use the discovery of physical laws to create material goods from disordered matter, which are then used for a variety of life-affirming purposes.

But in what way is low entropy beneficial, and how is it reduced? The second law of thermodynamics implies that the entropy of any system will never decrease over time unless affected by a change in its energy state. It is a fundamental fact of nature, and it permeates every facet of our lives. The concept of entropy is not simple, but it is highly relevant to the topic at hand, so I ask the reader to bear with me as I explain.

To illustrate entropy, consider a deck of playing cards that accidentally falls from a table onto the floor. Clearly, the cards become more disordered than they were before. Instead of being in a neat pack, they are scattered on the ground. Let us say all the cards were in a specific sequence when they were on the table, but now they are completely out of order. The cards have fallen into a random state. Moreover, without checking them, we can have very little knowledge of their present sequence. In short, the cards are *disordered*, they are *randomly* distributed, and the sequence they are in is *uncertain*. They are higher in entropy.

The second law of thermodynamics means that no object or group of objects becomes more complex or more ordered by itself. Most things, left to their own devices, become more disordered over time; they naturally decay. For example, ice melts, metal corrodes, and buildings fall into disrepair. More fundamentally, entropy increases as heat (energy) disperses and equalizes within a system. Heat always flows from hot to cold – never the other way around – and as it does so, the molecules in the system as a whole become more scattered, more random, and more disordered. Consider a lump of coal burning in a fireplace. Chemical energy stored in the coal is released in the form of heat and spreads throughout the room. When the coal has finished burning, the room and the fireplace are at the same temperature. But the molecules that were the coal are now more randomly distributed as soot and ash, and the air molecules in the room are warmer, in a slightly more excited state, and more disordered. Entropy has increased.

How does this relate to the pack of cards? Before the cards fall, they have potential energy, but this is released as kinetic energy which disperses the cards in all directions as they hit the floor. The dispersal of this energy causes entropy to increase, both in the cards and in the molecules of the surrounding air, which are heated microscopically by friction. In the case of melting ice, heat from the surrounding air flows into the ice, the temperatures equalize, and as they do so, the molecules in the ice become less ordered as they turn to liquid water. The air surrounding the ice becomes slightly cooler and more ordered, but never more so than the disorder created in the ice.[166]

Despite this seemingly inevitable process, entropy can be reversed, at least locally, where heat (energy) is made to do work instead of being allowed to disperse. For example, heat from the burning coal can be used to drive a steam engine, which can be used to power a loom that makes fabric. But the entropy reduction represented by the output of the loom can never be greater than the disorder created by the burning of the coal and the heat released to the air, precisely because no engine is 100% efficient. The cards that fall to the floor can be gathered up and put back in the right sequence. However, the production of the energy required to do it creates more disorder elsewhere than the order put back in the cards. In a similar vein, a freezer can turn water into ice, rusted metal can be sanded off and repainted, and the house can be

---

[166] Burning is an example of an exothermic processes in which heat is released and entropy increases in the surrounding air. Melting ice is an endothermic process in which heat is absorbed. Entropy increases in the ice but decreases in the surrounding air. Nevertheless, net entropy increases.

repaired. But every time energy is made to do work like this –
whether it is generated by a mechanical engine or a human body –
the order created can never be more than the disorder engendered
somewhere else.

If we examine the universe as a single closed system, the amount
of disorder is constantly increasing because heat from the galaxies
is spreading. In a few billion years, the galaxies will burn out, the
temperature of the universe will be slightly warmer than it is now,
and maximum disorder and randomness will prevail. However, as
long as heat radiates from concentrated energy sources such as
around stars, then that energy can be harnessed locally and made
to do work. As a consequence, order can be created. Indeed, while
the universe as a whole is becoming steadily more random, the
energy gradient that prevails around our sun allows for small
pockets of order to arise here on earth. And it is the sun that
provides nearly all the necessary energy for the most complex form
of order to exist – namely, life. Taken as a whole, the disorder
created in the rest of the universe by the radiating heat from the sun
is always greater than the order created on earth. But as long as the
sun keeps burning and life takes some of that energy to do work,
then entropy remains low in our small pocket of the cosmos.

Living things are self-sustaining biological engines which
harness energy on a continuous basis to remain alive and keep
entropy at bay.[167] Energy is made to do work, which is employed to
maintain the very engine that performs the work. Plants perform
this self-sustaining feat by capturing energy directly from the sun via
the process of photosynthesis. Light energy, in conjunction with
carbon dioxide and water, is converted into chemical energy in the
form of sugars and starches, which allows the plant to grow and
ultimately reproduce. Animals prevent entropic increases by

---

[167] In nearly all cases, energy comes either directly or indirectly from the sun.
There are some living things which derive energy from other sources, such as
organisms in deep sea vents which use geothermal energy, and
chemosynthetic bacteria which derive energy from inorganic chemicals.

consuming chemical energy in the form of other animals or plants, which is used to build proteins, carbohydrates and fats. Energy is then released via catabolism to provide for the maintenance and growth of cells, and to allow the animal to do additional work within its environment.

Energy sources are required precisely because life is a constant struggle against entropy and decay. When the biological engine stops working, it decays and dies, and entropy increases. Therefore, to sustain life, all living things must constantly consume. And thus, most species, including our own, have evolved a mechanism which drives them towards the creation of bodily order by incentivizing the consumption of energy sources. In humans and most animals, this drive is manifested in a psychological state called hunger. In addition, there are other basic drives, all of which come under the rubric of "felt uneasiness," the purpose of which is to maintain the life of the individual and avoid death. These include thirst, the feeling of extreme heat or cold, fear of danger, etc. Death is the reversal of order. As the body decomposes, it releases heat, and entropy increases. Since all living things eventually die, sexual desire is another basic instinct which most species possess, precisely so that order is maintained via the animal's offspring.

We cannot know exactly how non-human animals feel, but we can presume that their behaviors and instincts are similar to our own. Of course, human needs are more complex, and felt uneasiness drives us to action and not merely reflexive or instinctual behavior. But the basic outcome is the same – namely, the persistent push toward bodily integrity and reproduction, in opposition to the inevitable tide of increasing entropy. In short, life is about creating and preserving order. If this were not the case, we would cease to exist as a species. Life, therefore, is a system of *negative entropy* – a term first coined by Erwin Schrodinger in his popular book, *What is Life?* – which refers to the way in which all living things reduce entropy by feeding on free energy.[168]

However, because human beings have reason and can engage in human action, we can also harness other sources of energy besides that provided by food – for example, wood, coal, oil, hydroelectric and nuclear power, etc. – and use them to create order in matter external to our own bodies. Generally speaking, we call the various states of ordered matter "goods." These are then either consumed directly, or they are used indirectly as tools – capital goods – to produce more goods. For example, most of the food we eat is not plucked from the wild, as animals do, but rather planted and grown using various tools, which range from the simple plough to large and complex agricultural machinery. These capital goods require energy to build and operate, but they also require a production structure, all of which involves creating and maintaining order and reducing entropy. The more complex the form of these capital goods, the larger is the structure required and the greater the amount of work (energy) needed.

All consumer goods, from the most mundane to the seemingly bizarre, satisfy some need which is perceived as necessary to remove felt uneasiness, or create happiness, *ex ante*. Human beings are complex animals, and their needs are great and varied, and thus the goods they demand in an advanced society elicit the creation of a vast, highly organized – i.e., low entropy – structure of production. Our entire civilization is created and maintained by finding energy supplies, and then employing them in localized systems to create

---

[168] Schrodinger was criticized for using the term "negative entropy" instead of "free energy." However, he explains that the purpose of using this term was to convey the idea that entropy was "transferred" from the living body to the surroundings. He did not want people to think that simply by harnessing energy (instead of free energy) the entropy of the body could be reduced without it increasing elsewhere. He thought that "free energy" was too technical a term for the average reader, free energy being the amount of work performed, and equal to enthalpy minus the absolute temperature multiplied by the entropy of the system, $(G = H - TS)$. Schrodinger, Erwin (2012) [1944] *What is Life? The Physical Aspect of the Living Cell.* Cambridge University Press, p. 74.

order out of chaos so as to satisfy many needs from the most basic to the most esoteric. Virtually all material goods, whether they are gathered and collected as a natural resource, or created from various natural resources, or manufactured from a multitude of intermediate goods, involve reducing entropy by harnessing energy. By gathering or creating them, we create order out of chaos.

Finding Regularities is a Natural Inclination

While energy is necessary for the creation and maintenance of civilization, it is not sufficient. No advancement could be made without a basic knowledge of the laws of nature. This is a major factor that distinguishes us from animals. By studying and applying the regularities we observe in the material world, we are able to build the capital goods and ultimately produce the consumer goods we need to sustain ourselves.[169] It is this natural propensity to look for laws governing physical processes, combined with an instinctual drive to alleviate uneasiness and seek happiness, that gives rise to the creation of the highly-ordered material states that exist outside of our own bodies. There are, of course, some animal species that create ordered states in their environment purely by instinct. For example, birds build nests, spiders weave webs, bees construct hives, and so on. But we are the only species which actively creates novel objects by understanding and employing the laws of nature. We use this knowledge, not only to make the goods themselves, but in many cases to build the machines which harness the needed energy.

Even seemingly mundane goods require a knowledge of cause and effect, and hence a basic understanding of natural laws. Consider, for example, the knowledge needed to forge a hammer, make a bow and arrow, or build a plough. Taken to the extreme, our knowledge of physical laws leads to the massive low entropy

---

[169] There are exceptions in the animal kingdom, such as birds building nests, and beavers building dams, etc., although none of these involve using reason. Nevertheless, they also are creating order out of chaos for life-enhancing purposes.

condition of an advanced civilization.[170]

One cannot deny there exists a natural inclination to engage in actions that impose order in an otherwise disordered and uncertain material world, precisely because in most cases it is positive for life. Thus, while the will is free, humans do not choose entirely randomly. Clearly, through the process of natural selection, evolution has *not* given us a mind that makes choices in a solely haphazard and indiscriminate way.[171] Our will operates in conjunction with our evolutionary instincts, the most dominant of which is our natural desire to live. This is the strongest of all, and only rarely does the

---

[170] There is, however, one other component that makes a major contribution to the development of an advanced civilization, and that is the free market. When people arc freely able to express their will, and not prevented from doing so by individuals who deign to control the actions of others through force or coercion, capital has the best chance to accumulate. Where the market is not free, knowledge is of little use in building a great civilization. Fortunately, this desire to control others is not a universal human disposition since most people only wish to be left alone. Unfortunately, there exists a small minority of individuals who are disposed to oppress and are very often able to seize power and impose their will by interfering with the actions of the populace on a large scale. When this occurs, and the will of the majority is prevented from being expressed in action and free exchange, then inevitably the accumulation of capital becomes severely limited. This is an important issue that is the subject of a later chapter, but the point I wish to make here is that outside of the hampered economy, an essential capability and natural inclination common to most of humanity, excluding perhaps an iniquitous few, is that of ordering matter by observing cause and effect and applying reason. This is a capability that no other animal possesses.

[171] Language itself is a case in point. All languages are composed of basic phonemes which are grouped together form morphemes, and which form a finite number of words. Words can then be ordered to produce an infinite number of possible sentences according to specific rules of grammar. All languages have a common basic structure which is hardwired into the human brain, and while children learn specific words by hearing their parents speak, they have an innate sense of the correct ordering of verb and noun structures which is not learned. Steven Pinker claims that we have a natural language instinct that probably arose through the process of natural selection. According to that author, we understand sentences by breaking them down, parsing them into discrete units, and looking for order among the grammatical information.

will overcome it. Sometimes, a person who is severely depressed commits suicide. Occasionally, we hear of a mother who sacrifices her own life to save that of her child; or a soldier who puts himself in harm's way to save the rest of his platoon. But this kind of heroism is rare. The urge to live is paramount in all but a few cases.

Other instincts are easier to overcome. We can go on a fast, at least for a while. We can abstain from sex. And we can decide to endure extreme conditions, provided it does not lead to death. But most of our actions are geared towards life; they are life-affirming and tailored to creating order. Hence, while the will is always free to choose from a multitude of possibilities, usually we choose purposive actions which conform with our strongest instinct, which is to live. Only rarely are we faced with a decision to act immediately to avoid death, and so the vast majority of life-affirming action involves the creation of goods which we perceive as necessary to enhance our lives.

Of course, purposive actions can be destructive instead of constructive, and many actions (or inactions) are neutral. Not everything people do with regard to material objects is directed towards creating order. For example, sometimes it is necessary to destroy goods in order to recycle them, or even to dismantle whole areas of production so as to create new more efficient ones; the economist Joseph Schumpeter called this "creative destruction."[172] Additionally, disorder may simply be the result of a mistake. Moreover, some humans, particularly those with violent or psychopathic tendencies, are disposed to engage in wanton destruction, including violating the bodily integrity of others for material gain or pleasure. On a large scale, aggressions of this kind lead to war, which is the most ruinous human activity of all. But these kinds of destructive actions are the product of a lack of reason and are therefore anti-human. They occur because while evolution

---

[172] See the chapter "Creative Destruction" in Schumpeter, Joseph A. (1975) [1940] *Capitalism, Socialism, and Democracy*. Harper Collins, New York, pp. 81-86.

has given us an advanced brain, it is not infallible. Human beings are not perfect, and some are grossly imperfect.

Nevertheless, to the extent that human action is on balance life-affirming – otherwise we would cease to exist as a species – it is the case that creating order or reducing entropy in the material world to produce goods is a disposition that is fundamental to human existence. This occurs only because human beings have reason and the unique ability to seek and comprehend the laws of nature, at least to some degree. If we had neither reason nor the capacity to find regularities and interpret them, we would not be able to act. We could live only by instinct, as animals do.[173]

Life-affirming human action is purposive action, which through an understanding of physical laws, is directed at producing and maintaining low entropy states – namely, the low entropy condition of the human body and of the material goods in our environment. But as I shall next explain, the laws of the physical world are not the only kinds of laws we can apprehend to reduce entropy. And low-entropy material goods are not the only kind of orderly states that can be used for life-enhancing purposes.

---

[173] Mises states, "As with every instance of action, the recognition of the laws of nature is put into the service of man's efforts to improve his conditions." Mises, Ludwig von (1998) [1949] *Human Action: A Treatise on Human Action*. Ludwig von Mises Institute, Auburn, AL, p. 145.

9

Countering Entropy in the Mental World

Non-Material Goods

Not all goods that produce happiness are material in nature. Indeed, it might be said that the most successful actions in life are those which give rise to non-material goods, and which act on the mind directly. These include things like a good marriage, close friendships, education, art, music, etc. We do not normally think of producing and consuming goods like love or wisdom or beauty, but unless they are given to us unconditionally – as, for example, in the case of a parent's love for a child – we have to acquire them through thought and action. They have to be "produced" before they can be "consumed." Occasionally, we might derive contentment or satisfaction purely by happenstance – for example, by unexpectedly encountering a beautiful view while out for a walk – but even in these cases it is necessary to act in certain ways to make it possible. Equally so, it is necessary to act in a particular manner if we want to avoid the opposite of goods – namely, "bads" – that are displeasing, depressing, or dissatisfying. Ugliness, hate, ignorance, etc. are "bads" most of us want to avoid, precisely because they involve disorder, uncertainty, disutility, and a psychic loss.

There seems to be something about the lower entropy involved in beauty – whether it is because of its regularity, complexity, intricacy, or harmony – that directly affects human emotions in such a way as to create a more satisfactory mental state, and this is manifested as aesthetic pleasure. A regularity that is consistently found in nature is the so-called golden ratio, a classic example of which can be found in the spiral of the nautilus shell, which has a diameter that increases by exactly 1.618 times every 90 degrees from the tip to the base. The ordering of the leaves on plants often follows this pattern, as does the ratio between many different points on the human face. The golden ratio is also found in ocean waves, whirlpools, flowers, and many other natural phenomena. It exists because nature tends to optimize growth in such a way as to produce the maximum amount of order for the least amount of work, and this can be achieved with repetitive iterations in which each addition is in the same proportion to the sum of that which has gone before. Mathematically, this results in the ratio of approximately 1:1.618.[174] We tend to find objects that involve this proportion to be aesthetically pleasing, perhaps because in witnessing it, its regularity is mirrored in the mind itself. Because of this quality, the golden ratio is employed in classical architecture, feng shui, and fine art. Human faces which have proportions that most closely adhere to the golden ratio are generally considered particularly beautiful.

Music seems to be a very notable case where the order and complexity of the art form is reflected in the mind, usually in a positive way. Plato considered music to be the most powerful form of education because he thought that its harmonies could put order into the soul, even during the earliest stages of life. Confucius considered music to be such an important element of society that he taught that all education should involve it. Music was not merely a form of entertainment but was also a means for enhancing long-term social well-being by creating order. Unlike other forms of art, which derive meaning from a physical connection to the human or material world, or from a narrative that relates to that world, pure instrumental music is entirely abstract, and yet it can evoke very powerful and specific emotions depending on its theme. Perhaps the

---

[174] The golden ratio is derived from two quantities whose ratio of the larger to the smaller quantity is equal to the ratio of their sum to the larger quantity. Let $a/b = 1.618$. This implies $(a+b)/a = 1.618$. From this it follows that $(2a+b)/(a+b) = 1.618$ and $(3a+2b)/(2a+b) = 1.618$, etc.

resonance we feel with certain passages of music arises because the harmony and structure we hear have a direct correspondence with the kind of order or disorder in the mind associated with the experience.

Consider the rich and complex yet highly structured music of Bach's Goldberg Variations, or the dreaminess and breath of color conjured by the gentle melody and changing dynamics of a Chopin nocturne. Even music that is loud and discordant can be satisfying, provided it retains some melodic structure. Mussorgsky's classic *Night on a Bald Mountain* arouses dark, eerie, and menacing feelings that reflect the mental disturbances caused by genuine fear or discomfort, but perhaps the music is a reminder that life in general can be inauspicious, and in witnessing the abstract form, it puts legitimately frightening experiences that occur in the real world into a more measured light. Melancholy music seems to have a similar effect. In one study, it was found that because the sad impressions evoked by the melody are physically non-threatening, the music enhances mood by helping to resolve real events that have been encountered in the past.[175] By bringing the negative feelings to the forefront of attention, the dysphoric state can be controlled and ultimately reduced. Perhaps, in temporarily inducing a kind of mental entropy by means other than a genuine memory, the music shows that sadness is not something that has to be permanent.[176]

---

[175] Sachs, Matthew E., Antonio Damasio, and Assal Habibi (2015) "The Pleasures of Sad Music: A Systematic Review." *Frontiers in Human Neuroscience,* Vol. 9, p. 404.

[176] The same can be said for poetry. For many people, the rhythm, meter, cadence, and metaphorical connections in great poetry can create intensely pleasurable sensations. In one study of poetry readers, 40% showed visible goosebumps when listening to their favorite poems. Wassiliwizky, Eugen et al. (2017) "The Emotional Power of Poetry: Neural Circuitry, Psychophysiology and Compositional Principles." *Social Cognitive and Affective Neuroscience,* Vol. 12 (8), pp. 1229-1240.

Utility Versus Lasting Contentment

A good, by definition, induces a psychological condition called satisfaction or happiness, which affirms that the action taken to produce or obtain it appears to have been worthwhile. It is the anticipation of this mental state that provides the motivation for the action. Evolution has created in us this need for an elevated mental state – in both its anticipated and realized form – precisely to guide and endorse actions which are positive for life.

Nevertheless, it is necessary to distinguish between short-term psychic profit and long-term satisfaction. Not all actions and not all goods lead to overall contentment. Take the example of a methamphetamine addict. For such a person, meth is a good because it leads to a quick high, and it therefore has utility. When the addict acts to obtain and consume the drug, his preference for it over everything else is demonstrated in the very action he takes. It ranks highest on his value scale at that moment. But methamphetamine is very unlikely to lead to sustainable happiness. Many other "goods" can be included in this category. Promiscuous sex, gluttony, drunkenness, thrill-seeking, etc. might be pleasurable in the short run – even inducing euphoria in some cases – but actions like these can have definite downsides longer term. So, utility and long-term happiness are not necessarily synonymous.[177]

The human mind is governed by multiple forces pulling in various directions. On the one hand are the instinctual drives, those immediate desires and appetites that exist in the here and now – Hume called them the passions – which have evolved in us over the

-----

[177] It should be noted that in praxeology and Austrian subjectivism, no distinction is made between short- and long-term satisfaction, because we analyze the logic of action from the perspective of each exchange. We note that utility is derived, ex ante, for the actor, but we make no investigation concerning the degree of utility. In addition, we do not investigate whether or not the actor gains in utility, ex post. However, in this chapter, we are dealing not with praxeology. Instead, we are asking what kind of actions lead to immediate satisfaction, and how do they differ from those that lead to overall contentment?

millennia, and which no doubt exist in non-human species as well. On the other hand, there is reason, that uniquely human attribute which looks to the future. Reason recognizes that while submitting to the passions might well grant instant gratification, the long-term consequences can be negative overall.

Even if yielding to the desire has a positive outcome, reason can tell us that deferring consumption for the purpose of engaging in production often leads to greater satisfaction in the long run. The degree to which a person chooses to postpone consumption in order to receive greater returns at a later date is called "time preference," and it varies during a person's lifetime and from one individual to another.[178] As reason develops in the child, time preference usually becomes lower; that is to say, the person becomes more inclined to wait and to do so for lesser returns. By middle age, time preference is often at its lowest. For example, if you offer a small child one piece of candy today or two pieces tomorrow, it is likely the youngster will demand the candy right now. Essentially, this amounts to the rejection of a rate of interest of 100% per day! On the other hand, an adult may well defer consumption of, say, $100-worth of goods in the present if that amount of money can be invested in a business that will return $110-worth of goods in a year's time.

If the production of material goods involves creating order out of disordered matter, the production of long-term well-being, flourishing, and contentment – a condition the Ancient Greeks referred to as *eudaimonia* – seems to involve creating a more ordered and harmonious mind. This low-entropy mental state should be

---

[178] Rothbard states, "A fundamental and constant truth about human action is that man prefers his end to be achieved in the shortest possible time. Given the specific satisfaction, the sooner it arrives, the better. This results from the fact that time is always scarce, and a means to be economized. The sooner any end is attained, the better. Thus, with any given end to be attained, the shorter the period of action, i.e., production, the more preferable for the actor. This is the universal fact of time preference." Rothbard, Murray N. (2004) [1962] *Man, Economy and State with Power and Market.* Ludwig von Mises Institute, Auburn, AL, p. 15.

differentiated from utility, which is the degree of psychic satisfaction that arises only from particular cases of exchange, and which may or may not lead to a lasting positive condition.[179] From an evolutionary perspective, it seems that natural selection has exerted an influence on the human will to prefer the low-entropy condition, because an actor with a stable mind is more likely to lead a productive and successful life, and hence, more likely to pass on their genes. In the ancestral environment, low mental entropy would have become associated with happiness and contentment as a means to spur the individual toward actions that yield positive long-term outcomes.

For the individual actor, however, the process of attaining this condition involves a certain amount of self-control in overcoming potentially negative impulses. It involves thinking about future consequences and applying reason, which is something animals cannot do and do not need. Indeed, this is what it means to be human. To be sure, instinct is important in humans too, but because of our power to act, we realize that base desires often have to be tempered with some form of moderation lest they lead to potentially serious adverse consequences. As human beings, we have the ability to comprehend that acting in a life-affirming way often involves short-term sacrifice and avoiding immediate gratification because this leads to greater well-being and overall contentment in the long run. The fact that most of us have the ability to anticipate this long-term state and to strive for it, at least to some degree, is evolution's way of telling us that a mind low in entropy is positive for human life.

Short-Term Versus Long-Term Action

The production of virtually all goods – whether material or non-material – requires some kind of action in the physical world. And therefore, most actions involve an understanding of the laws of

---

[179] Again, this is *not* a praxeological statement. See the earlier footnote.

nature and the law of causality, at least to some degree, in order to derive utility from the good in question. But what about our long-term goals? What about our life considered as one long action? Short-term actions can satisfy an immediate desire, but to achieve low mental entropy and overall well-being, it is necessary for the actor to consider actions with a much longer time dimension consisting of multiple smaller actions that combine together with the goal of obtaining satisfaction far into the future.

For example, suppose I decide to eat a ham sandwich to satisfy my immediate hunger. It is a fairly simple matter to go to the refrigerator, pull out the sandwich – assuming it has been made – and place it in my mouth. (It is true there are a few steps involved – because even short-term actions can be broken down into smaller sub-components – but eating a sandwich is essentially a short-term affair that can be considered a single action.) However, if I set upon a goal of going to university and obtaining a degree, because I believe this will serve me well in terms of my long-term happiness, then this is an altogether different affair. For unlike the case of the ham sandwich, I will undoubtedly have to undertake thousands of smaller actions in order to achieve my desired end. The same is true if I want to sustain a happy marriage, cultivate lasting friends, have a rewarding career, become a successful entrepreneur, or maintain good health, etc.

Now, when it comes to eating the sandwich, all I need to do is follow some basic physical rules. This is also true with respect to each of the many tiny actions that are required to attain any distant goal. However, with respect to the latter, in order to string those actions together into one long action, in order to move consistently towards the right long-term goal, to not deviate or waiver and to not lose sight of the task I have set myself, I require something else. I need to find and apply an entirely different set of rules. We call these rules *self-discipline*.

Self-Discipline and Virtue

The rules we apply in this area are individual and self-imposed, unlike the physical laws of nature which are universal and immutable. Every individual has to determine them for himself. Put simply, we each have to choose an appropriate set of self-imposed laws to apply to our own long-term actions. The set of rules we follow does not govern our will, for that is an impossibility. Indeed, the will is the very entity that establishes and enforces the rules, or in some instances decides to abandon them, for good or for bad. Rather, we must impose them on our actions *via* our will. With luck, the consistent application of, and adherence to, the right kind of self-imposed laws leads to a flourishing condition. Unfortunately, it is often the case that the road chosen involves an absence of self-discipline, and this inevitably leads to the opposite situation: a life of turmoil, grief, and strife. Therefore, the question must be asked: How do we establish a code of conduct that leads to long-lasting well-being?

It seems the ancient Greeks might have had the right answer, embodied in the concept of virtue. For the Ancients, one lived a virtuous life, not necessarily to satisfy the gods or to gain admission to heaven, or to achieve the approval of others, or to increase one's standing in society. One did so for its own sake because virtue was an end in itself. In this context, "virtue" means excellence, the ability of anything to perform well given its inherent characteristics, this representing its highest good. Since man's characteristic function is the ability to reason, it follows that virtue consists in performing well according to rational principles, and in living a virtuous life, one attains the highest human good, which is *eudaimonia*, often translated as contentment, well-being, or flourishing.[180]

The Greeks outlined four cardinal virtues: wisdom, courage, moderation, and justice. Of these, wisdom is the only intellectual virtue. Above all else, wisdom is necessary to apply reason properly,

---

[180] Aristotle, *Nicomachean Ethics, Book 1*, Chapter 7.

for without the right kind of reasoning, there is little possibility of finding the appropriate code by which to live. But courage is required also because courage involves the steadfastness of character required to stand up to one's own bad impulses and to enforce the law one imposes on oneself. Without courage, our thoughts and actions become lawless and uncontrolled. Wisdom and courage act together to produce moderation, which the ancient Greeks viewed as a kind of mental calmness and order. Justice, the last of the four main virtues, is critical in the establishment of law and order in the community, which I shall consider in the next chapter. But with respect to our own actions, treating other people fairly, without being either too harsh or too lenient, is one of the most important virtues.

Plato's view on virtue was guided by his belief that the mind is divided into three parts which he labeled "appetitive," "spirited," and "reason."[181] The appetitive element, roughly corresponding to Freud's "id," encompasses primitive desires such as gluttony, sex, and avarice. The spirited component, analogous to the "superego," arises from social conditioning; it is the moral brake that subdues the self-centered desires. And the final element is reason, similar to Freud's "ego," which rules over the other two portions of the mind and acts as the final arbiter and decision maker. While appetite and spirit battle it out, reason decides which one to listen to. Plato thought that if the appetitive part gains the upper hand, then the person becomes impulsive and uncontrolled, but if spirit becomes

---

[181] This is described in The Phaedrus where Plato used the Allegory of the Chariot to describe the soul as being divided into three parts – reason, spirit and appetite – which he compared to a chariot being pulled by two winged horses. One of the horses is noble and obedient, and represents spirit; he loves honor, and is guided by glory. The other equine is unruly and obstinate, and epitomizes apatite; he craves bodily pleasures, such as food, drink and sexual gratification. The charioteer is reason, who tries to control the horses and make them work together by employing wisdom, vision and purpose. If reason succeeds, spirit becomes strength and magnanimity, and appetite becomes temperance. Ultimately, thus leads to harmony and justice.

too dominant, then the individual is constantly striving for unrealistically high standards. Thus, for harmony and order to prevail, reason must find a way to make spirit and appetite work together, and this requires great wisdom. If applied correctly, the right balance can be achieved.

While Plato thought virtuousness was a product of learning – and therefore much like any other branch of knowledge – Aristotle felt that obtaining virtue was not merely an intellectual endeavor; it also involved practice. For Aristotle, virtue is the correct psychological disposition with regard to one's own immediate emotional responses, and it is always found at the golden mean between the two vicious extremes of excess and deficiency. For example, in response to fear, the correct virtue is courage, and this lies somewhere between cowardice (the deficiency) and rashness (the excess). When we feel the desire for pleasure or wish to avoid pain, the golden mean is temperance, which lies between self-indulgence and complete indifference. In self-expression, the virtue is truthfulness, and not the vices of boastfulness or false modesty. In terms of beneficence, generosity is a virtue, but not the excess of extravagance or the deficiency of miserliness. The correct response to a feeling of anger is a controlled temper, not uncontrolled rage or pusillanimity, and so on.[182]

The Stoics, led by Zeno of Citium, thought that virtue consists in choosing habits that promote health, strength, and agility, and avoiding actions that lead to sickness, weakness, and low self-esteem. In order to be successful in this endeavor, prudence is required. However, according to Zeno, if one should fail, then one should accept one's fate with the utmost self-control, propriety, and magnanimity. The Greeks called this *apatheia* – commonly translated as equanimity or indifference – but, more precisely, as the freeing of

---

[182] See Chapter 31, "Aristotle's Ethics" in Copleston, Frederick S. J. (1993) *A History of Philosophy Volume I: Greece and Rome*. Doubleday, New York. pp. 332-350.

suffering through discipline.[183] In contrast, Epicureans subscribed to *ataraxia*, or tranquility, which is achieved by withdrawing from the public sphere and seeking a life that minimizes pain while maximizing pleasure. However, pleasure does not mean debauchery, because in the long run this inevitably leads to a greater degree of misery than enjoyment. Thus, the most sublime state is achieved through prudence and temperance. Like the Stoics, Epicureans believed prudence to be the source of much virtue.[184]

In Ancient Rome, all citizens were expected to aspire to personal virtues, such as comity, dignity, tenacity, frugality, respectability, prudence, gravity, and truthfulness. These qualities were at the heart of the *Via Romana* or Roman Way. In addition, Roman culture emphasized public virtues (often represented by deities) that included equity, mercy, justice, confidence, liberality, dutifulness, honor, and courage. Philosophically, many Romans were stoics. Epictetus, who was born a slave, became a great teacher of stoicism and greatly influenced the stoic philosopher and emperor Marcus Aurelius.[185] Some, like Cicero, combined various philosophical positions. Cicero was a syncretic who fused stoicism with epicureanism.

While most moral theories today concentrate on specific actions, ancient moral attitudes focused on the actor and on the attributes that a person needed in order to be moral. Modern moral theories, insofar as they have an objective foundation, are either consequentialist – as in utilitarianism – or they are deontological, in which case the source of right action comes from God, duty, or natural law. In contrast, the Ancients were concerned not so much with the particulars or their consequences, but rather with the state of mind of the actor. They saw morality in more general terms, whereby the pursuit of moral excellence was a goal in itself, in much the same way that one might seek to attain eminence in a particular

---

[183] On the Stoic ethic, see Ibid., pp. 394-400.
[184] On the Epicurean ethic, see Ibid., pp. 406-412.
[185] Ibid., pp. 428-437.

profession. In relatively small city states where people were expected to participate in public life, it was possible to recognize a virtuous person by his actions and attitudes, even if those actions were not always specifically spelled out. Nevertheless, the individual sought to lead a virtuous life, not just to gain the esteem of the community, nor merely for the benefit of the community, but also as a means to achieve *eudaimonia*.

Like the ancient Greeks, the 13th century philosopher and theologian Thomas Aquinas also considered human flourishing. In *Summa Theologica*, he asks, what good constitutes true happiness – the *summum bonum*? And he considers eight possible candidates, eliminating them one by one until he is left with what he regards as the highest good.[186]   Of the first four possible contenders, wealth and material things are good, but they are only a means to an end, and the ends they can buy are limited; a person who views money as the ultimate good leads a shallow life indeed. Honor might seem good, but it is merely a sign of virtue; it is not an actual virtue. Fame, on the other hand, exists only in the mind of others and is never everlasting. And power like wealth is only a means to an end. Moreover, money, honor, fame and power can all have harmful outcomes, says Aquinas, and the happiness they deliver is only partial at best. Of the final four candidates, bodily health is certainly good, but it is not the ultimate good, for it ignores the health of the mind. Pleasure is also good, but sensual pleasure is transitory at best, and real pleasure is merely a consequence of happiness, or at best synonymous with it; it cannot tell us the nature of happiness. This seems to leave only wisdom and virtue; wisdom being the good of the soul, and virtue being the good of the will. Like the Ancients, Aquinas agreed that they are a source of real happiness.

However, Aquinas goes one step further. The good of the soul, he says, cannot be the ultimate end, for while it is true that a good

---

[186] Aquinas, Thomas (1265-1274) *Summa Theologica*, First Part of the Second Part, Question Two, Articles 1-8.

mind or soul leads to happiness, it cannot lead to perfect happiness. And precisely because our desires for happiness are unlimited, there must be an unlimited good not yet considered. And for Aquinas, this is God.

No one ever manages to establish a code of conduct that produces perfect happiness. But to the extent that long-lasting contentment of some degree is achieved, it likely originates with virtue. Plato said, "know thyself," by which he meant, I think, that by fully understanding one's own mind, one can choose to apply a virtuous code of conduct that results in real happiness. With wisdom, courage, moderation, justice, and many other virtues, a disciplined mind and a happy life is accessible.

However, we live in a world today where the importance of real virtue is minimized. For many people, the temptation to throw out self-discipline and embrace licentiousness, and to seek happiness solely from material pleasures without engaging in any kind of virtuous action is too great. While hedonism of this sort might result in short-term satisfaction, it is unlikely to lead to contentment in the long run. Moreover, far too many people today think that virtue, if it has any relevance at all, applies only to how one's actions affect others.

Now, it is certainly the case that how we act towards other people is of great importance. This is particularly so with respect to justice, but it is also true when it comes to other positive acts such as benevolence, generosity, and kindness, for example. However, because there is a widespread belief that virtue has worth only insofar as it affects society in general, there are many individuals who think they can gain prestige and standing by falsely portraying themselves as benevolent or kind or just – and hence virtuous in the eyes of the community – even though they lack the wisdom, courage, moderation, and justice actually needed to *be* virtuous. But their sanctimonious and hypocritical displays – otherwise known as virtue-signaling – never lead to real happiness, because the greatest reward from virtue comes not from the praise or respect of others, and certainly not at all when the virtue is false. Rather, the real return is that which is given to oneself in the form of a harmonious and orderly mind, which originates only from within when the virtue is genuine, and this can come about only when it is directed by the appropriate self-imposed laws.

10

Countering Entropy in the Social World

Uncertainty in Interpersonal Relations

The human will be not governed by any physical law, and thus left to its own devices is free to initiate actions unhindered, good or bad, positive or negative for life. Nevertheless, one cannot deny that the will is designed to impose regularity and order in an otherwise disordered and uncertain world. *As a product of our reason, we are law-seeking and entropy-lowering beings.* Alone among all living things, it is our innate disposition to find rules and to employ this knowledge for the purpose of eliminating uncertainty and producing order in the physical world and in the mind. In the material world, we lower physical entropy in the form of goods that have utility. In the mind, we lower mental entropy, the ultimate expression of which is long-lasting satisfaction and contentment. In the former, we employ the universal and objective laws of nature. In pursuit of the latter, we find an individual code of conduct called self-discipline, which involves virtue.

But thus far, I have considered man only in isolation. I have considered action only insofar as it affects material objects and the actor himself. However, the potential for uncertainty and disorder also exists in our dealings with other people, and therefore laws that deal with this kind of entropy are important as well. Crusoe, alone on his island, need not concern himself with such things. But when Friday appears on the scene, the circumstances change because both these actors must face uncertainty in their relations with each other.

Suppose Crusoe decides to make a fishing net in order to trade with Friday for a bow and arrow. To accomplish this exchange, Crusoe certainly needs to have the appropriate level of knowledge to make a net of the right size and quality, but he also needs to understand the desires of Friday. This is a particular kind of understanding – *verstehen* in German – that is a subjective assessment we make about the thoughts of other human beings with whom we interact, and it is an essential element of every voluntary interpersonal exchange, no matter how mundane. Some people, such as successful entrepreneurs, are especially good at understanding the needs and wants of others, but for many it is hit and miss. Nevertheless, whatever the circumstance, there is always an element of uncertainty involved because it is never possible to determine objectively and conclusively the state of mind of someone else. As far as Crusoe is concerned, Friday might not like the net. Friday might decide he could make a better net himself and prefer to keep his bow and arrow. Hence, Crusoe's uncertainty. All exchanges involve uncertainty, and reducing it through *verstehen* is critical to interpersonal action.

But there is another kind of uncertainty involved in dealing with other people. For what if Friday were to steal the net instead? Can Crusoe be certain he will not? Or consider it from Friday's point of view. Can Friday be sure that Crusoe will not sneak into his hut in the middle of the night, murder him, and take his bow and arrow? Life is unpredictable in many ways, but one of the most unsettling is the possibility of undesirable and unpredictable physical acts of aggression. Uncertainty regarding voluntary exchange is alleviated by *verstehen*, but uncertainty regarding *involuntary* exchange is rather different. Ameliorating it does not necessarily involve empathizing with the aggressor, for very often the victim has no prior knowledge of the aggressive act. Yet clearly there is a definite need to reduce this kind of uncertainty in order to be able to go about one's business without concerning oneself about physical interference from other people.

While actions can be considered individually, all our actions are in essence one long concerted action to pursue and achieve happiness. One cannot deny this is true, for it is an oxymoron to claim one's final goal in life is to be *un*happy; a goal, by definition, is an anticipated state of affairs that increases happiness (satisfaction) over the present state. Some individuals are not successful in achieving their goals, and others discover *ex post* (after the fact) that a goal chosen was the wrong one. Occasionally, an action taken toward a goal might temporarily make the actor less happy, and sometimes the goal is simply relieving or avoiding pain. However, one cannot deny that the *final* goal of every human being is happiness.

Thus, reducing the amount of uncertainty concerning physical aggression in one's life as a whole – considered as one long action – is just as important, if not more so, than in the carrying out of any particular individual act. To be clear, certainty in general is not the goal. A slave might lead a life of certainty, but he does not usually lead a happy life. The slave can be certain that if he does not work hard enough or tries to run away, his owner will beat him mercilessly. What the slave wants is the certainty that he can down tools and walk away *without* the slaveowner using any kind of violence against him. But of course, of this, he is extremely uncertain. Thus, the objective is to increase the certainty that one can exercise one's will without being physically aggressed against or threatened, and this is required precisely so that one's goals in life can be acted upon, unhindered, to the maximum extent possible. Achieving this state of low mental entropy is the most fundamental and basic goal in life.[187] It underlies all other aims.

Uncertainty implies high entropy, whereas certainty is lower in entropy. And a society in which one is not under a current threat of

---

[187] For an interesting perspective on how uncertainty-related anxiety increases mental entropy, see Hirsh, Jacob B., Raymond A Mar, and Jordan B. Perterson (2012). "Psychological Entropy: A Framework for Understanding Uncertainty-Related Anxiety." *Psychological Review*, Vol. 119 (2), pp. 304-320.

violence, where one can exercise one's will more certainly, makes it easier to attain successful outcomes in the string of actions needed for a flourishing life. We set out in life with a series of goals, and we hope to accomplish them to the maximum extent possible without being blindsided by unpredictable events that might interfere with that process. Now, with regard to such capricious events, the relevant issue here concerns *not* such things as poor health, personal accidents, and natural disasters, for these can be resolved, if at all, only by a knowledge of physical processes. Nor is it the uncertainty concerning the motivation of actors in cases of voluntary exchange, for that can be resolved only by *verstehen*. Rather, the issue we are concerned with here is the general case of physical interference from other human beings; that is, unwelcome *involuntary* physical interpersonal actions that involve force or coercion.

Reducing Entropy in Society

Now, it is true that most human beings generally do not wish to murder or steal, or indeed commit any aggressive act against another person. Unfortunately, there are some individuals who do not mind doing so at all. Rousseau claimed that in a state of nature, man was naturally good but that the noble savage became corrupted by civilization. Freud made a similar case. But it is not civilization that corrupts man; on the contrary, civilization is the product that results from the cooperation of man in voluntary association. In truth, human beings, whether they lead a primitive existence or not, are not always good. They are fallible, they engage in folly and vice, and in some cases overt acts of aggression. Civilization is not the corrupting influence. On the other hand, Hobbes claimed that nature is red in tooth and claw; that it is man's natural disposition to be in a war of all against all in a competition for limited resources, and that outside of society, ordinary men live in permanent fear of a violent death. For Hobbes, life is "solitary, poor, nasty, brutish, and short,"[188] and the only way to preserve order is to institute a ruler who has absolute dominion over every person in society. Indeed, it is still a common position among many people today that without a strong government, society necessarily breaks down into warring factions where the winner takes all.

However, Hobbes' view of mankind is far too pessimistic. It is certainly true that most of nature is indeed in a war of all against all. With the exception of a few social species, the animal world is a zero-sum game because what one individual takes from nature, another is deprived of that same resource. But because human beings are rational animals and can engage in the division of labor, we realize we can act together in ways that increase the total production of goods over and above that which we could attain individually. We comprehend that cooperation can improve the lot of all. For human beings, life need not be a zero-sum game. Indeed, cooperation based on voluntary exchange and the division of labor is the very thing that creates a civil society.

Therefore, since human beings do not have an animal mind and possess at least a modicum of reason, they naturally search for a legal code that creates an orderly society, one that removes the kind of impediments engendered by aggressive and coercive acts. Indeed, as law-seeking and order-creating beings possessed of reason, it is entirely consistent with life and the goal of reducing

---

[188] The full quote is, "Whatsoever therefore is consequent to a time of War, where every man is Enemy to every man; the same is consequent to the time, wherein men live without other security, than what their own strength, and their own invention shall furnish them withal. In such condition, there is no place for Industry; because the fruit thereof is uncertain; and consequently no Culture of the Earth; no Navigation, nor use of the commodities that may be imported by Sea; no commodious Building; no Instruments of moving, and removing such things as require much force; no Knowledge of the face of the Earth; no account of Time; no Arts; no Letters; no Society; and which is worst of all, continual Fear, and danger of violent death; And the life of man, solitary, poor, nasty, brutish, and short." Hobbes, Thomas (2014) [1651] *Leviathan*. Digireads.com Neeland Media LLC. Kindle Edition. p. 56.

entropy to seek a system of law, applicable to everyone, that delegitimizes unwelcome acts of aggression. For such a system, not only eliminates any potential losses for victims, but moreover reduces the amount of uncertainty concerning the threat of violence in society as a whole. This is conducive toward attaining the lifelong goal of happiness that everyone seeks. The desire for a society such as this is not alien to human nature, as Hobbes contends. It is not man's natural disposition to devolve into animalistic behavior in the absence of an absolute ruler. On the contrary, the tendency to seek laws for the purpose of creating an orderly society is innate in everyone.

Of course, there will always be those who disavow this position. Undoubtedly, there are some who claim not to care one wit if they live in a lawless condition, because they believe they can thrive from disorder. But even criminals recognize the need for some level of law and order, if only in their dealings with one another. Moreover, criminals rely on the fact that everyone else lives in a state of voluntary cooperation governed by agreed-upon rules, for if no one observed rules of any kind, then the criminal would be put at just as much risk as everyone else. A person who argues in favor of true lawlessness is asking for a world without reason, for a dog-eat-dog world where there is only animalistic behavior; indeed, for the end of humanity. To the extent that most human beings are sufficiently intelligent and possessed of reason, very few would argue against a legal code at all, even if they might argue over the particular details, and even if they might personally choose to violate it from time to time.

Finding Universal Laws to Apply to Society

If the defining characteristic of humanity is employing reason to discover laws for the purpose of reducing uncertainty and creating order, and hence reducing entropy, then finding the right laws that produce the right kind of order in society – and not merely laws that suit oneself – must be one of the highest goals of humanity.

If such laws exist, they cannot be like the set of rules each person imposes on himself. Their formulation must be objective with objectively determinable outcomes because laws subjectively derived and applied to the whole of society would create uncertainty and disorder, the very thing one wishes to avoid. But they cannot be like physical laws that claim the existence of causal relations between things. Rather, they must command; they must tell people how they ought to act in their relations with each other. As such, they cannot be derived *empirically* by *observing* the regularities that exist, but rather must be *deduced axiomatically* to determine the regularities that *ought* to exist. Their propositions cannot be *synthetic a posteriori* but rather *synthetic a priori*, precisely because they have to be logically demonstrated from self-evident axioms as I shall explain. But they are laws of nature nonetheless; laws of human nature concerning justice; laws designed to create order and reduce entropy.

In the physical world, order is created by discovering the universal laws of natural science and understanding how they affect matter in response to human action. In the mind, order is created by finding an individual code of conduct called self-discipline that is based on virtue, and understanding how it affects one's thoughts. In the case of society, order is created by discovering man-made laws in accordance with a proper underlying principle of justice, and understanding how those laws affect human interactions when enforced. As regards the latter, justice gives rise to a legal code that is apparent to all who possess the necessary intuition of cause and effect with regard to their own actions, who can understand human nature in general, and who have the rationality to see how the law's application would improve their own happiness by creating order in society.

This is not to say that discovering the right legal code is easy. Discovering objective laws – whether they be the laws of the physical world, the laws of economics, or laws that conform with justice – is difficult. Before the scientific revolution, people had an intuitive sense of the operation of many physical laws – by observing regularities and attributing certain events to specific causes – but it took many hundreds of years to formalize them into the basic laws of classical mechanics. The scientific revolution swept away many erroneous judgments and superstitions that up to that point had clouded mankind's understanding of the physical world. In the field of human action, it was not until the end of the 19th century that classical economists like Carl Menger and Eugen von Bohm Bawerk discovered the laws of economics, but the methodology was only formalized in the 20th century by Ludwig von Mises, and even today there is considerable academic resistance in accepting its validity. In a similar vein, finding an absolutely true legal code concerning justice is not straightforward, and persuading people of its validity is not easy. There have been many legal systems that claim to be just, but arguing there is only one that is logically valid encounters considerable opposition. People do not like to be told their views are wrong; that their particular view of justice is arbitrary and inconsistent.

Thus far, I have *not* alluded to any notion of morality with respect to this legal code. I have suggested that its proper objective is the universally held natural desire to reduce uncertainty and create order caused by the threat of violence rather than to create a more moral society. The ground for this approach is that proposing an objective code on the basis of the latter raises the age-old question of which system should exist when there seem to be many different standards of morality that are subjectively held. For example, many people might say that prostitution is wrong and should be outlawed, while others might argue it is a victimless crime and should be perfectly legal. Some might aver that governments should be instituted to take from the rich in order to assist the poor, and that not doing so is immoral, while others might claim such government action is itself immoral because the assistance is given involuntarily by taxpayers through state coercion.

Even those who are generally considered to be common

criminals could dispute a system of justice that is implemented on purely moral grounds. If Peter robs Paul, a majority of citizens might certainly empathize with Paul, and claim that Peter's action is morally wrong. But Peter and others like him might argue that it is perfectly acceptable for the strong to take from the weak. There are some individuals – such as psychopaths – whose personal code of conduct grants them a license to engage in aggressive acts, and they have no qualms about doing so. While they might well acknowledge their personal morality is at odds with that of the majority of society, they can simply say, so what? No one can assert there is a single all-encompassing moral standard that is a universal feature of the human mind or that such a standard is a defining characteristic of mankind.

On the other hand, it *is* a universal disposition to want to reduce entropy in one's life because at some level, it is necessary for life itself. Anyone who genuinely strives for high levels of entropy in his life ultimately dies. He commits suicide. Of course, not everyone possesses the ability to reduce entropy in every circumstance. But no one can deny that the desire to do so is a defining characteristic of humanity in general, and that it is universal. Secondly, no one can claim that *reason* is not a universal feature of the human mind either. Indeed, it is a performative contradiction to argue against the case for reason because argumentation itself requires some form of reasoning. It is true that not everyone has the same level of rationality and not everyone's reasoning is correct. But no one can deny that it is a defining characteristic of humanity. Finally, no one can deny that finding laws of cause and effect by employing reason is a universal feature of humanity. As human beings, we could not act without the knowledge of such laws. We would be mere animals. Therefore, finding causal laws is also a universal human propensity.

Given the structure of the human mind, I maintain that it is axiomatic that human beings seek laws applicable to society for the purpose of lowering entropy in their lives. Those who argue against this principle – that such laws are not applicable to themselves – are arguing against their own actions and life itself. They might not like the laws, and they might not obey them, but they cannot logically deny that appropriate laws prevent uncertainty and disorder, and that this is good.

Some say the objective of the law should be to increase the overall level of utility in society, or "social utility."[189] But utilitarianism is a poor philosophy in which to ground the law because there is no cardinal measure of utility. Creating the greatest happiness for the greatest number of people might seem like a laudable goal, but it is not possible to add up psychic satisfactions or dissatisfactions individually, let alone compare one person's value scale with that of another.[190] For example, forcibly taking money from the wealthy to give to the less affluent might seem like a good idea because a dollar given to the latter would appear to engender a greater degree of happiness – or marginal utility – than the marginal utility lost by the millionaire who is forced to supply the money. But we cannot assume this to be true in every case, because it is impossible to measure anyone's psychological state

---

[189] Ronald Coase makes this utilitarian case in his paper, The Problem of Social Cost. The example given is that of a factory spewing smoke over a neighborhood. This of course represents an invasion of property rights for the homeowners, but, for Coase, property rights are not important for deciding the terms of settlement in the dispute. Rather, the issue is limiting the social cost while maximizing the social utility, and this is to be decided either by statute or by the judicial system as appropriate. See Coase, Ronald H. (1960) "The Problem of Social Cost." *The Journal of Law and Economics*, Vol. 3, pp. 1-44. For the alternative view, see Davidson, Laura and Walter E. Block (2021) "Epistemological Foundations in the Ethical Debate Concerning Fractional Reserve Banking and Borrowing Short and Lending Long." *Political Dialogues*, Vol. 30, pp. 243-271.

[190] Rothbard states, "Modern welfare economics is particularly adept at arriving at estimates (even allegedly precise quantitative ones) of "social cost" and "social utility." But economics does correctly inform us, not that moral principles are subjective, but that utilities and costs are indeed subjective: individual utilities are purely subjective and ordinal, and therefore it is totally illegitimate to add or weight them to arrive at any estimate for "social" utility or cost." Rothbard, Murray N. (1998) [1982] *The Ethics of Liberty*. New York University Press, pp. 202-203.

quantitatively. Human minds, and hence human happiness, can only be assessed subjectively. This is true for every situation in which a person is claimed to be disadvantaged relative to someone else.

Since utility is a purely subjective and ordinal phenomenon, no one can calculate what the overall effect of a law would be for society in utilitarian terms. Using coercion to take property from those who are deemed (subjectively) to have greater utility at their disposal than others or forcing certain actions upon those who are assumed for whatever reason to have greater happiness than others can assuredly do only one thing. It will, without question, make these individuals less happy without necessarily improving to a greater degree the lot of those who are the recipients of their "largesse." Only purely voluntary actions are guaranteed to increase utility in every exchange, at least *ex ante*.

The Universal Threat Axiom

How then can proper laws be deduced? It is clear no human being wants to be the victim of physical violence. It is certainly possible for someone to subject themselves to it deliberately in order to avoid worse consequences – for example, to defend others, or to preserve their principles or honor. But it is a contradiction to argue that anyone wants to be a victim of violence, since being a victim necessarily implies an interpersonal action that is not voluntary and a loss of utility. It is a violation of the will.[191]

But there is a difference between a physically aggressive act and a *threat* of such an act. With regard to the former, not everyone is subjected to aggression at any given time, and not everyone is averse to employing violence to obtain what they want. Therefore, an aversion to aggression in general is not a universal feature of the human mind. A threat, on the other hand, is forward looking and

---

[191] In using the term "victim," we imply that the violence is illicit. There are of course situations in which violence is not illicit; for example, in a boxing match.

may or may not have a physical consequence. But because a credible threat always implies a *probability* of aggression and because no one wants to be a victim, it follows that everyone would want to eliminate or reduce that probability. If they did not want to do so, then there would be no threat. This is axiomatic.

A threat might be direct, as in coercion or extortion, or it might be indirect, as might occur if one is present in a crime-infested area, for example. But in both cases, eliminating the threat by submitting to it results in a physical loss and a violation of the will. This is clear in the case of a direct threat, but it is also true if the threat is indirect. For example, if a woman is prevented from walking home alone at night because of a credible fear she might be mugged, her will has been violated. She is forced into an action she does not want. But resisting the threat, such as by fighting back, is also a violation of one's will. (There are some cases in which a person might actually want to be in a confrontation, and while this would not be a violation of the will, it would mean, by definition, the threat does not exist.)

It would seem the only way to have one's will *not* be violated is to ignore the threat and act upon one's original intentions regardless. But this necessarily means the probability of aggression remains. If the slave ignores his owner's threats and downs tools, he will face a high probability of aggression, as will the person threatened by a robber. The woman walking alone at night also faces a probability of violence.

Indeed, at any given time, while not everyone is being aggressed against, *everyone* in society is under a threat of aggression of some kind, even if that threat is very small. When living in *any* community, it is never possible to completely eliminate the probability of violence from other people. Only a person who lives alone on an island can make such a claim. No matter how peaceful it might seem, the mere fact that violence could arise implies a certain degree of uncertainty. Even if someone were to insist they felt no threat at a particular time and place, no one can be certain they would never be threatened with aggression at any time in the future. The possibility of being a victim of violence is applicable to every human being in society because it is a fact of life. There is always an element of uncertainty.

Therefore, it follows that the desire to eliminate (or at least reduce) the probability of physical aggression occurring to oneself is universal, not merely to prevent the physical loss that arises in particular cases of crime but, more importantly, to prevent the uncertainty that is caused by living with the threat of crime in general. Being a victim of a single act of aggression causes a loss of utility. But being forced to comply with an ongoing threat or otherwise live with uncertainty, interferes with the string of actions that might otherwise lead to the kind of long-term happiness or *eudaimonia* that is fundamental and universal. At the very least, by interfering with the will of the individual, it inhibits the pursuit of that goal.

Hobbes maintained that all men fear a violent death. This was an exaggeration. Hobbes lived during a period of civil war when violence was everywhere, and death was a manifest threat to just about everyone. But he was *not* wrong about people wanting to avoid being a victim of violence. One does not need to be in continual fear of one's life to desire the elimination of threats of violence in general. No one, not even those who engage in aggressive acts themselves, wants to be the target of aggression. Indeed, it is axiomatic that all people should want to reduce or prevent the probability of aggression occurring to themselves. I call this idea the *universal threat axiom*. The universal threat axiom exists because uncertainty implies an increase in entropy, and reducing entropy is a fundamental aspect of all life.

The Nonaggression Principle

Since human beings possess reason, it follows there must be a universal principle, the purpose of which is to reduce the probability of aggression as described by the universal threat axiom. Since violence from another human being can occur at any time and come from any quarter, only a general ban on aggression can accomplish this goal. However, a principle that delegitimized aggression and force under all possible circumstances would not permit redress and would amount to pacifism. Thus, logically, the only way to avoid this state of affairs is to delegitimize the *initiation* of aggression and the *initiation* of aggressive threats.

This idea can be summed up in one sentence, known as the *nonaggression principle*, as follows:

> It is illegitimate to initiate a physically aggressive act
> or threaten such an act against other human beings
> or their legitimately owned property.

We have yet to define property, but "aggression" means any involuntary acts involving force or fraud directed against the body or property of another person. It means only physical aggression. Under the nonaggression principle, there is no such thing as "psychological aggression" or "microaggression" or "verbal aggression." This is the case because these actions cannot be objectively determined as causing harm (see the next chapter). A key word here is "initiate" because if people have an exclusive right to their property, then clearly, they have a right to defend it from aggression. Therefore, using force in self-defense, including the defense of one's property against the initiation of force or threat of force, is legitimate. However, it must be proportional. For example, a homeowner does not have the right to kill someone who momentarily walks across his lawn. That "defense" would be disproportionate, and the individual concerned would be guilty of murder.

The rational justification for the nonaggression principle is neither deontological nor utilitarian. Nor does its justification lie in an alleged superior moral outcome. While these arguments have all been proposed by libertarians as a means of defending it, they cannot be logically demonstrated. They are simply matters of faith.

The justification for outlawing physical aggression lies in the fact that the degree of *social certainty* – not social utility – is maximized when physically aggressive acts are restricted. While it is true that outlawing initiations of force increases utility for the *individual* who would otherwise be a victim, the universality of the nonaggression principle rests on the fact that *all people* can be more certain they can go about their business without the Hobbesian threat of aggression. And because this increase in certainty is gained by everyone who is covered by the law, it necessarily increases social order, which is always positive for life.

Now it might be asked, how can we be sure that the degree of certainty is indeed increased throughout society? After all, certainty is a psychological state that is no more measurable in cardinal terms than utility. While this is true, it is not necessary to quantify every individual's feeling on the matter in order to evaluate gains and losses. This is because once the possibility of physical aggression has been eliminated (or at least reduced), the knowledge that it no longer exists (or is less likely to exist) is gained by everyone who apprehends it. The problem with utilitarianism is that it is not possible to calculate the overall outcome in terms of utility in all cases of involuntary exchange. While we know voluntary exchanges are always positive for the individuals concerned, we have no means to know whether or not they are always superior in terms of social utility. Perhaps, permitting certain kinds of involuntary exchange might produce greater social utility, but we simply do not know.

But social *certainty* is always greater, the larger the percentage of voluntary exchanges, and always less, the larger the fraction of involuntary exchanges. There is no ambiguity. Even the criminal can be more certain of the outcome should he violate the law! In some situations, uncertainty might remain, where, for example, law enforcement is weak or absent. But a legal code formulated on the basis of non-aggression does not *reduce* certainty under any circumstance. When physical aggression is prohibited, the probability of leading a peaceable, non-violent life is never lessened for anyone, with the sole exception of a person who initiates violence himself. Provided there is at least some enforcement, it is always raised to some degree. As a consequence, life-affirming order is increased throughout society. To put it simply, this is objectively, universally, and unequivocally good from a social perspective.[192]

Moral relativists and others who argue that aggression is justified under some circumstances might not like the nonaggression principle, but they cannot logically deny it produces a result that is universally good for the human race and for themselves. Even criminals who violate the principle cannot disagree with its validity. If it is adhered to and enforced, it accomplishes three important outcomes. Firstly, it eliminates the loss of utility for those who would otherwise be the victim of an aggressive act. Secondly, and more importantly, by creating a society where physical aggression is eradicated, it eliminates both direct and indirect threats, removes persistent uncertainty, and reduces entropy in the mind of every individual to pursue *eudaimonia* unhindered.

And thirdly, it creates an orderly society, such that the functioning of society as a whole is lower in entropy. In the economy, it results in a harmonious, purely voluntary free market based on nonaggression. The free market gives rise to a price structure that accurately reflects the demands of the consumers, given the availability and distribution of natural resources. This is important because the price structure coordinates the activities of entrepreneurs who are incentivized by profit and loss to allocate resources in the most efficient way possible to meet consumer

---

[192] Clearly, if all physically aggressive acts are outlawed, then the only interpersonal actions of a physical nature that are permissible are necessarily voluntary. And here we can say that in every such case, there is an overall increase in utility precisely because both sides profit; otherwise, neither side would make the exchange in the first place. But the justification for banning physical aggression does not rest on this idea. Libertarians sometimes assume that it does, which is a mistake. It is an error because, if it were true, then we could equally justify banning non-physical aggression on the grounds that only non-physical non-aggressive exchanges are guaranteed to benefit everyone (which they do). Rather, the only justification for outlawing physical aggression is that it objectively increases social order.

demand (see chapter 13). It does all this under circumstances of continuous exogenous change, creating the most orderly production structure possible. Indeed, Rothbard called the free market a "beautiful and orderly structure."[193]

Entropy In All Three Areas of Life

I have shown that human beings can reduce physical, mental, and social entropy by discovering and employing different sets of laws. But the three sets of laws I have considered – namely, the objective physical laws of nature, the self-imposed laws of self-discipline, and the objective laws that flow from the nonaggression principle – are each applied in *all three* areas of life.

For example, to lower physical entropy in the form of bodily integrity, a knowledge of physical laws is required. But reducing physical entropy also requires self-discipline to maintain the body in good health, and it requires the nonaggression principle to prevent its physical injury from violence. To lower mental entropy, self-discipline and virtue is required, as we have seen in the previous chapter. But the nonaggression principle is also needed to reduce the uncertainty concerning violence from others, in addition to which physical laws must be employed by every human actor to produce material goods that contribute to the goal of the actor's well-being. And finally, to obtain social order and a harmonious society, the nonaggression principle is essential. But self-discipline and virtuous action is also needed on the part of each individual for voluntary interpersonal actions to be successful, and the application of physical laws is required to implement the division of labor in the free market.

Thus, we see that all of these laws are used together to reduce entropy in ways that are entirely consistent with life and, in particular, with the life of a rational being.

---

[193] See Rothbard, Murray N. (2004) [1962] *Man, Economy and State with Power and Market.* Ludwig von Mises Institute, Auburn, AL, p. 569.

11

Objective Morality, Property, and Libertarian Law

Objective and Subjective Moral Propositions

Freedom implies morality. Since only beings with reason have free will, it is clear that only rational beings have the ability to acquit themselves morally. This is why animals are not subject to any kind of moral standard, and why the degree of moral conduct expected of children is less than that of adults. If a person lives alone on an island, he is subject only to the demands of personal morality. Robinson Crusoe has free will, but he need not observe interpersonal morality until Friday arrives on the scene.[194] Moreover, if we were all free-floating wraiths with no material lives, if nothing we ever willed was manifested in physical reality as an action, and if all our exchanges with others were never of a material nature, but rather will on will, and mind on mind, as in a computer simulation, the issue of morality would be moot. Furthermore, if we were nothing but a soul, with no body, no material needs, and no desires or passions, but *only* a will that was free, then not only would there be no need for moral commandments, there could be none. A free will governed by a law is contradictory.

However, in the real world of human relations where the will is manifested in interpersonal action, morality comes into play, for it dictates those actions we ought to do because they are considered good, and those we ought not to do because they are deemed to be

---

[194] This disregards the view that some forms of autarkic action undertaken in isolation are considered by some to be immoral.

175

bad. Most moral precepts, however, are subjective in nature; they depend on many different factors, not the least of which is how people feel about the particular situation at hand. For example, if most people believe in God, then the public might declare that going to church is a moral good. But unless it can be demonstrated conclusively to every rational being that going to church is indeed good – and by good, I mean positive for life in general – then it remains only a subjectively held moral proposition. It cannot therefore be mandated under an objective legal code discussed in the previous chapter. Indeed, there are many moral precepts which we might think of as being especially good, but which cannot be made part of a legal code precisely because it is not possible to demonstrate conclusively that they are life-affirming for all people in all circumstances.

I maintain, therefore, that morality is divided into two areas: subjective and objective. Objective moral propositions describe actions, including inactions, which are rationally determined to be conducive to life and which are universally good without question.[195] Subjective moral propositions describe actions and inactions which may be life affirming, but which cannot be demonstrated conclusively to be good for everyone in all situations.

I have argued that the legal code must be defined by objective moral propositions. But it is clear it encompasses only a subset of morality because it incorporates only those imperatives which are absolute, universal, and deduced objectively from first principles. Moral imperatives of this kind do not involve any prescriptions or proscriptions which are subjective, whether they claim to do good or circumscribe evil. And they do not exist simply to create a more moral society, whatever that might be. This idea goes against the grain for many present-day moral philosophers, who tend to be

---

[195] As Rothbard states, ". . . the natural law provides an objective set of ethical norms by which to gauge human actions at any time or place." Rothbard, Murray N. (1998) [1982] *The Ethics of Liberty*. New York University Press, p. 17.

relativists and reject out of hand any notion of absolutism. For these philosophers, the idea that an objective moral ethic can be deduced *a priori* is anathema. They maintain that morality is always subjective, and that therefore a legal code should command or prohibit actions on the basis of expediency or majority vote, or simply on the basis of what feels right at any given time and place. Nevertheless, since the legal code I have described exists solely to lower entropy, and since social order exists as a unitary phenomenon, it is clear that subjective laws that are particular to time and place or which vary according to the whim of certain individuals are inappropriate. Only a system of law with an objective foundation based on absolute principles can achieve the desired outcome.

The task at hand is *not* to decide upon a morally desirable social outcome first and then attempt to derive appropriate laws to achieve that outcome. Rather, the undertaking is to work from the bottom up and ask what kind of moral or immoral actions have an objectively *determinable* outcome, and therefore might be considered for inclusion in the underlying principle of law? And what kind of moral actions must be excluded because their outcome can only be subjectively assessed?

Positive Actions

We generally think of benevolence as being good from a moral perspective. Provided the action is voluntary for all concerned, benevolence is good for both the giver who gains satisfaction from the act, otherwise he would not choose to act, and for the recipient who profits in utility *ex ante*. But on the question of what *constitutes* doing good, it would be absurd to claim that what is good in one particular exchange is necessarily good in every other. While one person might appreciate a gift, another might consider it unnecessary or even an insult. An act of courtesy in one situation might be perceived as obsequiousness somewhere else. Acts that are intended to be benevolent are generally good but may not be so in every circumstance. Sympathy, compassion, generosity and kindness are, by definition, good, but the specific acts that constitute them and the sentiments they engender differ in every case.

The question of what comprises moral goodness in these cases is always determined subjectively according to the particular circumstances. The actor places himself psychologically in the position of the other person and attempts to make his best guess at what he would want if he were that individual. If the recipient is willing to accept the benevolence, then it is generally good. But because every situation is different, there can be no objective standard for goodness in this regard. Every case is unique. A universal principle mandating goodness cannot be formulated objectively in a way that would apply equally to all people in all places at all times. Positive acts like this can only be subjectively assessed.

Non-Physical Aggressive Action

On the flip side of the coin, many interpersonal actions are commonly considered to be morally bad. However, here we must distinguish between two kinds of supposedly harmful acts – namely, those that initiate physical aggression where the loss is material, and those that do not, where any loss is purely psychological. With regard to the latter, meanness, unkindness, disparagement, lack of compassion or sympathy, etc. are generally considered to be bad, but whether the action gives rise to a psychic loss or not is wholly dependent on the mind of the "victim." Harsh words that could reduce a sensitive person to tears might have absolutely no effect on someone with a thicker skin, who might even consider those words to be constructive criticism. Similarly, what one person feels is an inconsiderate or thoughtless action, another might simply brush off as inconsequential. The psychological loss exists only in the mind of the person claiming the loss. Moreover, the "victim" can *claim* to have suffered some harm, but there is no means of verifying it. Therefore, there can be no objective standard in this regard. A universal principle that prohibits unkind acts of this sort cannot be formulated rationally, any more than one that mandates positive acts.

Certain autarkic actions[196] and voluntary interpersonal exchanges also fall into the category of supposedly bad activities where it is claimed there is some objective harm. For example, drug use, prostitution, pornography, gambling, moneylending, and speculation are frequently condemned for religious, economic, or philosophical reasons. Often people will claim that harm is caused to one or both of the participants, or that "society" at large is damaged due to some nebulous corruptive force. But unless physical violence is involved in the exchange, the harm, if any, exists only in the minds of the onlookers who claim the activity is wrong because they find it personally offensive. The point is, at the time of the exchange, provided all participants are willing, no objectively determinable harm is caused.

Now some might ask, "Isn't it obvious the drug user is either going to harm himself with an overdose, or harm someone else to support his habit? Shouldn't we ban prostitution because this exploits women? Aren't those evil moneylenders exploiting the poor by charging exorbitant rates of interest?" The answer is, we do not know. It is never possible to determine with exactitude the long-term consequences of any action. We do know, however, that at the time of the exchange, provided there is no coercion involved, all parties necessarily attain a psychic profit, otherwise they would not have made the trade in the first place. No one has lost. On the other hand, since banning activities like these can only be accomplished with force against the will of the participants, a law that prohibits them will certainly cause a loss of utility. Outlawing these kinds of

---

[196] An autarkic action is an action where no one but the actor is involved, i.e., one that is not interpersonal. However, an autarkic action is still considered an exchange. This is because the actor exchanges his present state of affairs for one that he expects to be more satisfactory as a consequence of the action.

exchanges on utilitarian grounds interferes with the will of the parties concerned and runs into exactly the same problem we saw with so-called positive obligations.[197] In sum, while you or I might well decide to refrain from these kinds of acts ourselves, this is an individual decision that can only be made subjectively according to our personal standards. This is not a determination we should ever foist onto others.

Physically Aggressive Action

The case, however, is very different when it comes to involuntary interpersonal exchanges that have a physical aspect; in other words, actions that initiate physical aggression or violent intervention. These differ in one important respect from those described above. They have a physically harmful element that verifiably lowers utility for the victim in every case. Even though the loss cannot be measured in quantitative terms, it is verifiable as a loss, qualitatively, precisely because the harm is material and objectively clear, and not merely subjectively assessed. As such, actions like these are irrefutably antithetical to life in some way. The most obvious is murder. Another is assault. Kidnapping or false imprisonment involves a verifiable loss of utility because it prevents the victim from acting according to his will, which would otherwise increase his utility. Crimes which deprive the victim of material goods also represent a verifiable loss. Only these kinds of aggression against person and property are objectively determinable as being antithetical to life. Only these kinds of violations can be included in the nonaggression principle.

---

[197] Walter Block's book Defending the Undefendable shows how seemingly notorious persons like the prostitute, the ticket scalper, the slumlord, and many others, not only hurt no one, but on the contrary provide a benefit to those with whom they trade. Block, Walter (2018) *Defending the Undefendable.* Ludwig von Mises Institute, Auburn, AL.

Property Rights

What are the specific laws that flow from the nonaggression principle?

All physically aggressive acts involve violating the property rights of others. But what is property, and why do we have it? Scarcity is a fact of life. Most goods are limited, and therefore some rational method of who uses those goods or consumes them has to be determined. If goods were superabundant, as in the Garden of Eden, it would seem there would be no need to own anything. It would seem disputes could never arise. If I want to eat an apple, I do not have to ask anyone for an apple, nor do I need to buy one, nor do I have to steal one. I simply pick one from the tree. But even in the Garden of Eden, where there exist unlimited material goods, there is still scarcity – namely, the scarcity associated with my body and the standing room it occupies. Even in this land of plenty, my body is scarce because there is no other body I can inhabit.[198] When I say it is *my* body, I mean that I own it; it is my property. And what is ownership? It is, quite simply, the exclusive right to control, use, alter, and dispose of my property in any way I see fit.

Clearly, I own my body because it is the seat of my will. Someone else cannot claim my body, because only I possess a mind and a will that can control it. Another person might try to physically control me, but his mind alone cannot. He might use his mind to try to influence mine, but ultimately all my actions are my own.[199]

---

[198] See Hoppe, Hans-Hermann (2004) "The Ethics and Economics of Private Property," in Enrico Colombatto (ed.), *Companion to the Economics to Private Property*. Edward Elgar, London.

[199] It might be said that one mind can effectively control another through so-called mind control techniques, such as brainwashing, propaganda, hypnosis, etc. However, no mind can completely control another without some kind of physical intervention. It is not possible to telepathically control a person's will. A person's decisions can certainly be influenced by various techniques, especially when he is not aware of them, but without physical intervention of some sort, the ultimate decision to act or not act still rests with the subject.

Thus, I am the exclusive owner of my body, and this is true whether I like it or not. In other words, I cannot alienate my will. This is the *axiom of self-ownership*. I have a natural and exclusive right to my body, and anyone else who attempts to control it, or attack it, or force it to do something against my will is committing an aggressive act, provided of course I have not initiated an aggressive act myself. And because I have a natural property right in my body, any physically aggressive act against it by someone else must be considered illegitimate and a violation of the nonaggression principle. Thus, assault, torture, murder, rape, kidnapping and slavery all must be outlawed.

Of course, we do not live in the Garden of Eden, and in the real world there are many other things that are scarce, which means it has to be decided who owns them. Somehow, we have to allocate property rights to limited resources in a way that is consistent with the nonaggression principle. This means that the rights themselves must be objectively determined and universally applied. Universality implies that rights are equally applicable in all possible cases concerning the stated class of objects covered by the law – in this case property – and that they are time- and place-invariant. Objectivity means that the rights are deduced axiomatically from first principles.

Logically, there are only two ways to accomplish universality. The first is for every person to have an equal share in every good. This arrangement amounts to a system of universal joint ownership or absolute communism. But it is clearly unworkable. Firstly, there are some things a person must own exclusively. Every individual must own his or her own body, for the reasons stated above. Secondly, if everyone had an equal say in how other people should act, then no one could initiate any action without first gaining the permission of all. However, this results in an absurdity because giving permission is itself an action that would require the permission of all, and so on *ad infinitum*.[200] Thirdly, certain resources, like the food one puts into one's mouth cannot be owned jointly, since in the act of consumption, it cannot be shared. At that point, one must have absolute control over it. Fourthly, if everyone had an equal aliquot property right in every material good, then no single good could be controlled, used, altered, or disposed of without the approval of everyone. Even if just one individual were to dissent, it would violate that person's share in the property right of the good in question.

No society could be organized on these grounds because, if rigorously applied, all action would grind to a halt. A universal system based on communistic principles such as this would soon break down, and the result would be endless disputes, conflict, and disorder. Moreover, a system of universal joint ownership is far from being objective. An equal property share in all resources might seem reasonable, but there is no rational way to justify this method of organizing society, because it is neither deduced axiomatically from first principles nor inferred from observing regularities in human nature. Rather, it simply asserts that it is just. In reality, the assertion is made on an emotional and subjective basis. It assumes that all people have precisely the same motivations and desires.

The solution, and the only other alternative that complies with the basic principle, is to establish equal property rights; not an equal *share of property* but rather an equal *right to own property*. This fulfills

---

[200] Hoppe states, "Every action of a person requires the use of some scarce means (at least of the person's body and its standing room), but if all goods were co-owned by everyone, then no one, at no time and no place, would be allowed to do anything unless he had previously secured every other co-owner's consent to do so. Yet how could anyone grant such consent were he not the exclusive owner of his own body (including his vocal cords) by which means his consent must be expressed? Indeed, he would first need another's consent in order to be allowed to express his own, but these others could not give their consent without having first his, and so it would go on." Hoppe, Hans-Hermann (2004) "The Ethics and Economics of Private Property," in Enrico Colombatto (ed.) *Companion to the Economics to Private Property*. Edward Elgar, London.

the principle of universality because it can be applied equally to all persons without exception, and yet it suffers none of the practical problems associated with universal joint ownership. It is also objective because the rights are deduced *a priori* from the axiom of self-ownership. This deduction is made as follows:

Since I own my body, anything I do with it by way of my actions is necessarily an extension of my body and my will. If I use my body to create order out of disorder – a process called labor[201] – and I use my labor on matter in a state of nature – i.e., a material resource not owned by anyone – then, logically, whatever I create becomes an extension of me; in other words, it becomes my property, for me to use as I see fit. In Lockean terms, I have "mixed" my labor with it, I have a property right to it, and it becomes mine.[202] This much is clear. Today, very few natural resources are completely unowned. (Exceptions include the oceans and parts of Antarctica, although even in these cases, claims exist.) But in the days when vast swaths of land were unowned, it was possible to lay a claim to the land or the natural resources on it via the process of original appropriation or "homesteading."

Homesteading is the principle that whoever uses the resource first makes it his or her property, but this right is only established if

---

[201] Labor involves lowering entropy by doing any of the following: gathering, improving, creating, tending, organizing, investing, combining resources, etc. Does a service like psychological counseling lower entropy? Yes, if the goal is to increase satisfaction and happiness for the person seeking the service. Happiness is a more ordered state than unhappiness. A psychologically impaired state is disordered. Some actions might temporarily increase entropy, but if the goal is to create order, then it is still labor – e.g., spreading seeds on the ground to grow crops. However, anything that is designed to create disorder – for example, vandalism, war, etc. – is not labor.

[202] Locke states, "The labour of his body, and the work of his hands, we may say, are properly his. Whatsoever then he removes out of the state that nature hath provided, and left it in, he hath mixed his labour with, and joined to it something that is his own, and thereby makes it his property." Locke, John (2015) [1689] *Two Treatises of Government and A Letter Concerning Toleration*. Digireads.com Publishing, Kindle Edition. p. 111.

it involves mixing one's labor with it; otherwise, it remains unowned and in a state of nature.[203] Merely declaring virgin territory to be one's property is not legitimate. One cannot lay claim to the whole of the moon by mere declaration, for example. Traversing virgin land does not constitute ownership either, except for the very limited purpose of appropriating the land on which the traveler temporarily stands. Virgin land becomes property only when it is improved in some way by, for example, enclosing it, farming it, building on it, etc.[204] However, if the property subsequently becomes unused and abandoned, it returns to a state of nature for someone else to homestead. When Crusoe arrives on an uninhabited island, he does not own any part of the island simply by declaring it to be his. However, the berries he picks from a tree become his because he uses his labor to collect them. If he waters the tree and tends to it, then it also becomes his property, and if he fences in a group of trees and makes the fenced area into an orchard, then that too becomes his property.

Today, there are few natural resources that are not already claimed, and most produced goods are also owned. Therefore, if people wish to acquire property, either for the purpose of adding their labor to it, or investing in it, or directly consuming it, then they

---

[203] Rothbard states, ". . . all resources, all goods, in a state of no-ownership belong properly to the first person who finds and transforms them into a useful good (the "homestead" principle) . . . the first to find and mix his labor with them, to possess and use them, "produces" them and becomes their legitimate property owner." Rothbard, Murray N. (1998) [1982] *The Ethics of Liberty*. New York University Press, pp. 56-57.

[204] Locke states, "And though all the fruits [the earth] naturally produces, and beasts it feeds, belong to mankind in common, as they are produced by the spontaneous hand of nature; and nobody has originally a private dominion, exclusive of the rest of mankind, in any of them, as they are thus in their natural state: yet being given for the use of men, there must of necessity be a means to appropriate them some way or other, before they can be of any use, or at all beneficial to any particular man." Locke, John (2015) [1689] *Two Treatises of Government and A Letter Concerning Toleration*. Digireads.com Publishing, Kindle Edition. p. 110.

must acquire it from someone else in some way. And clearly, if owning property means the exclusive right to control and dispose of it, then its acquisition from another person must be voluntary, otherwise it would involve an aggressive act that violates the property right of the owner. Hence, the only legitimate method of acquiring owned property is through voluntary exchange or gift. In the case of the former, this means either an exchange with one's labor or an exchange of one kind of property for another. In the case of a gift, it means a gift by a living person or as a bequest. Logically, any other method of acquiring property is involuntary and therefore illegitimate. Thus, all forms of theft, including larceny and embezzlement (simple theft), robbery (theft with force), fraud (theft by deception), and extortion (theft by coercion) must be outlawed. In addition, any other action which violates the rights of the property owner, including unauthorized use or vandalism, is illegitimate.

A property-rights system based on these principles is objective because it is based on the natural property right that every person has in his or her own body, and in legitimately owned property external to the body acquired through non-aggressive means. It is consistent with the nonaggression principle. Collectively, it eliminates or reduces certain impediments in a way that permits free and life-affirming action. No other system can achieve this. A legal code which establishes different laws for different groups, or laws unequally applied, or laws that take property from one group to benefit another, is neither universal nor objective. Laws of that kind are man-made, arbitrary, and subjective, and they violate the nonaggression principle.

Libertarian Law

The legal code that proscribes the specific acts mentioned above, I shall hereinafter refer to as *libertarian law*.[205] I could have called it

---

[205] The term "libertarian law" first appears in Rothbard, Murray N. (2006)

the "natural law" or the "common law," but these terms have different meanings to different people, depending on the particular ethical philosophy within which their use arises. For example, "natural law" can be used very broadly to mean any moral theory that comprises moral realism, but it can also have more specific meanings, as in the case of Aristotelian natural law, stoicism, or the natural law of Cicero or Aquinas. While most interpretations refer to natural law as arising spontaneously or naturally and fulfilling some common purpose without positive intent, other definitions take it to mean a form of divine law, as in the case of Islamic natural law. The definition of "common law" is even more vague. Historically, it has referred to law based on ancient usage and custom, but modern interpretations imply legislation based on precedent that arises not from tradition or habit but rather from judicial rulings. Therefore, given the different definitions of these terms and to avoid confusion, I shall simply call this legal code libertarian law.

Libertarian law, which is based on the nonaggression principle and the concept of property rights, is logical and objective. Moreover, it is discoverable as a law of human nature. It allows every person to act legitimately according to his will without violating the property of anyone else. It also allows the maximum possible freedom. It does not give rise to *absolute* freedom, which would allow people to be free to commit aggressive acts; rather, it allows people to be *free from* aggressive acts. It thus ensures peace and tranquility, all of which is conducive to leading a happy and purposive existence.

Libertarian law is not a complete moral doctrine, nor is its purpose to increase society's morals. It addresses only the issue of physical aggression. Its only purpose is to say how the individual must *not* act. It has parallels with the Negative Golden Rule, which

---

[1973] *For a New Liberty: The Libertarian Manifesto*. Ludwig von Mises Institute, Auburn, AL, p. 286.

states, "Do *not* do unto others that which you would not have them do unto you."[206] It circumscribes – i.e., sets limits – to the complete set of permissible action by explicating those actions which are absolutely impermissible. It deals only with violations of the nonaggression principle and does not judge other actions, even if they engender strong moral sentiments. A person can be labelled as being mean, a liar, and selfish, but unless that individual has aggressed against the property of another – physically – then the determination of "guilt" is a sentiment, based on a feeling, and libertarian law has no comment. (This is not to say the libertarian has no comment, a point of confusion which often entails the libertarian being unfairly branded as unfeeling.) But if the mean, mendacious, and selfish individual decides to embezzle or steal or rob from another, then this becomes an altogether different category of moral infraction which libertarian law condemns.

In demarcating the range of impermissible actions from everything else, libertarian law is *negative*. The term "negative law" simply means the law only says what a person must *not* do. It does not say what anyone should do positively. It therefore lies in opposition to "positive law," which compels individuals to do certain things. As a matter of logic, because such compulsion always involves the initiation of force or threat of force by the authority in power, it follows that all of positive law – and this includes virtually every statute law – violates the principle of nonaggression. Even if certain positive laws might appear well-meaning, they are necessarily and objectively morally bad from this perspective.

Some people accuse libertarianism of being callous and uncaring, but this is wholly unjustified criticism. Libertarian law does not prevent, in any way, human beings from being benevolent, generous, caring, empathic, or virtuous. Indeed, to lead a complete and moral life, virtuous and compassionate actions toward others

---

[206] There are certain exceptions when the interaction is voluntary. For example, a surgeon might have to perform surgery on a patient, which he would not want done to himself.

are of the utmost importance. However, what libertarianism does say is that the application of virtue is subjective; it is up to the individual to decide how to act positively toward other people. And it says that any attempt to codify positive virtues into law is *necessarily* an aggressive act that violates libertarian law. Positive law (statute law) always involves the lawmakers and their enablers committing one of the aggressive acts mentioned above, against those on whom the law is imposed. I shall have more to say on this in a later chapter, but for now it should be noted that, more often than not, statute laws are created to give the appearance of virtue, without those who support the law having to make any significant sacrifice themselves. Such laws often make a display of being compassionate and constructive, while in reality they are always aggressive and destructive.

Unlike physical laws, which are immutable and apply to material objects, libertarian law requires the exercise of a collective will for it to come into force, and relates only to rational beings. The determination to implement it, or not, rests with us. We have a choice in the matter. But the law exists nevertheless as a product of the rational mind, and it waits for our decision to put it into effect. There is a paradox here. Reason only arises because we have free will, but free will gives us the choice to ignore the nonaggression principle and embrace other methods of organizing society. It would seem this possibility acts against reason. How can reason act against itself? Reason is the defining characteristic of mankind. It elevates us above all other living things, but our reasoning is not perfect, and hence sometimes we fail. Just as the individual sometimes fails to embrace self-imposed laws grounded in virtue that produce happiness, so too can society choose an inappropriate legal system that leads to disorder and chaos. But if life exists by creating order out of chaos, and if the defining characteristic of human life is to employ reason to do so, then the further we drift from libertarian law, the more we regress. An argument against libertarian law is an argument against the future well-being and development of the human race.

Libertarian law is the apotheosis of a rational society. Suppose for a moment we were not the only rational beings on earth. My thesis is that any sufficiently rational group – human or not – whose driving force is to survive against the tide of entropy would ultimately adopt libertarian law. The fact that no human society has fully embraced it thus far is merely a reflection of the fact that it will take time for it to be recognized as the means to reach the maximum degree of human flourishing. The institution of slavery took thousands of years to be abolished and is still prevalent in some parts of the world today. But enlightened societies eventually realized there was a better way. And so it will be with libertarian law. It is true, of course, that throughout the ages, kings, presidents, legislators, dictators, and tyrants of various sorts have imposed their own kind of law on society – at odds with the nonaggression principle – so that they or a select group can benefit at the expense of the population at large. But even the most despotic rulers recognize that social cooperation is needed at some level, otherwise their society degenerates. Most humans cannot survive as solitary animals in a dog-eat-dog world because human bodies are simply not equipped to handle nature "red in tooth and claw" outside of a group. Even the most primitive hunter gatherers engage in social cooperation and the division of labor to some degree.

To the extent that we choose a legal code that enhances social cooperation rather than undermines it, we do so *not* merely because it is our natural disposition. Nor because we have evolved to be moral beings. Rather, we do so because we have evolved to be rational beings. And the more rational the society, the more likely it is that self-governance in compliance with libertarian law is the outcome. Conversely, the more we, as a society, ignore this principle and distance ourselves from libertarian law, the more it implies we have regressed to a lower form of humanity. The challenge is to recognize and then censure the few humans who would willingly subvert cooperation for their own purposes.

That we sometimes fail in this endeavor and are not always consistent, is merely a reflection of the fact that we do not have perfect reason, and that we are driven to a greater or lesser extent by animalistic instincts inherited from our evolutionary past, which are also not infallible. But just as physical laws exist, waiting to be discovered and exploited, so do objective moral laws. The code of justice I have called libertarian law also exists in nature waiting to be identified and capitalized upon.

12

The Epistemological Status of Justice

Historical Views of Principles of Justice

In the annals of human history, there have been many different perspectives regarding principles of justice and the kinds of laws that should exist. While virtually all legal systems have some common elements, it is clear that much of what is claimed to be just with regard to law is particular to time and place. I have argued that justice in this context should never be relative or subjective. Rather, it should be universal, rationally determined, and limited to prohibiting actions which are objectively rights violations, namely, initiations and threats of physical aggression involving violations of the rights of persons or their property. However, more often than not, justice has been based purely on subjective moral sentiment. Therefore, it comes as no surprise that there has been little consensus on the kinds of laws that have been deemed to be just.

In Plato's dialogue, *Republic*, Socrates asks, how do we know what is just?[207] Polemarchus responds by saying that justice is giving each man his due – in other words, an eye for an eye. Thrasymachus, the sophist and cynic, says that justice is whatever the strong decide is in their best interest and that the law merely serves to dupe the weak to do the bidding of the rich and powerful. Glaucon, however, takes the opposite view. He claims that laws are enacted by men to protect the weak from the powerful, for without laws to restrain bad

---

[207] For an excellent summary, see Guthrie, W. K. C. (1975) *A History of Greek Philosophy: Volume IV*. Cambridge University Press. pp. 439-443.

intentions, any person given enough power will commit evil acts. For Glaucon, people regularly find their will frustrated by the will of others, and therefore justice exists in order to keep the peace. Socrates (who in the dialogue reflects Plato's thoughts) does not dispute that the law preserves the peace, but he rejects the idea put forward by the others that justice is a purely human creation. Rather, he thinks it is eternal and absolute, and that we have to find it by acquiring the right kind of knowledge. Justice, according to Plato, should be left to experts who, like navigators, steer the ship of state safely into port. However, Plato's conclusion is that society should be run in a dictatorial fashion under a totalitarian-like system.[208]

By way of contrast, Aristotle in *Nicomachean Ethics* lays out two concepts of justice.[209] Firstly, there is the notion of the law itself, which Aristotle claims is derived from the set of authoritative rules of conduct that conform to established principles. Secondly, there is the idea of the proper application of justice, which he defines as the mean between two extremes – namely, defect or excess. Justice so administered is a major virtue, according to Aristotle.[210]

There have of course been many other conceptions of justice since the time of the Ancient Greeks, and most have been at odds with each other. For example, at various times, religious scholars have claimed that laws should be based on divine command, either because God knows what is morally good, or because anything which God commands *must* be morally good. Thomas Hobbes maintained that justice and the law should be left completely at the discretion of an all-powerful sovereign, without whom a war of all

---

[208] For Plato's views on justice and the ideal state, see Ibid., pp. 444-455.

[209] For Aristotle's view on justice, see Guthrie, W. K. C. (1981) *A History of Greek Philosophy: Volume VI.* Cambridge University Press. pp. 370-376.

[210] See Chapter 9.

against all is inevitable.[211] Utilitarians, such as Jeremy Bentham[212] and John Stuart Mill, claimed that the objective of the law should be to produce the greatest good or happiness for the greatest number of people, but never fully answered how that could be accomplished.[213] More recently, John Rawls created a theory of justice based on "fairness," which asked people to imagine what kind of laws they would want if they came into society behind a "veil of ignorance" with no preexisting knowledge of their position and status beforehand.[214]

Many people today contend that rules should exist to attain "social justice," the idea being that the law should address supposed inequities in power and wealth. Advocates of distributive justice schemes contend that resources should be allocated according to certain subjective criteria, usually with the goal of achieving what is perceived to be some kind of equal outcome. In this regard, Marxists and socialists claim that goods should be distributed "from each according to his ability to each according to his need." Neo-Marxists, on the other hand, claim that in order to achieve social justice, laws should exist to transfer wealth and power from certain "privileged" groups to less privileged ones, in which privilege, or the

---

[211] Hobbes states, "And because the condition of Man . . . is a condition of War of everyone against everyone." Hobbes, Thomas (2014) [1651] *Leviathan*. Digireads.com Neeland Media LLC. Kindle Edition. p. 58.

[212] According to Bentham, "By utility is meant that property in any object that tends to produce benefit, advantage, pleasure, good, or happiness . . . or (what comes again to the same thing) to prevent the happening of mischief, pain, evil, or unhappiness to the party whose interest is considered, if that party be the community in general, then the happiness of the community, if a particular individual, then the happiness of that individual." Bentham, Jeremy (1907) [1789] *An Introduction to the Principles of Morals and Legislation*. Oxford at the Clarendon Press, London. p. 2.

[213] Mill states, "Utility, or the Greatest Happiness Principle, holds that actions are right in proportion as they tend to promote happiness, wrong as they tend to produce the reverse of happiness." Mill, John Stuart (1863) *Utilitarianism*. Parker & Son, London. p. 9.

[214] Rawls, John (1971) *A Theory of Justice*. The Belknap Press of Harvard University Press, Cambridge, Mass.

lack of it, is said to exist on the basis of an identity associated with race, sex, sexual orientation, gender identity, or religious affiliation.[215]

From the time of the ancient Greeks to today, all these ideas about justice and the law are at variance with one another because their underlying suppositions about morality differ. Hence, there has been no consistent methodology by which principles of justice can be derived. There has been no consensus. All too often – indeed in almost every case in every era – advocates of a particular system simply extract from their moral or political background those principles they *feel* are appropriate to turn into law. They consult their particular ideology, pick and choose those actions they consider to be good or bad, or those they believe will lead to beneficial or detrimental outcomes – often with reference to themselves – and then promote laws that encapsulate their particular position, whatever that might be.

To be sure, some philosophers have resorted to a more rational methodology in determining what is just. In this regard, Locke's classical liberalism and Kant's categorical imperative come to mind. Nevertheless, virtually every legal framework and every political structure has incorporated aspects of moral and political thinking that are clearly subjective and particular. Throughout history, in determining the nature of justice, there has been a consistent failure to exclude underlying subjective premises and, more particularly, a deficiency in differentiating them from those that are objective. Part of the reason for this is that many philosophers and legal scholars

---

[215] Philosopher Stephen Hicks describes justice in the postmodern era as follows: "As there are no universally valid legal principles of justice, arguments become rhetorical battles of wills . . . All decisions are inherently subjective and driven by preference and politics. The law is a weapon to be used in the social arena of subjective conflict, an arena driven by competing wills and the coercive assertion of one group's interests over those of other groups." Hicks, Stephen R. C. (2011) *Explaining Postmodernism: Skepticism and Socialism from Rousseau to Foucault (Expanded Edition)*. Ockham's Razor. Kindle Edition, Loc. 721-725.

conclude that it is all very well to ground justice in moral principles, but it is impossible for any aspect of morality to be completely objective, and therefore it is perfectly appropriate for the law to be made up on the fly. Others are convinced that their particular brand of morality is completely objective, even though it is not, and decree laws that most people would find abhorrent; indeed, some of the most execrable theocratic dictators might be included in this category. Yet others presume that laws should be fashioned according to the peculiarities of time and place without reference to any moral standard at all.

The system of justice I have proposed in this book is based on moral principles, but only those that are objective, rationally deducible, absolutely true, timeless, and therefore applicable to every human being equally. It is a system of justice that is based on one all-important axiom – *the nonaggression principle*. Strict adherence to this principle leads logically through a process of deduction to a superstructure of law – *libertarian law* – that involves individual freedom, property rights, voluntary interpersonal exchange, contract, and restitution for victims of aggressors.

To be clear, libertarian law has little or nothing to do with the Libertarian Party, nor is it a system of law that is "fiscally conservative and socially liberal." Many people roll their eyes when they hear the word "libertarian." They assume that libertarians are selfish libertines who care nothing about those less fortunate than themselves, or that they are isolationists. Or they claim that libertarianism is a utopian system. None of this is true. In fact, a libertarian society – that is to say, a genuinely free society – would almost certainly be more egalitarian, more compassionate, more charitable, more socially conservative, more peaceful, and definitely *less* utopian in its goals than any socialist scheme ever tried or proposed. Much of the misconception regarding libertarianism is a result of grossly distorted claims, not to mention outright propaganda, by those in positions of power who hate freedom simply because they want to hold onto that power. The truth is that most people have never really thought all that hard – or more precisely, never been encouraged to think all that hard – as to why libertarianism is the only valid way to order society.

While many elements of libertarian law have been incorporated in systems of justice from time to time – as in the common law of England for instance – lamentably, very few societies have adopted all of its ramifications fully. One exception, perhaps, was Celtic Ireland,[216][217] which was a genuinely free society from about the 7th to the 17th century, after which it came under the jurisdiction of the English crown. Over the centuries, many political economists and philosophers have promoted systems that adhere fairly closely to libertarian law. John Locke, in the second of his *Two Treatises of Government* suggested a free society based on individual property rights and contract theory that included many libertarian elements. Thomas Jefferson, who drew heavily on the works of Locke, included its premises in the U.S. Declaration of Independence, wherein it states: "We hold these truths to be self-evident, that all men are created equal, that they are endowed by their Creator with certain unalienable Rights, that among these are Life, Liberty and the pursuit of Happiness."[218] During the 19th century, the anarchist Lysander Spooner embraced a version of the nonaggression principle in *No Treason* (1867) in which he denounced the State, and Gustave de Molinari outlined a method for the production of security in a free society that would operate according to this same principle.

But it was the economist and political theorist Murray Rothbard who fully deduced the logical consequences of justice based on the nonaggression   principle   and   thereby   completely   described

---

[216] Ibid., pp. 286-290.

[217] Peden, Joseph R. (1977) " Property Rights in Celtic Irish Law." *Journal of Libertarian Studies,* Vol. 1 (2), pp. 81 - 95.

[218] The term "life, liberty, and pursuit of happiness" was substituted by Jefferson in place of the more well-known (at the time) triad of "life, liberty, and property." See Rothbard, Murray N. (1998) [1982] *The Ethics of Liberty.* New York University Press, p. 23.

libertarian law. He did so most notably in two works. In the first of these, *For a New Liberty* (1973), Rothbard demonstrated that throughout history the biggest aggressor of all has been the State, and he proposed a radical reorganization of society in which the government is expunged and every individual has the inherent right to genuine freedom returned. Then, in *The Ethics of Liberty* (1982), Rothbard described in more detail the ramifications of the free society and showed how freedom as a natural right might apply to a range of practical problems.

Positive Law

Under libertarian law, the only legitimate laws are those which are based solely on objective moral grounds and which are consistent with the nonaggression principle. Logically, all other laws are unjust, and therefore not laws at all, precisely because they violate the bedrock moral maxim. They are invalid. Regrettably, however, the dominant position held by most legal scholars today is that legal validity arises as a consequence of social facts of some kind. In this perspective – known as legal positivism – law and morality are conceptually distinct, and thus laws do not necessarily have to comport with any moral principles at all. Under legal positivism, the vast bulk of law originates either from social convention or from an authority such as a legislature, or it is made extemporaneously by judges from the bench. And thus, invariably – whether its authors realize it or not – it is based upon the subjectively held convictions of either the society at large or the particular individuals who hold sway over the legislative or judicial process.[219]

Posit for a moment that a kind of mass hysteria took hold and a majority of people decided to denounce certain middle-aged spinsters for communicating with the devil, and a law was passed to condemn these unfortunate persons to death. Or suppose the

---

[219] See "Natural Law Versus Positive Law" in Rothbard, Murray N. (1998) [1982] *The Ethics of Liberty.* New York University Press, pp. 17-20.

legislature passed a law allowing certain privileged individuals the right to counterfeit money but made it a crime for anyone else to do so. Or imagine a law where certain young men are picked at random by a lottery and then sent off to a faraway land to be subjected to an ordeal akin to Russian roulette.

At one time or another, all these laws were passed in America, either because the masses clamored for them, or because a few individuals in positions of power thought, subjectively, they would be a good idea, or because it benefited them personally. According to the standards of legal positivism, they were all legal, but it is clear they were not objectively just nor were they required to be. Under the nonaggression principle, all laws would have to adhere to objective standards of justice, and thus not only would the particular laws mentioned above be unjust, but moreover, they could not even be considered to be law. Indeed, judged according to this standard, the entire body of statute law – all of which is based upon nothing other than subjectively held belief – would be illegitimate.

Sadly, far too many people today believe that all moral and legal issues are subjective and relative. This is not to say the entire moral ambit is axiomatic or objective; indeed, it is the case that many ethical questions can be answered only on subjective grounds. But what is most pernicious is the belief that a system of law can include such subjective propositions. Even among those who subscribe to realist ethical theories, there has been a consistent failure to weed out subjectively held assumptions from conceptions of the law. Among the anti-realists – i.e., the subjectivists and nihilists – the situation is even worse, for they do not believe that a rationally-deducible system is even possible, and certainly not one that is necessarily true. And finally, there are the non-cognitivists. Convincing them that universal moral truths apply to the law is the hardest of all because they assert that true or false moral statements have no meaning at all.

Hume's Is-Ought Problem

Why are so many people reluctant to acknowledge that objective moral statements are possible? Much of the problem stems from the false belief that universal and objective propositions apply only to the physical world. This misconception is epitomized by the famous "is-ought" problem, first raised by David Hume in *A Treatise of Human Nature* (1739). Hume noted that a statement about what *is* the case must be derived from objective factual premises. This is certainly true in the world of physical objects. For example, the statement, "the car *is* accelerating" describes an objective fact based on observation. Additionally, the statement "force *is* equal to mass multiplied by acceleration" is a universal law concerning objective facts, also derived empirically. On the other hand, a moral statement about what *ought* to be the case – for example, one *ought* not to steal – is of a different kind. Hume maintained that this difference arises because such statements have no objective factual premises – by which he meant there can be no empirical observation supporting them – and thus their truth cannot be determined. If their truth is indeterminate, said Hume, then no moral laws can exist.[220]

---

[220] Hume's famous quote on the "is-ought problem" is as follows: "In every system of morality, which I have hitherto met with, I have always remark'd, that the author proceeds for some time in the ordinary way of reasoning, and establishes the being of a God, or makes observations concerning human affairs; when of a sudden I am surpriz'd to find, that instead of the usual copulations of propositions, is, and is not, I meet with no proposition that is not connected with an ought, or an ought not. This change is imperceptible; but is, however, of the last consequence. For as this ought, or ought not, expresses some new relation or affirmation, 'tis necessary that it shou'd be observ'd and explain'd; and at the same time that a reason should be given, for what seems altogether inconceivable, how this new relation can be a deduction from others, which are entirely different from it. But as authors do not commonly use this precaution, I shall presume to recommend it to the readers; and am persuaded, that this small attention wou'd subvert all the vulgar systems of morality, and let us see, that the distinction of vice and virtue is not founded merely on the relations of objects, nor is perceiv'd by reason." Hume, David (1739) *A Treatise of Human Nature.* John Noon, London. p. 469.

Hume's objection to the existence of universal natural moral laws is based on two fallacies. The first is that all moral statements must exist within a single category; either they are all objective or all subjective. And for Hume, they are all subjective. The second is that all natural laws must necessarily have factual premises. But this is also false. It is true that many moral statements are subjective. It is also the case that there are no moral propositions that can be determined by experience alone. But some moral truths are universal and can be determined objectively by deduction from self-evident axioms, *a priori* – namely, from the axiom of self-ownership and the axiom of action, along with a few empirical observations concerning human nature.

To wit, it is axiomatic and self-evident that all human beings have free will and the will cannot be taken away; it is inalienable. It is also self-evident that we act according to our will, and action is purposive and directed towards the production of goods which increase utility and happiness. Additionally, it is clear that human beings have a natural propensity for actions and behaviors that perpetuate their lives, otherwise *homo sapiens* would cease to exist as a species. This is manifested in a will to live and in actions that are life-affirming. But it is also the case – as a matter of empirical reality – that life is a constant struggle against entropy and decay, and that life-affirming actions are those which reduce or inhibit entropy. Therefore, all genuinely good actions, in addition to increasing happiness, also create order or reduce disorder; specifically, order in material objects and in the body, order within the mind, and finally order in society. Enduring happiness is merely nature's way of telling us we are on the right track.

To act positively, we seek regularities. We seek laws of the physical world, self-imposed rules, and laws applicable to society, all of which produce material, mental, and social order. However, because the world is uncertain and human beings are not infallible, not all actions result in outcomes that are genuinely good. They might *seem* good *ex ante* or immediately *ex post*, but they nevertheless result in unhappiness in the long run. This is particularly the case when it comes to instituting universally applicable *positive* laws that are deemed to do good in society at large. Happiness is a psychological condition, endowed in us by nature, that signifies order within the mind, which is positive for life. But because the outcome of good actions can be assessed only subjectively, no universal positive laws can be demonstrated to increase happiness overall, either qualitatively or quantitatively. Any argument to the effect that they can is erroneous, and any attempt to institute laws along these lines is bound to fail. This was the failure of utilitarianism, a failure that arose because interpersonal comparisons of utility and happiness cannot be made.

In contrast, physical aggression demonstrably lowers utility on the part of at least one person in every case, and according to the universal threat axiom, the threat of aggressive acts creates uncertainty and disorder in people's lives. Therefore, laws that prohibit all initiations of physical aggression or physically aggressive threats must be universally good. Negative laws of this kind reduce uncertainty for everyone and necessarily increase the degree of order in society at large. They are objective and just. All other laws prohibiting or mandating positive or negative actions are unverifiable with respect to utility and are therefore subjective and unjust.

G. E. Moore's "Naturalistic Fallacy"

The term "naturalistic fallacy" does not have the same meaning as the "appeal-to-nature fallacy," the assertion that something is morally good if it is natural and morally bad if unnatural. Rather, Moore's naturalistic fallacy maintains that it is impossible to ascribe moral goodness (or badness) with reference to a natural property such as pleasure. According to Moore,[221] this is because goodness is

---

[221] See Moore, George Edward (1922) [1903] *Principia Ethica*. Cambridge University Press. pp. 10-17.

a non-natural simple quality that cannot be uniquely defined.

In order to understand why he feels this is the case, it is necessary to explain what "open" and "closed" questions mean in this context. An open question arises when something being defined cannot be reduced to a tautology, and the question of what it is has multiple possible answers. For example, in seeking to define "green," the question, "what is green?" might be answered by saying "grass is green." But one could also say "leaves are green." Moreover, grass could be yellow or brown, and leaves could be red, etc. Therefore, the question of "what is green?" is an open question because there is no single way to describe what the experience of green is exactly. It cannot be uniquely defined as something else. The definition is unsettled.

On the other hand, a closed question arises when the thing being defined can be explained simply in other terms, and the question of what it is can be resolved. For example, a bachelor is defined as an unmarried man. In this case, the question of "what is a bachelor?" is a closed question, precisely because there are no alternative answers with respect to the bachelor's marital status and sex. The terms "bachelor" and "unmarried man" mean the same thing, and the definition is therefore settled.

Moore's argument is that "good" is a simple non-natural quality and cannot be expressed as something else that has the same meaning, because the question of "what is good?" is an open question. One could say "pleasure is good." But someone else might say "work is good," and a sadist might even say "torture is good." Moreover, it could be said that pleasure is not always good, and neither is work, and most people would define torture as bad. But the point is that describing "good" in terms such as pleasure or work or torture does not settle what it is. We cannot pin down the definition of goodness, says Moore.

But is Moore right? Certainly not in the social sphere of interpersonal relations, for as we have seen, social order is indeed definitively good. A sadist might claim that torture is good because engaging in it gives him pleasure, but he cannot claim that it would be good for society, or for himself, if everyone practiced it. For if torture were permitted, then this would increase the degree of entropy in society as a whole – as manifested in social uncertainty – which would be universally undesirable. As mentioned in chapter 10, the universal threat axiom implies that the desire for less uncertainty is universal, and that no one, not even someone who engages in crime, wants to be under increased threat and uncertainty. Thus, social order is the very definition of social good. Even though social order cannot be measured, it always increases when the nonaggression principle is observed. Therefore, both the nonaggression principle and the social order it produces are unquestionably good.

With respect to what constitutes "good" for the individual, this of course must be decided by the person himself. As mentioned in chapter 9, self-discipline and virtue are likely to lead to long-term happiness. But there is no guarantee that these qualities are necessarily considered good by everyone, or indeed that everyone prefers long-term happiness over short-term gain. Psychopaths probably do not feel that way. Nevertheless, if low mental entropy is equivalent to a state of enduring happiness, it follows that low mental entropy must be good for the individual. No one can argue that they want to be unhappy because, by definition, happiness is universally desirable. How one goes about achieving that state is up to the person himself, and whether or not it leads to the flourishing condition known as *eudaimonia* is never certain. But if it is achieved, then it must be considered good by the person who experiences it.

In many animal species, happiness is simply a feeling that has evolved to indicate to members of the species that their behavior is positive for their continued life and reproduction. Many positive instinctual behavioral responses are no doubt associated with pleasurable feelings and have been reinforced through the process of natural selection. Human beings are no different in this regard. Conversely, pain and dissatisfaction indicate precisely the opposite;

that the behavior is detrimental and is likely to result in disordered and harmful physical consequences.[222] Now, evolution is never perfect, and no doubt there are many occasions when the feelings are delusory. A hard-core addict might feel happy when he takes the drug, at least temporarily, but the action of taking narcotics is probably not conducive in the long run to his continued existence, assuming he wants to live. But, in general, without the drive to achieve happiness, there would be no motivation for action at all, and it is likely that *homo sapiens* would cease to exist. Whether or not the continued existence of mankind is considered good from the perspective of everyone is beside the point. It is certainly good from the point of view of someone who wishes our species to thrive.

Libertarianism and Morality

It is worth repeating here that libertarianism does not deny there are many moral claims that have a singularly subjective component. For example, compassion, generosity, kindness, benevolence, tolerance, beneficence, empathy, mercy, and truthfulness are all generally considered to be morally good, whereas meanness, selfishness, greediness, intolerance, stinginess, heartlessness, and mendacity are usually thought of as being morally bad. But in each case, the question of the act that constitutes them is a judgment based on sentiment and feeling. In general, the particular elements that would qualify a person's action to be described in these terms is never precisely given – even if we claim to know what they are in

---

[222] There are circumstances where we endure short-term pain and/or avoid immediate gratification precisely to achieve long-term gain. An example might be working out at the gym to improve one's physique. If this is considered from a praxeological perspective, it as an exchange – i.e., the labor (disutility) of working out in order to achieve the goal – in this case, an athletic body. However, from a psychological perspective, we endure short-term pain (and/or avoid short-term gratification) in order to achieve longer-term satisfaction because generally speaking this is better, not always, of course, but as a general rule. And I submit it is better because the end state is low mental entropy.

a specific case – and the degree to which a person's character in general can be said to align with them is never quantifiable. Put another way, with respect to these particular traits and many others, it is entirely subjective how we assess the moral worth of the individual's action or character as a whole. When we label the action or the person as being good or bad, it is merely a feeling, a sentiment.

But this emphatically is not the case when it comes to the issue of justice; for with respect to actions which violate the nonaggression principle – such as murder, rape, robbery, theft, fraud, assault, kidnapping, extortion, etc., – we leave the arena of sentiment altogether and enter the realm of objectivity. This is not at all to suggest these crimes engender no emotional response in the victims or the public at large. Clearly, in most cases they do, at least to some degree. Nor does it mean there is no subjectivity in determining whether or not a person might have committed a crime. In many instances, the determination of guilt involves an examination of the evidence, where impressions and opinions play a role. No, what this means is, if a person has committed one of these crimes – even if it is a relatively minor one – then *the action* involved is objectively, absolutely, and unequivocally morally bad; no bones about it. It is, categorically, a moral transgression.

Falsifiability and Objective Confirmability

In order to be classified as scientific, scientific laws have to be falsifiable – that is, the possibility must always exist that they may be disproved from further empirical evidence.[223] If that possibility does not exist, then they are not scientific. Religion and astrology are not scientific, because no evidence can be presented to disprove their claims. But since morality and justice do not rely on evidence to

---

[223] The term "falsifiability" as a criterion for demarcating scientific theories was introduced by the philosopher Karl Popper. For the basic definition, see Popper, Karl (1961) *The Logic of Scientific Discovery*. Basic Books, New York. pp. 40-42.

determine their laws, this raises the question of how we know whether laws that claim to be just are in fact just.

One possible answer is that their moral truth-claim is valid simply because "moral" and "just" mean the same thing – as in the statement, "this law is moral and therefore just." But this obviously gets us nowhere, because the proposition is a tautology and only trivially true. Another might be their truth is based on some kind of faith. Divine command laws are like this. They say, "this law is just because God deems it to be good." Utilitarian laws are also based on a kind of faith. They say, "this law is just because we believe it to be for the greater good of society." Utilitarian laws have the same validity as religious commands because they cannot be proved or disproved empirically or by other means. No one can read the minds of those who have supposedly benefited (or those who have potentially lost) from the application of utilitarian laws, let alone quantify and calculate the net effect. Utilitarians who claim they can are basing that claim on personal belief.

However, the legitimacy of any law prohibiting physical aggression does not rely on any type of faith. Rather, it rests on the fact that involuntary aggressive acts necessarily result in an objective loss of utility in ways that non-physical aggressions do not. In simple terms, the outcome of physical aggression can be seen. While evidence of guilt is sometimes murky, evidence of the harm itself is always clear. On the other hand, when the harm is merely psychological and subjective, the disutility cannot be established objectively, the harm is *not* clear, and laws prohibiting such "harm" are not just.[224] A similar situation arises with positive laws because

---

[224] For example, if a man asks a woman out for a date, and she rejects his offer, she may have harmed him psychologically. But she has a right to do so. If someone buys a loaf of bread, that raises the price of bread for everyone else by an infinitesimal amount. Everyone else could be said to be harmed, but no one's rights are violated.

objective confirmation of the supposed "good" created by such laws is not possible; hence they are also not just. Thus, *objective confirmability* is the *sine qua non* of just laws in much the same way as falsifiability is the essential element of scientific laws. If the outcome of a law lacks the ability to be confirmed objectively, then that law is not just. Laws that outlaw initiations of physical aggression *are* just precisely because eliminating these aggressions not only verifiably and objectively reduces disutility for potential victims, but crucially lowers uncertainty concerning involuntary acts within the community at large, all of which increases societal order and is positive for life.

13

Violent Intervention in The Market

The State as Violator of the Nonaggression Principle

The nonaggression principle is universal and objective. It is absolute. The initiation of physical force or the threat thereof is antithetical to life. There are many people who do not like this principle, and there are others who frequently violate it, but no one can logically argue against it, because to do so is to deny the order, harmony, and confidence necessary to pursue life itself and to embrace instead the chaos, discord, and uncertainty that results ultimately in death. It is to deny the very thing one needs in one's own life, at least to some degree. To argue against it represents the ultimate hypocrisy.

It should be clear by now that the biggest violators of the nonaggression principle are not individual criminals who commit isolated aggressions against small numbers of people, nor is it organized gangs who commit felonies on a larger scale. By far the worst aggressions originate from the State in the form of statute laws and various other governmental actions.

No statute law or ordinance is ever voluntary. Assuming the law is enforced, the officials responsible coerce compliance with the threat of either the loss of property or liberty. Assuming one complies, then one suffers a direct loss of utility. When faced with non-compliance, the officials implement force and aggression by making good on the threat whenever possible. If one ignores the government's edicts, then one must live with the uncertainty that

211

comes with knowing one might be arrested, fined, or imprisoned at any time. But if a person decides to set upon a course of resisting the government, then no matter how minor the violation, eventually that individual will almost certainly forfeit his life if he continues to resist, due to the overwhelming amount of force and violence the government can bring to bear.

A Typology of Violent Intervention

In what ways does the government violate the nonaggression principle? In his book, *Power and Market*, the great economist, historian, and libertarian philosopher Murray Rothbard laid out the typology of violent intervention in the market.[225] Rothbard noted there are three different ways in which the government initiates force in this area. The first of these involves coercing individuals to refrain from or perform certain actions which affect no one other than the actors themselves. This is termed *autistic intervention*. Examples include prohibiting the use of certain products or mandating speech codes. The second is *binary intervention*, in which the government forces individuals to perform certain tasks in its favor. Unlike autistic intervention, the government extracts some kind of material benefit from the subject, thus creating a hegemonic relationship. This is the same kind of relation that exists between a master and his slave, and it includes activities like conscription, taxation, and compulsory jury duty.

The third and final type of violent intervention in the market is what Rothbard calls *triangular intervention*, where force is used to interfere with voluntary interpersonal exchanges. Examples include laws that restrict the sale of certain kinds of goods, laws that require special permits or licenses, laws that prevent certain services between consenting individuals, and laws that mandate the terms on which goods or services should be sold. The last of these includes

---

[225] Rothbard, Murray N. (2004) [1962] *Man, Economy and State with Power and Market*. Ludwig von Mises Institute, Auburn, AL, pp. 1057-1061.

price controls, where exchanges are prevented from taking place at either above or below a fixed rate.

What can be said about the effects of these various kinds of intervention? The first thing to note is that, in every case, a coercive exchange takes place between the State and the subject. In the case of autistic intervention, the subject is either prevented from engaging in an action that would have returned a psychic profit, or he is forced to perform an action that results in a psychic loss. This is clear because whatever is forced necessarily violates the will. The difference between autistic and binary intervention is that in the case of the latter, the loss involves a transfer of goods or services from the subject to the government or to those who benefit from the government's policies. In triangular intervention, either one or both of the parties involved in the interpersonal exchange suffer a loss of utility.

The party that always benefits, either materially or psychically, is the government, or more accurately, the government officials responsible for the intervention, and those who are the recipients of the government's "largesse," including its workers and private individuals who are the beneficiaries of its laws. While this includes welfare recipients, by far the greatest amount of the pelf is reserved for those who are politically well-connected and therefore have the means to influence legislation in their favor.

Misconceptions Concerning Free-Market Capitalism

A commonly held view is that without some kind of government intervention in virtually every area of life, society breaks down into "anarchy" and chaos. The truth is precisely the opposite. When the nonaggression principle is upheld, all exchanges between human beings are purely voluntary, and as a consequence the degree of order is maximized. A free market does not at all imply a free-for-all. It does not mean the absence of laws. It simply means that according to the law, people can pursue their goals in life to the maximum extent without interference, provided they do not interfere with the will of anyone else. The result is not chaos but rather order and harmony.

Another common misconception is that capitalism has to be constrained, otherwise it leads to exploitation. Here, we must be very careful in the terms we use because the word "capitalism" is often ill-defined. The problem is that Western economies are often referred to as "free market" or "capitalist" when in fact they are nothing of the sort. They are more accurately called crony-capitalist, mercantilist, corporatist, economically fascist, or socialist.[226] While many people think these terms represent systems that lie at opposite extremes, in fact they describe political and economic regimes that are fairly similar inasmuch as they all involve violent intervention in the market to a greater or lesser extent. As such, they are indeed exploitative. However, in the true sense of the word, capitalism simply means a system of organizing society in which the means of production are privately owned. In other words, a truly capitalist system is the same as a free market, and in a genuinely free market, no one is forced or coerced or threatened to do anything against his or her will.[227]

The idea that free-market capitalism involves exploitation is due to the erroneous Marxian concept that capitalists supposedly exploit workers by not giving them their full due from the product of their labor. But this argument is false, because it is based on the disproved labor theory of value.[228] Anyone who saves and invests is a capitalist, and they exploit no one. The interest they receive, which Marxists

---

[226] See DiLorenzo, Thomas J. (2021) "The Rise of Economic Fascism in America." *Mises Wire*, (Sep 3, 2021).

[227] See Gordon, David (2022) "What's in a Name? Why the Definition of Capitalism Matters." *Mises Wire* (Mar 18, 2022)
Mises, Ludwig von (1979) [1958] *First Lecture: Capitalism* in Economic Policy: Thoughts for Today and Tomorrow, Ludwig von Mises Institute, Auburn, AL, pp. 1-15.

[228] See Murphy, Robert P. (2006) "The Labor Theory of Value: A Critique of Carson's Studies in Mutualist Political Economy," *Journal of Libertarian Studies*, Vol. 20 (1), pp. 17-33.

condemn, is simply a reflection of time preference, which exists because, all things being equal, people prefer a given satisfaction sooner rather than the same satisfaction later. This is axiomatic. Capitalists are rewarded with interest precisely because they are prepared to wait. Interest arises from the fact that capitalists advance money to producers, with which the latter buy factors of production, and the capitalists are rewarded at a later date with a premium derived from the sale of the finished products.[229] In a hypothetical free market in equilibrium, interest is the difference in costs. Workers are paid the going rate like any other factor of production, but since in a free market all exchanges are voluntary, including all exchanges with labor, there can be no exploitation. Indeed, true free-market capitalism is the *least* exploitative system possible.

As the great Austrian economist Ludwig von Mises showed (and later reiterated by Murray Rothbard) the free market is a beautiful and harmonious system that coordinates the demands of the consumers with all the resources that are necessary for their production, and it does so without any central planning. The key to this miraculous arrangement is the network of prices that results from the supply and demand of goods in the production structure. One can envisage this structure as a pyramid, with consumer goods at its base, capital goods – machines and intermediate products – in the middle of the structure, and original factors – i.e., natural resources and labor – at the apex. When the demand for a particular consumer good increases, the price rises, and this provides the profit incentive for entrepreneurs to engage in greater production of that good. But this also means the demand for the inputs increases, thus raising their prices and providing the motive for entrepreneurs to produce more of those capital goods. A similar process takes place at each higher level of the production structure until the price

---

[229] Rothbard, Murray N. (2004) [1962] *Man, Economy and State with Power and Market*. Ludwig von Mises Institute, Auburn, AL, pp. 345-348.

signals reach the original factors.[230] Meanwhile, at every stage, resources are transferred into the newly energized line, causing the supplies to increase and prices to move in the direction of equilibrium. At the same time, a reduction in the supply of capital goods and original factors in other production lines causes their prices to rise.

Hypothetically, if no further changes in consumer demand or other external factors were to take place, all the prices within the entire production structure would, after some time, come into a final equilibrium. But of course, in reality, the demand for goods and services constantly changes, in addition to which the supply of the original factors rises or falls as new discoveries of natural resources are made, and changes in the supply of labor occur. Moreover, advances in technology and better methods of production can also take place. All of this means that within any specific area of production, the prices never reach a final equilibrium, as each new external change – in consumer demand, original factors and technology – alters the incentives for the entrepreneurs.[231] But this

---

[230] As Rothbard explains, "Therefore, the value scales of the consumers determine, given the stocks of original factors, all the various results of the market economy that need to be explained: the prices of the original factors, the allocation of original factors, the incomes to original factors, the rate of time preferences and interest, the length of the production processes in use, and the amounts and types of the final products. In our changing real world, this beautiful and orderly structure of the free-market economy tends to be attained through the drive of the entrepreneurs toward making profit and avoiding loss." (Ibid., p. 569).

[231] Mises calls this hypothetical general equilibrium "the final state of rest" and contrasts it with the day to day clearing of the market which is termed the "plain state of rest." As Mises explains, "This final state of rest is an imaginary construction, not a description of reality. For the final state of rest will never be attained. New disturbing factors will emerge before it will be realized. What makes it necessary to take recourse to this imaginary construction is the fact that the market at every instant is moving toward a final state of rest. Every later new instant can create new facts altering this final state of rest. But the market is always disquieted by a striving after a definite final state of rest." Mises, Ludwig von (1998) [1949] *Human Action: A Treatise on Human Action*. Ludwig von Mises Institute, Auburn, AL, p. 246.

is precisely what is required, because the constant flux in prices provides the key information that entrepreneurs need in order to concentrate production in areas where prices are rising above their anticipated equilibrium point, and withdraw from those places where prices are doing the opposite. And within this beautifully coordinated, orderly, and harmonious system, resources are allocated at every stage of the production structure in such a way that the demands of consumers are met in the most efficient manner possible.

However, as Mises showed in his 1920 essay, *Economic Calculation in the Socialist Commonwealth*,[232] in a socialist planned economy, where a central committee dictates how resources are to be allocated, the entire market system breaks down precisely because none of the prices within the structure accurately reflect the needs of the consumers, balanced against the supply of the original factors and capital goods. In the free market, entrepreneurs constantly calculate where best to increase production based on expected profits, and where to withdraw because of anticipated losses. But the socialist planners cannot calculate, and not merely because they cannot be in myriad places at once or because they do not have the necessary information. Even if they had the information, they still could not calculate, precisely because there is no genuine competition. The profit and loss incentives that provide the necessary forces to constantly move prices in the direction of equilibrium are absent. As a result, there is no rational method by which to allocate resources.

Inevitably, as was the case in the Soviet Union, this situation creates vast surpluses of some goods and severe shortages of others, and a moribund economy that is chaotic and disordered. The more the government intervenes in the economy, the worse it becomes. This is precisely what one would expect in a socialist system, based

---

[232] Mises, Ludwig von (1990) [1920] *Economic Calculation in the Socialist Commonwealth*. Translated by S. Adler, Ludwig von Mises Institute, Auburn, AL.

on our understanding of the consequences of violating the nonaggression principle. The greater the violent intervention in the market, the greater is the degree of disharmony and social entropy.

While we think of Western economies as having a free market, the sad fact is they are nothing of the sort. While businesses are not as severely hampered as in the Soviet economy, they are nevertheless subject to myriad rules and regulations, which represents a considerable degree of violent intervention that distorts the price structure. As a consequence, it is axiomatic that the economy is far more disordered and discordant than it need be, there is far more uncertainty, and people in general are far less happy than would otherwise be the case.

Violent Intervention from Money Creation

What is clear is that when the market is genuinely free and all exchanges are voluntary, the outcome of each exchange is always positive for the individuals concerned. On the other hand, in a milieu of violent intervention, there are winners and losers. But the greatest economic damage from government aggression is the distortion that takes place within the market itself.

Consider the following voluntary exchange between Alice and Bob. Suppose Alice owns several bronze sculptures, and Bob owns a painting, and Alice agrees to exchange one of her sculptures for the picture. Assuming the exchange takes place, Bob has demonstrated that the marginal utility he gains from one of the bronzes is greater than the marginal utility he gives up from the painting; and for Alice, the valuations are reversed, *mutatis mutandis*.[233] Both have profited, psychically, from the exchange, at

---

[233] It is important to note that when an exchange takes place, the valuation of the good acquired by the actor is never equal to the value the actor places on the good given up. An exchange only takes place when the former is valued more than the latter. Thus, in voluntary interpersonal exchange, the valuations made the actors are necessarily the opposite of each other, otherwise the exchange would not take place. Only in involuntary exchanges

least *ex ante*, otherwise neither would have made the trade in the first place. But we cannot say by how much, precisely because the profit that Alice and Bob experience is only the increase in satisfaction they each acquire, and satisfaction is a psychological state that is not measurable in numerical or cardinal terms. It is ordinal only; we can say only that Alice preferred the painting to one of her sculptures, and Bob preferred the sculpture to the painting.

Valuations are always subjective. They are based on the subjective preferences of the actors. In the example above, the valuations which exist between Alice and Bob have no monetary component, because the transaction is one of barter. But in a money economy, subjective valuations are translated into cardinal money prices, in which money becomes the common medium of exchange for all goods and services traded. This is convenient because in a barter economy, it is often difficult to find someone with whom to trade when the good one wishes to sell might not be needed by any potential seller of the good one wishes to buy. Money solves the problem of this "double coincidence of wants."[234] It greases the wheels of the market, and it has great value performing this function. But how should we assess this value? What is the value of money itself? If Alice wants to sell one of her sculptures for money, how does she know how much to ask for it?

The answer is that she looks at the prices at which other comparable goods have sold for money in the recent past, and this serves as a guide for the transaction she is about to make. The value she places on the sculpture is the marginal utility she would give up in selling one of them (assuming they are all the same). The value she places on the money in this exchange – let us say she asks $100 – is the marginal utility of the goods she can buy with $100. Both of these valuations are subjective. But with respect to the latter, the *knowledge* of the kind and quantity of goods she can buy with $100

---

are the valuations not opposite.

[234] See Chapter 2, "The Origin of Money" in Mises, Ludwig von (1953) [1912] *The Theory of Money and Credit*. Yale University Press, New Haven. pp. 30-34.

is dependent on the existing price structure in the market, and this is objective. Technically speaking, the price structure is a present objective representation of the subjective valuations of all the market actors who have traded goods in terms of money in the immediate past. As such, it serves as an indispensable guide as to how the market is valuing money in terms of goods and services, and therefore how much the money can buy. It acts as the starting point for all future exchanges to take place, without which it would be impossible to assess (subjectively) how much money to exchange for any good.[235]

From the foregoing, it is clear that when the government intervenes in the market, it necessarily distorts the price structure. This is because prices no longer represent the past valuations of money (in terms of goods and services) that have arisen as a consequence of the intersubjective preferences of market actors engaged in voluntary exchange. Rather, they represent valuations that ensue from coercive exchanges that do not accurately reflect market-based preferences. In this regard, all interventions, even those which exist in so-called "capitalist" economies, entail precisely the same kind of deleterious effects as those which arise under purely socialist systems, albeit to a lesser extent.

---

[235] Because money has value as a medium of exchange, and not as a consumer or capital good, it would be impossible to assess the value of money subjectively without this price structure. An exception would be commodity money such as gold. But even in this case, the value of gold as money would be far higher than its value as a commodity only, and therefore, it would be impossible to assess the value of gold as money without an existing price structure. One might ask, how is money first valued if its value is dependent on previous exchange ratios? The answer was provided by Mises in his Regression Theorem. (Ibid., pp 114-122.) The first value of money as a medium of exchange is the value it had as a commodity in barter, such as gold. From then on, it is valued as a medium of exchange. One can expect that as the medium of exchange becomes more widely used, its value in that function will increase, ceteris paribus. While paper money obviously cannot originate in barter, it nevertheless attains its value from being originally linked to the commodity money. Mises's other great insight was to realize that money has marginal utility like any other good.

However, the problem is greatly exacerbated when the government intervenes, not merely in specific exchanges, but rather in the creation of money itself, for then the entire market becomes corrupted.[236] There are two principal ways in which money-creation occurs. The first is when the government permits banks to engage in fractional reserve lending.

In the *absence* of fractional reserve lending, commercial banks would be allowed to lend their customer's deposits, but *only* those that they receive in the form of time loans. They would *not* be permitted to lend money from demand deposits or current accounts, because the ownership of that money remains with the depositors, who are free to withdraw it at any time. The fact that such deposits are redeemable on demand means that depositors retain ownership, for if a person has full control over something, even if it is temporarily being held by someone else for safe keeping, then by definition the depositor still owns it. It is his. A demand depositor's funds are *not* owned by the bank, and the bank should not be free to do with that money as it pleases.

However, banks find that under normal circumstances, only a small percentage of depositors ever request the full return of their funds at a given time, which means a substantial portion of their customers' deposits typically remain on the banks' books. How tempting it is for the bank to lend that money out, and earn interest from it, even though they do not own it! And this is precisely what the government allows them to do under fractional reserve banking.[237]

---

[236] For an excellent description of the ways in which government intervention affects money, see Rothbard, Murray N. (1990) [1963] *What Has Government Done to Our Money?* Ludwig von Mises Institute, Auburn, AL.

[237] For an explanation as to why money creation from fractional reserve banking is unethical, see Davidson, Laura and Walter E. Block (2010) "The Case Against Fiduciary Media: Ethics is the Key," *Journal of Business Ethics*, Vol. 98 (3), pp. 505-511. Also, see Hoppe, Hans-Hermann, Jorg Guido Hulsmann, and Walter E. Block (1998) "Against Fiduciary Media." *Quarterly Journal of Austrian Economics*, Vol. 1 (1), pp. 19-50.

Suppose bank A has $1 million in the form of demand deposits. Under fractional reserve banking, the bank need retain only a small portion of this money, say 10%, in case some of the depositors ask to withdraw their funds. But the remaining 90% can be lent out to borrowers in violation of the property rights of the other depositors who, for the most part, remain ignorant of the fraud. That money – $900,000 – is then spent by the borrowers and eventually deposited into the accounts of customers at other banks. For the sake of simplicity, let us say it is all deposited in various accounts at bank B. Bank B must keep 10% of this money as a fractional reserve, but can lend out $810,000 to other borrowers who spend it, after which the money is deposited at bank C, and so on. Each time the money is lent out, there are two ownership claims, or titles, to the funds – namely, the claims of the depositors, and those of the persons who receive the money after it has been lent and spent. When the original money has been lent and spent numerous times, the total amount of money created out of thin air will be $9 million. (i.e., 900,000 + 810,000 + 729,000 + . . .) and the money supply will have increased from $1 million to $10 million.

Another way in which money is created is by direct intervention by the central bank, which simply prints it – or more accurately creates money as an accounting entry – through its open market operations.[238] Under this scheme, the central bank is permitted by the government to purchase bonds and other securities on the open market and pay for them with the new money it creates. These funds then find their way into the reserves of the commercial banks, enabling a new round of fractional reserve lending. Suppose the minimum required ratio for commercial bank reserves is 10%. For every dollar issued by the central bank, the commercial banks will multiply this amount by approximately ten times. For this reason, money issued by the central bank is sometimes called "high-

---

[238] Rothbard, Murray N. (1990) [1963] *What Has Government Done to Our Money?* Ludwig von Mises Institute, Auburn, AL, pp. 37-42.

powered money" because it forms the base of a pyramid of money creation in which the supply of money is vastly increased.

It will be noted that in creating money *ex nihilo*, the commercial banks and the central bank engage in an activity that can accurately be called counterfeiting.[239] If an ordinary person created money in this way, it would rightly be considered a felony. But the fact that banks are legally permitted to counterfeit money makes it no less of a crime. How does producing money in this way violate the nonaggression principle? Counterfeiting is clearly harmful when it involves consumer or producer goods. If an oil painting is represented as a Monet when in reality it is a Davidson, then the person to whom it is sold has suffered a loss of utility. It is a clear transgression of the nonaggression principle because it is theft by deception, which is fraud. The same is true for other tangible goods that are fraudulently sold, such as phony watches, jewelry, pharmaceuticals, and auto parts, etc. The case is less clear with money, only because money is not consumed or used up in any way. Rather, its utility lies as a medium of exchange and not as a consumer or producer good. Provided the forgery is good – and of course in the case of bank-issued money, the forgery is always perfect – it can be further exchanged without difficulty. It does not have to perform any other function. But this makes the crime of counterfeiting money no less serious.

Firstly, by increasing the money supply, it devalues the money of almost everyone who does not counterfeit. The exceptions include those who receive the money first, such as the investment houses which sell bonds to the central bank, and the borrowers of money from commercial banks who are able to spend the money before prices have risen. The people who are most victimized by this crime

---

[239] Jesus Huerta De Soto notes that in addition to counterfeiting, banks also commit fraud by "issuing a false receipt unbacked by a corresponding deposit." Huerta de Soto, Jesus (2006) *Money, Bank Credit, and Economic Cycles*. Translated by Melinda A. Stroup, Ludwig von Mises Institute, Auburn, AL, p. 245.

are those on fixed incomes and those who lend money in the form of genuine time loans. A time loan differs from a demand deposit in that the lender relinquishes ownership until the money is repaid. But if in the meantime, the money supply has been artificially inflated and devalued by central bank or commercial bank money creation, then the lender suffers a loss.[240]

However, by far the most pernicious effect of money inflation concerns the interest rate for loans. In the *absence* of any kind of money creation, the rate of interest at which money is lent is a reflection of social time preference.[241] Recall that time preference is the degree to which an investor is prepared to delay satisfaction in return for greater returns at a later date. A low time preference means a greater willingness to wait, or to put it another way, a greater willingness to accept lesser returns for a given period of waiting. In terms of production, the social time preference is an indication of the extent to which investors in general are prepared to wait for finished products, given the potential financial returns on those products. In the free market, competition among investors (lenders) who supply money, and among producers (borrowers) who demand money, results in a market rate of interest which reflects the social time preference.

But when the money supply is inflated, the additional influx of funds artificially lowers the market rate below the rate that would otherwise exist, and this distorts the production structure by

---

[240] As Rothbard states, "Particularly hard hit by an inflation, of course, are the relatively "fixed" income groups, who end their losses only after a long period or not at all. Pensioners and annuitants who have contracted for a fixed money income are examples of permanent as well as short-run losers. Life insurance benefits are permanently slashed . . . Also suffering losses are creditors who have already extended their loans and find it too late to charge a purchasing-power premium on their interest rates. Rothbard, Murray N. (2004) [1962] *Man, Economy and State with Power and Market*. Ludwig von Mises Institute, Auburn, AL, p. 992.

[241] Huerta de Soto, Jesus (2006) *Money, Bank Credit, and Economic Cycles*. Translated by Melinda A. Stroup, Ludwig von Mises Institute, Auburn, AL, pp. 284-291.

deceiving entrepreneurs into investing in projects of a term longer than would otherwise be the case.[242] The problem with this state of affairs is that the free market's finely-tuned and harmonized structure becomes broken precisely because the interest rate does not accurately reflect money's true supply and demand.[243]

Normally, in order for the market rate to fall, consumers must temporarily restrict their consumption of goods in order to free up investment funds. This is what is meant by market actors having a lower social time preference. But in the absence of reduced consumption, and with a simultaneous shift of resources into longer-term production lines, a dangerous state of affairs starts to brew. For a while, everyone can live high on the hog. People can consume without having to make any sacrifices, and businesses boom. However, this cannot last, for it soon becomes evident that the resources are simply not available to complete the projects, given the high consumption level. Businesses, particularly those whose products have a long time to completion, find they can no longer make ends meet. The investments thus become *mal*investments, and the unavoidable result is a recession.[244]

The recession is in fact the curative for the boom because it causes resources to be reallocated from longer to shorter production projects, but not without considerable pain for most businesses. As a consequence, the internal data of the production structure, including the market rate of interest, begins to reflect again the social time preference. Prices move back in the direction of equilibrium. However, in response to the recession, the inevitable reaction by the government, in concert with central and commercial banks, is to engage in a new round of money printing which repeats

---

[242] Ibid., pp. 347-384.

[243] The supply and demand of present money in terms of money repayable in the future, and more broadly, the supply and demand of present goods in terms of goods produced in the future.

[244] See also "Credit Expansion and the Business Cycle" in Rothbard, Murray N. (2004) [1962] *Man, Economy and State with Power and Market.* Ludwig von Mises Institute, Auburn, AL, pp. 994-1004.

the boom-bust cycle all over again.

The process of booms and busts I have briefly sketched here is known as the Austrian business cycle and was first fully elucidated by Ludwig von Mises.[245] Business cycles have existed for centuries – indeed since the advent of fractional reserve banking – but they became far more pronounced when central banks were created. This was due to the influx of high-powered money and the fact that central banks could engage in "monetary policy" which enabled officials to increase the money supply by design, far and above that which could be achieved by commercial banks alone.

This interference in the free market is without a doubt one of the worst kinds of violent interventions that governments commit. It is an egregious violation of the nonaggression principle. As mentioned previously, as the value of money declines, it causes a direct loss of utility for the vast majority of individuals who use money. The winners are the borrowers who receive newly created money early on, the banks who receive interest on this money, and the central bank and government officials who direct monetary policy. Secondly, as a consequence of recessions, it causes further losses to businesses, entrepreneurs, investors, and labor. All of this represents a large increase in material entropy.

But thirdly, by distorting the interest rate and creating booms and busts on a continuing basis, the business cycle causes enormous uncertainty for savers, investors, businesses, and consumers. It is a significant long-term threat to almost everyone. With an interest rate largely determined by unpredictable increases in fiat money creation, and a production structure in constant turmoil, savers

---

[245] Mises first discussed the Austrian business cycle in Mises, Ludwig von (1953) [1912] *The Theory of Money and Credit*. Yale University Press, New Haven. pp. 346-366, and subsequently in Mises, Ludwig von (1998) [1949] *Human Action: A Treatise on Human Action*. Ludwig von Mises Institute, Auburn, AL, pp. 547-583. For a very detailed explanation of Austrian business cycle theory, see Huerta de Soto, Jesus (2006) *Money, Bank Credit, and Economic Cycles*. Translated by Melinda A. Stroup, Ludwig von Mises Institute, Auburn, AL.

cannot plan for the future, investors in stocks and bonds fear their investments could be wiped out or severely curtailed at any minute, business owners worry if they are the next to be bankrupted, and consumers can never know how much they are going to have to pay for goods and services. This uncertainty creates social anxiety and a loss of *eudaimonia*, and represents a huge increase in mental and social entropy. From a long-term perspective, it insidiously destroys the dreams of millions. Ordinary people are prevented from planning out their lives adequately in this environment of random job destruction, market turbulence, and perpetual financial uncertainty. They are inhibited from attaining the kind of enduring happiness which would otherwise be available.

The apotheosis of money creation and the cause of perhaps the greatest uncertainty, along with soaring social anxiety and entropy, is the hyperinflationary phenomenon which Mises termed the crack-up boom.[246] In the first phase of this event, prices start to rise relatively slowly, and consumers and producers are generally reluctant to spend because they anticipate the price inflation is merely temporary, and the cost of goods and services will either level off or decline. But then as prices continue to rise, uncertainty mounts as market actors consider the possibility that the trend is permanent. Thus, they start to spend. But the spending drives up prices further, causing even greater anxiety, and so they spend more. At this point, it becomes clear that given the increasingly high cost of living, there appears to be a shortage of money. Thus, the government engages in further rounds of money printing, which only serves to raise prices more. The economy now enters the final stages of the hyperinflation, in which money printing and spending reinforce each other in spiraling out-of-control price increases. In the final death throes of the economy, a panic-driven despair grips the public as people are forced to spend their money as soon as they

---

[246] Mises discusses the cause and the effect of the crack-up boom in Mises, Ludwig von (1998) [1949] *Human Action: A Treatise on Human Action.* Ludwig von Mises Institute, Auburn, AL, pp 423-425 and pp. 541-542.

receive it, for now they realize that even if they hold onto their money for mere minutes, it falls in purchasing power.

Such was the fate of the peoples of Weimar Germany, Hungary after World War II, Zimbabwe, Venezuela, and many others. The collapse of the economy, which affects the vast majority of the population, destroys lives and causes misery on a massive scale, not just financially, but in every other possible way. Only war can inflict greater damage.

War

Of all the ruinous violations of the nonaggression principle, war represents the ultimate destruction of order. It is beyond the scope of this book to discuss the effects of war in any great detail, but I mention it here because without a doubt it is the worst act that a government can initiate. In every respect, war increases material, mental, and social entropy. It destroys the bodily integrity of those killed and injured. It ruins capital goods and infrastructure. It causes random and indiscriminate killing of innocent civilians and the destruction of their property. And it causes high uncertainty and anxiety for those who survive.

Wars are always initiated and fought by individuals, even though they are almost never described that way. For the most part, war consists of serial violators of the nonaggression principle who compete with each other for dominance through further aggression. Wars between nations are usually characterized as "country A attacks country B." A more precise description would be "the government of A attacks the government of B." But in reality, the truth is, "the officials of country A coerce or propagandize their citizens to attack the citizens of country B, and the officials of country B coerce or propagandize their citizens to attack those of country A." In wars between nations, even a supposedly peaceful nation attacked by a belligerent aggressor remains an aggressor against its own citizens, even though it might not be the initiator of the war.

In civil wars, the situation is much the same. Competing groups of aggressors fight for control of the government, or to put it another way, they fight for the "privilege" of attaining a monopoly on the use of violence against their own citizens.

The only legitimate conflicts are some revolutionary wars where the combatants seek to reduce or eliminate the power of a government. Such was the case in the American Revolution, which properly could be called a war that was fought in self-defense against an oppressive ruler. On the other hand, the French Revolution, the Russian Revolution, the Chinese Cultural Revolution, the Iranian Revolution, and many others, merely replaced an oppressive regime with one that was equally or even more tyrannical.

14

The Meaning of Free Will

It is clear there are certain eternal truths that are axiomatic, rationally deducible, and absolute, and yet they are *not* mere tautologies. These truths consist of synthetic *a priori* propositions, and include the principle of non-aggression, the axioms of action and self-ownership, the propositions of geometry, arithmetic, mathematics, and Austrian economics, among others. They can be recognized and understood by any person who has the will to find them through self-discovery and learning. A truth does not necessarily have to be deduced through logical reasoning, for it might be intuitive or self-evident. But to be understood it does require a certain intellect. In this context, intellect does not mean a high-order intelligence, nor does it imply a superior knowledge about worldly matters. Rather, it signifies a capacity of the mind to appreciate and grasp something that is a fundamental and universal, and to comprehend its significance and importance.

There are further truths concerning virtue and beauty which are also timeless. However, because many virtuous and aesthetic qualities act upon the emotions, and logically valid statements concerning them cannot be demonstrated *a priori*, it is easy to refute the claim that universally true propositions exist in this area by simply declaring, "I disagree." Throughout the ages and in different parts of the world, there have been disparate standards of virtue and beauty, which would seem to render their assessment entirely subjective.

And yet it seems clear there are fundamental principles concerning them which are ubiquitous. If certain kinds of action are practiced, and certain sensory manifestations are contemplated, there arises a higher order state of mind, and this is universal. Not everyone has the will or the intellect (in the sense mentioned above) to discover and apply true virtue, or to seek and appreciate true beauty. And there are many who claim to be virtuous or to have an aesthetic sense even though they possess neither of these qualities; virtue-signalers and pseuds are abundant, particularly in the postmodern world! But provided the fraudsters and their false claims are disregarded, there are universal elements which endure.

Whereas a person might be only dimly aware of a truth, or not appreciate its relevance, it suddenly becomes manifest and clear when the intellect is brought to bear. The intellect does not imply a long process of discovery, although that might indeed be required to find the truth. Rather, it involves the ability to see with the mind's eye, and it operates in that flash of understanding when one becomes fully aware of a truth's meaning and implications. It is the final stage of understanding. The moment when we grasp a fundamental principle is a moment of pure joy, and its understanding is permanent because the truth itself is eternal. Once we have seen the light, we cannot unsee it. We keep it within us.

No mortal person has the intellect to know everything that is true. Only a divine mind or God-like intellect can hold all truth in one place. But perhaps it is the case that when our intellect comes to appreciate a fundamental truth, we align our mind with the divine. In many Abrahamic religions, the origin of truth is God. Jesus said, "I am the way, the truth and the life: no man cometh unto the Father, but by me."[247] In Buddhist doctrine, there are two kinds of *satya* or truth – namely, the ordinary and conventional truths of phenomenal reality, and the absolute truth which describes ultimate reality and transcends everyday experience. In Hinduism, truth is

---

[247] *King James Bible*, John 14:6.

unchangeable, absolute, beyond phenomenal experience, and unaffected by time and space.

In this book, I have attempted to present an argument that has relied largely on discursive reasoning, supported by some empirical evidence. I have tried to avoid any religious, spiritual, or mystical connotations, but I shall now venture into that area in an attempt to bring together what I have presented so far. I stated in an earlier chapter that the human mind is limited in what it can know and understand. While there is much we can learn and have yet to discover, there are some aspects of our existence which no amount of empirical evidence or reasoning can explain. Nevertheless, it is a harmless diversion to speculate on such matters.

I shall describe a possible cosmological model, a representation to illustrate how the spiritual and transcendental components might be organized in relation to human existence. I emphasize there can be no proof or rational explanation for what follows.

Central to everything is absolute and universal truth. I shall call this the Truth. The Truth is indivisible and timeless, and like the sun, radiates out for all those who are prepared to see. Its origin, however, is transcendent and beyond being, or if you like, God. God is infinitely complex, perfectly ordered, impossible to understand, and beyond knowing, except as manifested in the Truth. This is the world of the spiritual, which lies in opposition to all that is phenomenal.

Most of the time, however, we are concerned only with mundane material matters. For most of us, our mind or soul is not preoccupied with the spiritual. But the phenomenal reality of the physical realm, including the reality of our own bodies, which we perceive when we look out at the world around us and away from spiritual affairs, is not as it really is; all the objects of the material world do not appear to us as things-in-themselves. They are like the shadows on the wall in Plato's Allegory of the Cave, or the three-dimensional representation of reality that is observed in the consciousness tunnel, a world framed by the lens of the mind's pure intuitions and concepts of space, time, and causality.

Moreover, every living thing in our everyday experience decays. Physical existence is temporary due to the effects of entropy. Entropy is everywhere and inevitable because it is the process by which we mark time. Indeed, it is the "arrow of time," for if there were no entropy, there could be no order in which events take place. It is how we tell the difference between perceptions that are reversible and those which are not, and as such, it is a key component of experiencing cause and effect. Thus, in looking out at the material world and away from the spiritual, everything, including our own bodies, appears ultimately to decay and die. Entropy is always present. But this too is not as it really is, for time and space exist only in our minds.

As we delve into the nature of the physical world, finding evermore fundamental particles, it becomes harder and harder to describe matter in terms that can be explained and understood to be operating according to physical laws. Indeed, the "hard problem" is not consciousness, which is a substance with which we are all intimately familiar, but rather matter itself. For how can we describe the fundamental essence of matter in terms of itself when we have no idea what that essence is? It is like looking at an image in a mirror within mirror. The image recedes forever into the background. And this is why it seems possible, and even probable, that matter can only be explained as a form of consciousness. Consciousness, not matter, is the ultimate reality. The physicist and Nobel laureate Max Planck implied this when he said:

> Consciousness, I regard, as a fundamental. I regard matter as derivative from consciousness. We cannot get behind consciousness. Everything that we talk about, everything that we regard as existing postulates consciousness.[248]

---

[248] Interview by J. W. N. Sullivan "Interviews with Great Scientists: VI - Max Planck" in *The Observer Newspaper*, 25 January, 1931, p. 17, column 3.

In addition, he stated:

> I would like to observe that my research on the atom
> has shown me that there is no such thing as matter
> in itself. What we perceive as matter is merely the
> manifestation of a force that causes the subatomic
> particles to oscillate and holds them together in the
> tiniest solar system of the universe . . . we must
> assume that this force that is active within the atom
> comes from a conscious and intelligent mind. That
> mind is the ultimate source of matter.[249]

Nobel laureate Erwin Schrodinger also suggested it when he wrote:

> But although I think that life may be the result of an
> accident, I do not think that of consciousness.
> Consciousness cannot be accounted for in physical
> terms. For consciousness is absolutely fundamental.
> It cannot be accounted for in terms of anything
> else.[250]

More recently, philosopher David Chalmers states:

> Perhaps the intrinsic properties of the physical world
> are themselves phenomenal properties. Or perhaps
> the intrinsic properties of the physical world are not
> phenomenal properties, but nevertheless constitute
> phenomenal properties . . . If so, then consciousness
> and physical reality are deeply intertwined.[251]

Suppose the basic unit of all material substances in the

---

[249] "Das Wesen der Materie (The Nature of Matter)," a 1944 speech in
Florence, Italy, Archiv zur Geschichte der Max-Planck-Gesellschaft, Abt. Va,
Rep. 11 Planck, Nr. 1797; as quoted Braden, Gregg (2008) *The Spontaneous
Healing of Belief.* Hay House, Carlsbad, CA., p. 212.

[250] Interview by J. W. N. Sullivan "Interviews with Great Scientists: IV – Erwin
Schrodinger" in *The Observer Newspaper*, 25 January, 1931, p. 16, column 2.

[251] Chalmers, David J. (2003) "Consciousness and its Place in Nature" in S. Stich
& T. Warfield (eds.), *Blackwell Guide to Philosophy of Mind* (Blackwell, 2003).

noumenal realm – as things-in-themselves – is indeed consciousness. Objects appear to us as matter because when we look out at the phenomenal world, that is how they are presented to us in space and time. But if all forms of matter possess certain quanta of consciousness, it is clear there must be different levels of this substance as it is manifested in the physical realm.

At the base level is inanimate matter, above which is plant life, but neither have sufficient quanta to possess perception or awareness. Next are simple animals, which may or may not have perception depending on the organization of their neural connections. Above these are animals which do have perception and awareness, and finally human beings who are self-aware.

As humans, we are unique because we have a brain with sufficient quanta of conscious substance that, in being self-aware, we can experience our own mind as a thing-in-itself. It is the one object in the universe we encounter in the noumenal realm. Therefore, we also have free will. Moreover, by having a will, we can turn away from the material toward the spiritual, at least for a while, and discover the Truth.

If we unleash the intellect to face Truth, then space, time, and causality disappears. There is no entropy. We momentarily detach ourselves from all that is material and find truths that transcend space and time, and which have no cause except to say that they must emanate from God. These truths are not empirical in nature, because empirical evidence is an aspect only of the realm of phenomena. Rather, they are self-evident or intuitive or discursive. They are the fundamental truths concerning justice, morality, virtue, the principle of non-aggression, the action axiom, the axiom of self-ownership, beauty, and no doubt many others. And when the intellect apprehends them, it is an awakening, a realization that we are grasping a fundamental essence of life, something that is genuinely good that unites us with an archetypal mind and with other souls. We become one with God. Everything is order.

In finding truths, we observe an *essence* of the noumenal realm, but it is not the noumenal world itself, because, with the exception of our own mind, we are incapable of experiencing anything as it is in itself. We cannot experience other conscious entities. If it were possible to encounter all matter as noumena, we would have to step outside the world of phenomena and observe the material world looking inward. But from our vantage point, which is inextricably tied to matter, we can only escape the material by turning toward God. And in facing God, what we experience is *not* the noumenal realm but rather the spiritual world of absolute Truth, which is the essence and *animating force* of the noumenal realm.

The force that operates noumenally is not gravity or electromagnetism or the strong or weak nuclear forces, all of which function in space and time and are associated with the law of causality. Rather, the force is absolute Truth. Truth is eternal, or more correctly, timeless. It has no time dimension, no extension, and no cause other than itself, and it originates from a place of perfect order. Metaphorically speaking, truth is the light, radiating out from the center. Truth is the primary force, and it operates on the primary unit which is consciousness. And while we cannot feel its force on other minds and other conscious entities, we do experience its power on our own mind.

The purpose of Truth is to make consciousness unite with God in a state of perfect order. In noumenal reality, where there is no multiplicity, the universe is one; but from the phenomenal perspective, Truth is manifested as the animating forces of the universe to produce cause and effect upon material objects and living things. And yet, from within this seemingly chaotic world, we observe order being created in the form of life.

Because humans have an intellect that can understand the Truth, and a mind that is self-aware, we can feel the true vitalizing force of the universe as it acts upon our own consciousness, and it gives us joy. Most of the time, the outcome of the will – our action – is directed against matter to produce order in our own bodies and in material things external to ourselves. But when we turn to find the Truth, we experience a higher spiritual state of order. And this brings us closer to God.

God represents the ultimate order, the origin of all Truth, where there is no time and no entropy. The will wants to create order because it wants to be one with God. It does this in the material world, but the effect is merely temporary precisely because entropy and time are a continual presence. The utility we derive from material goods provides satisfaction, but the satisfaction is usually fleeting, and it has to be maintained through constant action. It is a perpetual struggle, and it fails ultimately in death.

But the greatest happiness is found when we use our will to turn in the direction of God, when we employ the will to find self-discipline and virtue – which is the basis of all personal morality – when we exercise goodness in all its forms, and when we abide by the nonaggression principle in our dealings with other people. The will to do this is grounded in love. It is love of the Truth, and in doing this we unite with God, and join Him in all that is good and everlasting.

As the great medieval philosopher and theologian Thomas Aquinas noted, the ultimate happiness is found when we turn our love to God, Himself, because He is the ultimate good and the source of all that is True.

Index

About the Author

Laura Davidson is an accomplished author, researcher, and multi-disciplinary thinker who has established herself as an influential figure in the fields of economics, philosophy, and libertarian ethics. Her work is characterized by a rigorous approach to complex issues and has been published in numerous peer-reviewed journals.

Davidson is a recipient of the prestigious Lawrence Fertig prize in economics from the Ludwig von Mises Institute, which recognizes her outstanding contribution to the field of economics in the Austrian tradition. In addition to her writing, she is a frequent speaker at libertarian and economic research conferences, as well as other venues, where her presentations have been praised for their clarity and originality.

Davidson is a graduate of Oxford University, where she studied earth science and developed an understanding of the natural world and its complexities. Her intellectual curiosity subsequently led to an interest in the social sciences. Through her recent research and writing, she seeks to promote a more integrated and holistic understanding of the world we live in, one that takes account of both the natural and social dimensions of human experience.

While stressing that the social and natural sciences employ very different methodologies, she realizes that they can inform and enrich each other through a shared commitment to logical reasoning. Her work has received widespread recognition, and she continues to be a prominent voice in the ongoing conversation about the intersection of science, philosophy, and economics.

www.ingramcontent.com/pod-product-compliance
Lightning Source LLC
Chambersburg PA
CBHW071413090426
42737CB00011B/1448